AQUINAS AND THE CRY OF RACHEL

Aquinas and the Cry of Rachel

THOMISTIC REFLECTIONS ON THE PROBLEM OF EVIL

John F. X. Knasas

The Catholic University of America Press Washington, D.C.

Copyright © 2013
The Catholic University of America Press
All rights reserved

Library of Congress Cataloging-in-Publication Data
Knasas, John F. X.
 Aquinas and the cry of Rachel : Thomistic reflections
on the problem of evil / John F.X. Knasas.
   pages cm
 Includes bibliographical references and index. ISBN
978-0-8132-3490-8 (pbk)
 1. Thomas, Aquinas, Saint, 1225?–1274. 2. Good
and evil. 3. Theodicy. I. Title.
 B765.T54K586 2013
 214—dc23   2013031213

For Adelė Dirsytė

Contents

Abbreviations xi | Introduction xiii

CHAPTER 1. THE CRY OF RACHEL   1

    Maritain's 1942 Marquette Aquinas Lecture   2

    Maritain's *The Person and the Common Good*   9

    Camus's *The Plague*   12

CHAPTER 2. JOY   16

    Being as the Good and the Eruption of Willing   18

    Being and Philosophical Psychology   25

    An Ordinary Knowledge of God and Metaphysics   31

    Metaphysics as Implicit Knowledge   35

    Being and the Intellectual Emotions   41

CHAPTER 3. *QUANDOQUE* EVILS   45

    Aquinas's Rationale for the Corruptible Order   46

    The Corruptible Order and *Quandoque* Evils   53

    Bracketing *Quandoque* Evils between Goods   57

    A Caveat in Understanding the Subject of the Consequent Good   61

    The Effect of Human Providence upon the Frequency of *Quandoque* Evils   69

CHAPTER 4. NATURAL CORRUPTIONS   74

    Death as a Natural Corruption   75

    Natural Corruption as Nondefinitive   79

    Ambiguity of "*Praeter Intentionem*" and "*Per Accidens*"   87

    God and the Evil of Punishment (*Poena*)   94

    Other Interpretations   95

    Abraham and Isaac   110

    Conclusion   119

CHAPTER 5. PRELIMINARIES TO AQUINAS AND THE CONTEMPORARY DISCUSSION   122

    C.G. III, 71: "If Evil Exists, God Exists"   122

    William Rowe on Cosmological Reasoning   133

    De Ver. X, 12, ad 10m: "If not God from Justice, then God from Some Other Effect"   141

    Summary of Aquinas on the Existence of Evil   145

    A Strategy   152

CHAPTER 6. THE THOMIST AND THE CONTEMPORARY DISCUSSION: PERSONALIST THEODICIES   153

    Marilyn McCord Adams and "Horrendous Evils"   155

    William Hasker: Personal Satisfaction and World Approval   158

    John Hick: Creation as a Gymnasium for the Development of Our Virtues   161

    David Ray Griffin and the Denial of Genuine Evils   167

    The Brothers Karamazov   178

    Thomistic "Natural Desires" of the Human Person   182

CHAPTER 7. THE THOMIST AND THE CONTEMPORARY DISCUSSION: COSMOLOGICAL THEODICIES 194

    Diogenes Allen and Suffering as an Experience of God   195

    David Hume and *Dialogues concerning Natural Religion*, X and XI   201

    William Rowe and "Pointless Evils"   206

    J. L. Mackie and Further Objections to a Cosmological Theodicy   209

    Mackie's Fourth Criticism and Aquinas on the Causality of Human Choices   214

    Aquinas and Plantinga   220

    The Avoidance of Determinism   225

    The Avoidance of Divine Culpability   231

    A Thomistic Free Will Defense?   244

    Richard Swinburne: Nature as a Necessary Display Case for Our Knowledge of Good and Evil   245

    Bruce Reichenbach: Developing Plantinga and Swinburne   252

CHAPTER 8. CONCLUSION AND COMPARISON TO BRIAN DAVIES AND ELEONORE STUMP 263

    Brian Davies's Apophatic Treatment of the Evil Problem   264

    Eleonore Stump and the Love of God   276

    The Consolation of Rachel   286

Bibliography   293 | Index   301

Abbreviations for the Works of Aquinas

Unless noted, all translations are my own.

C.G.	Summa contra Gentiles
De Ente	De Ente et Essentia
De Malo	Quaestiones Disputatae de Malo
De Pot.	Quaestiones Disputatae de Potentia Dei
De Ver.	Quaestiones Disputatae de Veritate
In de An.	Commentary on the De Anima of Aristotle
In de Trin.	Commentary on the De Trinitate of Boethius
In Meta.	Commentary on the Metaphysics of Aristotle
In Phys.	Commentary on the Physics of Aristotle
In Sent.	Commentary on the Sentences of Peter Lombard
ST	Summa Theologiae

Introduction

In this postmodern age in which the limits of human rationality are emphasized, Thomism can come across as too strident and too full of hubris. Though Thomism cannot compare to the comprehensiveness of Hegelian philosophy, the vast number of articles on a vast number of topics in Aquinas's writings has provoked the sly comment to Thomists, "So, you think that Aquinas has all the answers?"

If the Thomist keeps calm, the Thomist can easily respond that actually Aquinas himself admits that he does not have all the answers. For example, on the topic of whether the world was created in time or from eternity, the philosopher comes to a standstill. Either manner of creation is a possibility as far as the philosopher can tell from the philosophically available evidence. Which possibility is true is only known from the creator telling us how the creator did it. All the Christian medievals thought that they possessed this communication from the Bible in which they believed.

In Aquinas's philosophical thought other cases of stalemate exist. I will argue that among these other cases is the problem of evil. The problem is an apparent contradiction between the fact of evil in the world and an omnipotent, omniscient, and all-good creator of the world. Such a creator is usually understood to be equivalent to the God of the Judeo-Christian tradition. Hence, on the obvious meanings of the divine attributes, one would think that God has the ability, awareness, and motivation to eliminate evil. So, if there is evil, is there God?

Aquinas has no philosophical answer to the evil problem, not because he is unable to formulate a comprehensive theodicy, but because he can formulate too many. Just as the philosophical discovery of a creative cause in Aquinas's metaphysics leads Aquinas to neutralize Bonaventurian arguments for the world's creation in time, and to neutralize Averroistic arguments for the world's creation from eternity such that either could be true, something else Aquinas's metaphysics discovers makes us wonder how the evil problem is solved.

That metaphysical discovery concerns the human person. Usually the problem of evil makes God the focus of the drama. Hence, many current theists attempt to solve the problem by trimming the sails of one or the other of the divine attributes. For example, God's goodness and knowledge are left intact but his omnipotence is modified. The modification consists in free creatures having a freedom whose exercise is simply the creature's prerogative. Hence, if God creates free creatures, humans for example, God cannot be in full control. Even though God may want the good, we may decide not to cooperate with the divine plan.

But for Aquinas the traditional understanding of the divine attributes remains while the focus is shifted to the human person. Aquinas deepens the shopworn understanding of the human as a rational animal. The human is a rational animal because the human is a metaphysical animal. The human is ineluctably an intellector of being. Being is an intelligible object, a commonality, perceived in all the things that we sense and in ourselves. Moreover, it is perceived not apart from the differences of all those things but precisely within those differences. As so perceived, being is an object of unspeakable richness.

The intelligible object of being has implications for its intellector. First, as intellecting being the human is invested with a dignity unmatched by anything else in its experience. But, second, by intellecting being analogically, that is, as a sameness within the differences of things, the human never perfectly draws being to itself. This complex fact about the human establishes an important baseline for discussions of human destiny as they bear upon solving the evil problem. By its natural abilities, the human is geared to pursue knowledge of being in a material world shot through with contingency. In this perspective there is the acceptance that one may not succeed in realizing human perfection though there remains the hope that someone else will. Yet this may not be the entire story. The same intellection of being establishes the possibility, remote though it may be, of a direct knowledge of being in the creator. Since Aquinas's metaphysics reaches the creator as a cause whose nature is that of being, metaphysics also shows that human destiny may involve a stage in which being steps forth and introduces itself to the human intellector. That possibility for human destiny would offer other explanations of evil.

What this situation means for the Thomistic metaphysician is that contemporary cosmological theodicies, in which evil is explained by reference to the good of the whole, and personalist theodicies in which evil is explained by some good accruing to the sufferer, will always fight themselves to a draw. From a strictly philosophical perspective, the Thomist will claim that theodicies are necessarily multiple because the philosophical understanding of the human allows God multiple possibilities in which to realize human destiny. Closure on these possibilities would be found only in religious belief.

Just as Aquinas's proofs for God should not be studied apart from his assertions that philosophy proves God in metaphysics, so too his reflections on evil should not be taken up apart from his metaphysical understanding of the human as an intellector of being. But in the latter case the development of wisdom does not lead to one answer but to many possible answers. This ignorance is a rich ignorance. It purchases these valuable practical conclusions. If the Thomist is a believer, for example a Christian, this metaphysical confusion leaves the Thomist with a profound gracious wonder at the gift of faith and its awesome truth that the creator has called us to himself in the most intimate manner possible. If the Thomist is not yet a believer, this same confusion at least leaves the Thomist, despite vicissitudes, in peace of mind to shoulder the responsibility of traveling the roads of religion and of listening and weighing their claims of revelation from the Absolute.

1

The Cry of Rachel

Reiterating the thought of Georges Sorel, Jacques Maritain remarked: "If philosophers lived up to their calling in the new age into which we have entered, the crucial work for them would be to renew the theory of evil, that is to say, by examining it more profoundly."[1] The philosophers Maritain especially had in mind were Thomists. And with many thinkers exploiting evil as the Achilles heel of classical theism, is the urgency of Maritain's remark any less today?[2] Maritain addressed the problem of evil with a singu-

---

1. Jacques Maritain, *God and the Permission of Evil* (Milwaukee: Bruce Publishing Co., 1966), 4.

2. See David R. Griffin, *God, Power, and Evil: A Process Theodicy* (Louisville, Ky.: Westminster John Knox Press, 2004). For a popular presentation of the process perspective, see Harold S. Kushner, *Why Do Bad Things Happen to Good People?* (New York: Avon Books, 1981). At the outset, a distinction ought to be made in the "problem of evil." First is the issue of *whether* there can be both evil and an all-good, powerful, knowing God, and second is the issue of *how* this can be so. Aquinas solves the first quite easily. At *C.G.* III, 71, Aquinas even asserts that evil proves the existence of God; since evil is a privation in a being and God is the first cause of beings, then if evil exists, God exists. For more on this claim, see my chapter 5. Logically speaking, the second how-issue can remain problematic without need to go back on the resolution to the first. For these two senses of the problem, see my

lar relentlessness.³ His first formal treatment of the issue was his Marquette Aquinas Lecture of 1942. Twenty years later in his *God and the Permission of Evil*, he was still arguing the point. Maritain's treatment won him high praise.⁴ Certainly anyone who read Maritain observed the honesty and sincerity with which he faced the issue. Maritain realized that the stakes were high and expended himself to clarify the matter. In the following monograph I wish to join with Maritain by examining the theory of evil more profoundly.

MARITAIN'S 1942 MARQUETTE AQUINAS LECTURE

I wish to begin with Maritain's critique of a Thomistic text on physical evil. As I will note, the critique's use of Rachel wailing for her lost children is, in the minds of other contemporary discussants, an archetypal form of the evil problem. Also, Maritain's critique illustrates a crucial ambiguity whose clarification is valuable for discerning a truer resolution of the evil problem.

The Thomistic text upon which Maritain focuses is *ST* I, 48, 2: "Whether evil is found in things." For Maritain the text is a failure philosophically. For its argument to follow, the text must be taken up in a larger theological context. The body of the text goes as follows:

> The perfection of the universe requires that there should be inequality in things, so that every grade of goodness may be realized. Now, one grade of goodness is that of the good which cannot fail. Another grade of goodness is that of the good which can fail in goodness. These grades of goodness

---

"Aquinas and Finite Gods," *Proceedings of the American Catholic Philosophical Association* 53 (1979), 93–94. In his *Why Does Evil Exist?* (Hicksville, N.Y.: Exposition Press, Inc., 1974), 67, Cohn Connellan acknowledges the same "whether" versus "how" distinction in the evil problem.

3. For an indexing of Maritain's treatments of evil, see Charles Journet, *The Meaning of Evil*, translated by Michael Barry (New York: P. J. Kenedy, 1963), 295–296.

4. Speaking of his extensive use of Maritain, Journet remarks, "An apology must be made for the constant quotations from his works—but we consider these to be rich and coherent, traditional yet full of innovation, and containing the most penetrating teaching on evil written in our own times from the Christian viewpoint." Ibid., 14.

are to be found in being itself [*in ipso esse*]; for there are some things which cannot lose their being [*suum esse*], as incorruptible things, while there are some which can lose it, as corruptible things. As, therefore, the perfection of the universe requires that there should be not only incorruptible beings, so the perfection of the universe requires that there should be some which can fail in goodness and which sometimes [*interdum*] do fail. Now it is in this that evil consists, in the fact that a thing fails in goodness. Hence it is clear that evil is to be found in things in the way that corruption also is found; for corruption itself is an evil.[5]

In sum, God permits evils for the perfection of the universe. Evils are a concomitant of corruptible things. And corruptible things belong to the perfection of the created order. Now according to Maritain, this text poses a danger to Thomistic commentary. The danger is that the text will be regarded "in a merely philosophical sense, and as a satisfactory answer given by the philosopher."[6]

But Maritain finds the philosophical explanation unsatisfactory. Maritain confronts the perfection of the universe solution with the Biblical personage of Rachel. The full text that Maritain has in mind is from Matthew 2:16:

Then Herod, seeing that he had been tricked by the Magi, was exceedingly angry; and he sent and slew all the boys in Bethlehem and all in its neighborhood who were two years old or under, according to the time that he had carefully ascertained by the Magi. Then was fulfilled what was spoken through Jeremias the prophet, "A voice was heard in Rama, weeping and loud lamentation; Rachel weeping for her children, and she would not be comforted, because they were no more."

Though human agency is responsible for the death of these innocent children, Maritain intends Rachel to be any mother who suffers the loss of a child from any source, human or natural. What consolation can the philosopher give this parent? Little or none.

---

5. *ST* I, 48, 2c; Anton Pegis, ed., *The Basic Writings of St. Thomas Aquinas*, vol. I (New York: Random House, 1945), 467.

6. Jacques Maritain, *St. Thomas and the Problem of Evil* (Milwaukee: Marquette University Press, 1942), 8.

4   The Cry of Rachel

Maritain poignantly writes, "Tell her this thing was necessary in order that every degree of being should be filled, and she will answer that she cares not one whit for the machine of the world,—let them give back her child!"[7] Appealing to a mother's intuition, Maritain effectively embarrasses any "perfection of the universe" reply to this tragedy. What can be the value of the perfection of the universe in comparison to the existence of this young and innocent human being? There is nothing more precious. Is there not? Does God not see and understand this? If God does, why does God permit such gross transgressions in his created universe? To speak of the perfection of the universe as somehow excusing God only entails that God is value-blind or insensitive to value even a created intelligence can acknowledge.

Maritain also gives Rachel's reply a Thomistic elaboration. What is wrong with that reply to Rachel is that it considers the human being to be a mere part of the whole universe and hence expendable for the universe's perfection. But human beings are *persons*.

> In that light not parts but real *wholes*; for the person signifies in itself, wholeness. Neither man nor even the angel are persons in the perfect and absolute state, but they are in a real sense persons,—however wretchedly that condition of person is realized in man.... And from this point of view the existence of evil in things injects into being an incongruity from which nothing can console us. *Et noluit consolari.* (And she refused to be consoled.) ... The suffering of a man is the suffering of a person, of a whole. Here he is considered no longer as part of the universe, but insofar as he is a person he is considered as a whole, a universe to himself; to suffer that pain as part of the universe in the perspective of nature or of the world taken as God's work of art, does not do away with the fact that as far as the person is concerned it is an utter anomaly.[8]

Maritain's thinking is this. Like the universe, the human person is a whole, so for itself. The person's extinction, then, is in principle not redeemable and not consolable. Justifying a person's destruc-

7. Ibid., 9.
8. Ibid., 11–12.

tion by good brought about elsewhere just misses the point, for the justification treats a whole as merely a part of a larger scheme.

But in virtue of what is the person such a whole, a universe unto itself? The self-sufficiency and autonomy of the person is rooted in freedom. Maritain speaks of "the moral and spiritual relations of created persons to one another and with God, which relates to the universe of *freedom* and presupposes the world of nature, but is quite distinct from it."[9] In *The Person and the Common Good* Maritain provides some Thomistic texts for the above.[10] They are both from the *Summa contra Gentiles* and concern God's governance of the rational creature for itself and not for anything else. In this respect the rational creature is like a whole. Because of its self-determination, this special providence is appropriate to the rational creature.

From such thoughts, Maritain criticizes the traditional explanation of evil. That explanation is insensitive to the "utter anomaly" of the person suffering and dying. With a sense of the person's dignity, a reader cannot help but experience the explanation as "insufficient," "enigmatic," "hanging in the air," and "discordant."[11]

After critiquing the traditional explanation, Maritain begins the positive work of filling its lacunae. Maritain first argues for the human's creation in the state of grace.

We see there the most profound reason of suitability for the elevation of the intelligent creature to the supernatural order; I say reason based on fitness! Not on necessity, nor on justice. God could, without the least injustice, have created man in a state of pure nature, man would have been defrauded of nothing which his nature as such demands; but in actual fact God has created man in a state of grace; let us say that in actual fact he

---

9. Ibid., 10.
10. Jacques Maritain, *The Person and the Common Good* (Notre Dame, Ind.: University of Notre Dame Press, 1966), 19, n.8.
11. For these characterizations of Aquinas's explanation, see Journet, *The Meaning of Evil*, 54, 239–40. In *God and the Permission of Evil*, 1–2, Maritain mentions his approval of Journet's book.

would not have created nature if He had not destined it for grace,—and this word carries us very far. Very far from Leibniz.[12]

Later, Maritain repeats, "God, in actual fact, would not have made nature if He had not destined it to grace."[13] How, then, does Maritain answer Rachel's cry? Maritain asserts that sorrow and suffering are the retinue of the intellectual creature's free refusal of supernatural beatitude. Maritain writes:

> Without fallible freedom there can be no created freedom; without created freedom there can be no love in mutual friendship between God and creature; without love in mutual friendship between God and creature, there can be no supernatural transformation of the creature into God, no entering of the creature into the joy of his Lord. Sin,—evil,—is the price of glory.[14]

In other words, "sin ... [is] not permitted for the greater perfection of the machine of the world, but for the consummation of a work of love which transcends the whole order of the world."[15] So to Rachel Maritain's reply is that sorrow, suffering, and death are the results of man's refusal of God's love. God has willed to love us; in fact God created humans, that is, Adam and Eve, in what theologians call the supernatural "state of innocence." But man refused God's love. The consolation is that God still loves us and will bring us to him.

As gripping as Maritain's critique of 48, 2, is, analysis of Maritain's position reveals some inconsistencies that invite deeper reflection. For Maritain, 48, 2, fails as a piece of philosophy. Its reasoning comes to wreck on the understanding of the human as a person. In the perspective of that understanding, Maritain's complaint is uncompromising—the death of a human as a person is an "utter

---

12. Maritain, *St. Thomas and the Problem of Evil*, 13. Maritain's problem with Leibniz is that Leibniz makes all evils suffered by free agents "simply instrumental in regard to the universal order." For Maritain's texts, see Journet, *The Meaning of Evil*, 52.
13. Maritain, *St. Thomas and the Problem of Evil*, 17–18.
14. Ibid., 19.   15. Ibid., 18.

anomaly." Since 48, 2, is a philosophical argument, Maritain's complaint should also be philosophical. And it seems to be. For the dignity of the person Maritain appeals to human freedom. Human freedom is a thesis of Maritain's Thomism. Also, even though Rachel is a Biblical personage, Maritain makes it clear that he intends Rachel to stand for all mothers, not simply for mothers who believe in Biblical revelation. Hence, in the apparently philosophical perspective of the human as person, 48, 2, treats the human inappropriately. As a person the human is a whole; but 48, 2, considers the human as a part. Sticking to the human as a person, one cannot explain evil by viewing the human as a part of a larger whole. Rather, one must realize that the human somehow has only itself to blame for the evils that it suffers. This thought creates the opening for the introduction of original sin and the person's spurning of the creator's love.

Yet Maritain's position includes some back peddling that can only confuse the reader as to his actual position. As "utterly anomalous" as death is for the human person, Maritain insists that the human's desires not to die and not to suffer are "conditional and inefficacious."[16] Still within the perspective of the human as person, not within the perspective of original sin, Maritain describes the desires as only a profound "reason of suitability" and of "fitness" for the elevation of the intelligent creature to the supernatural order. As quoted above, for Maritain these desires create no reason for supernatural elevation based upon "necessity" or upon "justice."

Hence, the reader would pose the following questions. First, if in the philosophical perspective of person, human death is an utter anomaly, why is the desire not to die and not to suffer conditional and inefficacious? Should not the desires be the opposite? In other words, why does not the human as person provide a reason for supernatural elevation that is based upon necessity and justice? Does not "anomalous" mean inconsistent, contradictory,

16. Ibid., 12.

and improper? Do not those meanings of "anomalous" imply that a divine refusal of supernatural elevation is inconsistent, contradictory, and improper?

Second, granting Maritain's avowal that the human as person provides only a fitting but not necessary reason for supernatural elevation, how can Maritain claim to know that God would not have created nature if God had not destined it for grace? A philosopher can reason only on the basis of the natures known by natural reason. If the nature of the human as person provides only a reason of fittingness, then all the philosopher can claim is that perhaps creation includes the offer of supernatural elevation.[17]

Third, if the concept of the human as person does not eliminate the possibility of a state of pure nature, since as Maritain says supernatural elevation is only fitting and not necessary, then what is fundamentally wrong with the reasoning of 48, 2? Rather, 48, 2, would be explaining evil from the possibility that Maritain grants. Also, does not the same possibility undercut his usage of Rachel? Given that the state of pure nature would have "defrauded" the human of nothing, is not Rachel overreacting?

In sum, if Maritain's remarks about inefficacious and conditional human desire and about the possibility of pure nature are to be taken seriously, then Maritain should remove his mention of Rachel and erase his remark of "utter anomaly." But Maritain does neither. Hence, this reader is confused. Which of the above textual sets expresses Maritain's position? If the philosopher grasps the human as person, then the gratuity of the supernatural is removed. If the theologian knows the truth of the human as person, then Maritain is not giving a philosophical critique of 48, 2.

---

17. "If [God] wills to make a man, He must give him an intellect. But if there is anything which is not necessary for that which God wills, then that thing comes from God, not as something due, but simply as a result of His generosity. Now, the perfections of grace and glory are goods of this kind, because nature can exist without them inasmuch as they surpass the limits of natural powers." *De Ver.* 6, 2c; Thomas Aquinas, *The Disputed Questions on Truth*, vol. I, translated by Robert W. Mulligan (Chicago: Regnery, 1952), 264–65.

MARITAIN'S *THE PERSON AND THE COMMON GOOD*

Yet not long after, in *The Person and the Common Good* (1946), Maritain revisited the understanding of the human as person. Maritain's treatment is noteworthy for a number of reasons. First, it provides Thomistic texts. The texts derive from the *Summa contra Gentiles* III, 111 and 112 in which Aquinas argues that in God's providence rational creatures are governed for their own sake. Second, the remarks about the person only cement in the reader's mind the previous questions.

On the one hand, in a lengthy but important note 7, Maritain in part says:

> Using a distinction established further on, we may say that as individual or part, the intellectual substance is first willed and loved for the order of the universe and the perfection of the created whole; as person, it is first willed and loved for itself. Yet, like every creature, it differs from God, or Personality in pure act, more than it resembles Him. Hence, absolutely speaking, it is part or "individual" more than "person" and before it is a "person." (It is this that Kant failed to see.) It follows therefrom that, absolutely speaking, the intellectual substance is loved and willed for the order of the universe of creation before being loved and willed for itself. This in no wise hinders it, in contrast to irrational beings, from being really for itself and referred directly to God.
>
> Let us add that if we pass to the supernatural order, the order of formal participation in the deity, this priority of the universe of created nature over the person is reversed. Each person is here willed and loved for its own sake, that is, to find bliss in God (He truly died for each of them), before being willed and loved for the order and perfection of *this* world or of the universe of nature and creation.[18]

Here it seems clear that the philosopher does not consider the human as a person, hence as a whole. First, Maritain mentions the

---

18. Maritain, *The Person and the Common Good*, 17–18. I want to mention that in this spot Maritain's thoughts exactly express what will be the thesis of my own book. A reader might remember these remarks of Maritain as the reader goes on to consider my own remarks.

mistake of Kant. In his *Groundwork for the Metaphysics of Morals*, Kant delineated a view of the human in which it was always wrong to treat the human as a mere means to an end.[19] For Maritain Kant's view fails to realize that every creature differs from God more than it resembles God. In light of this difference, the human is more part than whole and so is loved and willed for the order of the universe. Second, at the start of the second paragraph Maritain says that by passing to the "supernatural order," we reverse the priority of nature over the person. Now the person is willed and loved for the person's own sake. As the term "supernatural" indicates, this pivot to the human as person is a theological consideration. If the notion of person is theological, then Maritain's Marquette Aquinas lecture critique of 48, 2, was not philosophical but theological. But is that fair? Should not the critique of a philosophical position be philosophical also?

But an answer to that question does not seem to matter. Unfortunately, when Maritain goes on in chapter 3 to describe expressly the consideration of the human as individual, or part, and as person, or whole, Maritain produces confusion for the reader. Maritain presents the distinction between individual and person as "belonging to the intellectual heritage of mankind."[20] He speaks of the "philosophical discovery of personality"[21] to which the most apposite approach is through the self-donation that characterizes love. It is noteworthy that within this philosophical context Maritain claims that "the person is directly related to the absolute."[22]

---

19. "For, to say that in the use of means to any end I am to limit my maxim to the condition of its universal validity as a law for every subject is tantamount to saying that the subject of ends, that is, the rational being itself, must be made the basis of all maxims of actions, never merely as a means but as the supreme limiting condition in the use of all means, that is, always at the same time as an end." Immanuel Kant, *Groundwork of the Metaphysics of Morals* II (German Academy ed., vol. 4,. 440), translated by Mary Gregor (Cambridge: Cambridge University Press, 1998), 45.
20. Maritain, *Person and the Common Good*, 34.
21. Ibid., 38.
22. Ibid., 42.

Finally, to cement the impression that the chapter 3 discussion of person is philosophical, Maritain follows the above with the remark: "Finally, we turn to religious thought for the last word and find that the deepest layer of the human person's dignity consists in its property of resembling God—not in a general way after the manner of all creatures, but in a proper way." He goes on to speak of the effects of grace. My point is that only now in chapter 3 does the discussion of the human as person become theological. Previously, the discussion should have been philosophical.

So is the notion of the human as a person, as a whole, philosophically attainable? Note 7 of chapter 2 appears to say no, chapter 3 appears to say yes. This oscillation repeats the wobbling noted in the Marquette lecture. In the lecture the claims of personality are presented as known to all mothers. Also, to develop the understanding of the human as person, Maritain uses the philosophical theme of human freedom. Nevertheless, in the end our philosophical consideration of the human seems to sink to the level of the individual, to use language from *The Person and the Common Good*. Maritain concedes that the consideration uncovers only reasons of fittingness for supernatural elevation.

Maritain's inability to make up his mind about the philosophical or theological character of the human as person when he critiques 48, 2, is not a reason to dismiss him but a reason to think more profoundly. As I will note, some excuse for the wobbling is found in the Aquinas texts cited by Maritain, though Aquinas will be much more clear than Maritain.[23] But the true source goes deeper. The notion of being, the *ratio entis*, can become associated with things in a way that invests those things with the preciousness of being itself, which is also the *ratio boni*. Yet because this is an allocation of preciousness by association, the recognition lingers that one has overstepped one's claims, that things do not quite deserve

---

23. For my discussion of Aquinas's arguments at *C.G.* III, 112, see "A Caveat in Understanding the Subject of the Consequent Good" in my chapter 3.

this dignity. In sum, there is a deep psychology at work here. I will argue that becoming aware of that psychology goes a long way to understanding why evil is a problem.

CAMUS'S *THE PLAGUE*

Maritain's employment of Rachel seems prescient, since Albert Camus and Anthony Flew will employ the same scenario in their work. In his novel, *The Plague* (1947), Camus describes the agonizing death of a young boy. To Rev. Paneloux's observation that "perhaps one should love what we cannot understand," Camus has the Dr. Rieux respond, "No, Father, I've a very different idea of love. And until my dying day I shall refuse to love a scheme of things in which children are put to torture."[24] Camus's mention of "a scheme of things" echoes Maritain's "machine of the world" to which innocent life seems sacrificed. Likewise in his 1964 essay, "Theology and Falsification," Anthony Flew claims that a reasonable person cannot logically combine the thoughts of God as our loving father with our suffering excruciating pain. Only an exercise of Orwellian "doublethink" enables the religious intellectual to retain his faith in a loving God in the face of a heartless and indifferent world. An example of what Flew has in mind is: "But then we see a child dying of inoperable cancer of the throat. His earthly father is driven frantic in his efforts to help, but his Heavenly Father reveals no obvious sign of concern."[25] Again, it is as if God cares more for something other than the child. How could this be? Is there anything more precious than a child?

The persistence of this form of the problem of evil, viz., the suffering and death of the young and innocent, accounts for the focus of this book as expressed in the title. Though I will probe arguments, logical analysis will not characterize my treatment. Rath-

---

24. Albert Camus, *The Plague*, translated by Stuart Gilbert (New York: Alfred A. Knopf, 1948), 196–97.

25. Anthony Flew, "Theology and Falsification," *New Essays in Philosophical Theology* (New York: The Macmillan Company, 1964), 108.

er, deep and honest philosophical analysis of the human psyche will be the dominant target. Why? When Rachel looks at her slain children, when Dr. Rieux accompanies the child through his death throes, when the father looks down at his son prostrate with throat cancer, their cry and despair are not the conclusions of syllogisms. Their reaction of despair is a response to a perception that is frustratingly elusive to hold in a contemplative gaze. Perhaps the perception is so fleeting because its object is so piercing. Nevertheless, such a perception is, I think, more than a sense reaction. The intellect is involved as well. What we have in the reactions of these personages appears to be the opposite of Kant's mention of awe upon looking at the starry sky.[26] Aquinas says something similar to Kant in acknowledging an implicit knowledge of God.[27] From some perceptions we take the thought of God while from others we have anti-theistic attitudes.

Of the three authors, Camus provides us with the best description of the state of mind. The plague has abated and the populace of Oran has returned to normalcy. As Dr. Rieux walks the city, he mediates on what he sees:

Among the heaps of corpses, the clanging bells of ambulances, the warnings of what goes by the name of fate, among unremitting waves of fear and agonized revolt, the horror that such things could be, always a great voice had been ringing in the ears of these forlorn, panicked people, a voice calling them back to the land of their desire, a homeland. It lay outside the walls of the stifled, strangled town, in the fragrant brushwood of the hills, in the waves of the sea, under free skies, and in the custody of love. And it was to this, their lost home, toward happiness, they longed to return, turning their backs disgustedly on all else.

---

26. "Two things fill the mind with ever new and increasing admiration and awe, the oftener and more steadily they are reflected on: the starry heavens above me and the moral law within me." Immanuel Kant, *Critique of Practical Reason*, "Conclusion," in *Critique of Practical Reason and other Writings in Moral Philosophy*, translated and edited by Lewis White Beck (Chicago: The University of Chicago Press, 1949), 258.

27. C.G. III, 38. For an extended comment, see "Being and Philosophical Psychology" in my chapter 2.

As to what that exile and that longing for reunion meant, Rieux had no idea. But as he walked ahead, jostled on all sides, accosted now and then, and gradually made his way into less crowded streets, he was thinking it has no importance whether such things have or have not a meaning; all we need consider is the answer given to men's hope.

Henceforth he knew the answer, and he perceived it better now he was in the outskirts of the town, in almost empty streets. Those who, clinging to their little own, had set their hearts solely on returning to the home of their love had sometimes their reward.... And for some time, anyhow, they would be happy. They knew now that if there is one thing one can always yearn for and sometimes attain, it is human love.... And as he turned the corner of the street where Grand and Cottard lived, Rieux was thinking it was only right that those whose desires are limited to man and his humble yet formidable love should enter, if only now and then, into their reward.[28]

One can rail that like Flew, Camus is an atheist with an axe to grind. Moreover, one can note that his use of Rev. Paneloux to effect a caricature of the Catholic Church's position, viz., all suffering is the result of personal sin not original sin (as noted above by Maritain), need not indicate any malice on Camus's part.[29] Camus had little formal knowledge of Catholicism. So, I regard these thoughts as the thoughts of an honest man. Also, they are not idiosyncratic. We have all visited this state of mind. And so I maintain that no syllogism about evil will ever be effective until this psychology is addressed. What is the psychology?

The psychology consists in experiencing an excruciating joy in what one knows will cease to exist—the fragrant brushwood, the waves on the sea, free skies, human love. It consists in a desperation caused by an apparently insane combination of unspeakable preciousness and disregard. What is common to all these ordinary but poignant instances is transiency. When happiness is found in something as passing as the above, reality cannot but appear to

---

28. Camus, *The Plague*, 270.
29. On the primitive Catholicism to which Camus was exposed, see Jean Onimus, *Albert Camus and Christianity*, translated by Emmett Parker (Tuscaloosa, Ala.: University of Alabama Press, 1970), 31–37.

rest on nothingness. If one's delight is taken in the scents of the brushwood, then one cannot but experience nothingness in their removal. The passing of the all is the presencing of nothing. Of course, the realist and down-to-earth man can grab one by the collar and shake one back to one's senses. The cloudless sky is just the cloudless sky, waves are simply waves, love is just love. Yet in one's heart, one knows that this is a lie. It is so good that these things exist, and so sad that they pass. As was said of Rachel, she refused to be consoled because her children were no more. So despite the matter-of-fact realist, something needs to be addressed. It would appear that a philosophical determination of what provides joy is called for. Next, explanation is required of how joy becomes inextricably combined with transient things so that their passing is a cause for sadness. Only after exploring this preliminary psychology can the mental space be opened in persons like Camus, Rachel, and Flew for an investigation of Aquinas's apparently dispassionate remarks on why evil exists.

2

Joy

My thesis is that the problem of evil is generated by an inappropriate aggrandizement of persons and other things. There is in human consciousness an object of unspeakable preciousness. It is the notion of being understood as the good. But because the notion of the being is so spontaneously abstracted from sensible things, it can lie unnoticed in our conscious life. Nevertheless, because of certain features of sensible things, for example, their smallness or largeness either in size or in time, the contemplation of things can unwittingly enlist the already abstracted notion of being. This association with being can invest a thing itself with the preciousness of being so that the thing's loss rings as "utterly anomalous." The solution to the problem of evil is to become clear-sighted about what fundamentally gives us joy—being. Only through the apportionment of being to other things do we find joy in them. In other words, as precious as anything is, it is not the be all and end all. For example, as intellectors of being we have a particularly intimate relation with the good itself. But that cognitive union never suffices to render us the good. In the end we remain by our natures parts of the created whole, although principal parts. The fundamental object of our joy remains being and our joy in and love of others and ourselves derives from a relation with being. Hence, as understandably difficult as the death of a loved one is, it is really selfish to be overcome by despair; for if being has been extinguished in one instance, it continues to call for love and respect in others. Is it not unseemly to deny that truth by complaining that one has nothing else left to live for?

That our joy in things derives from joy in being is reflected in the thesis that happiness is the last end and that everything is willed for the sake of the last end. But, as I will explain in the next section, the object of the will, viz., happiness or the last end, is the *ratio boni* or the *bonum in communi*. These expressions designate the *ratio entis* in another guise. It is also reflected in the thesis that angels, who are more excellent creatures than we, by a natural love first love God more than themselves. The reason given is that God is identical with the *"bonum commune"* (*ST* I, 60, 5, ad 5m). But as just noted, the common good is another way to speak of being. Third, Aquinas insists (*ST* I-II, 2, 6, ad 1m) that in respect to final causality, no difference exists between acting for the vision of God or acting for the delight in that vision. If we look for the reason of delight's final causality, then we consider "the good which is the object of delight and so is its principle and gives to it a form." Aquinas presents the good as causing something in which the good becomes present, so that the something caused by the good is a final cause, a point of attraction. Finally, time after time Aquinas explains various evils by appeal to the notions of whole, the greatest of which is the intelligible whole of being, and part. Even the incident of the sacrifice of Isaac Aquinas resolves (*ST* I-II, 94, 6, ad 2m) by noting that original sin reduces humans to an ungraced state in which, as parts, we suffer the death of nature as established by the author of nature.

In my opinion, the problem of evil calls for a philosophical psychology that can explain how the correct object of our joy can become incorrectly identified with something else. As I will argue, this explanation will reveal why many react negatively to Aquinas's various reflections on why evil exists. But my purpose is to defend Aquinas's reflections as only *possible* explanations for evil. In my opinion, Aquinas does not believe that philosophy knows the definitive answer to the question of why evil exists. The philosopher has no definitive answer because the philosopher has *too many* possible answers. The situation that I am envisaging is parallel to Aquinas's view about philosophy's impotence on the question of the world's beginning in time or not. By his religious faith, Aquinas knows that the former is the truth. But by his reason alone, Aquinas cannot make up his mind. The arguments of the two sides in the debate fail to be conclusive. The Bonaventurians claimed that reason could demonstrate the world's temporal inception as taught by Scripture. At *ST* I, 46, 2, Aquinas thinks reason cannot demonstrate the world' temporal inception and neutralizes the arguments. The Aristotelians claimed that reason could prove that the world and motion were eternal, without a temporal beginning. At *ST* I, 46, 1, Aquinas thinks reason cannot prove the world and motion are eternal and neutralizes the supposed proofs. Aquinas thinks that a creator could cause either an eternal world or a temporal world and that nothing that the metaphysician knows about the existing world or about the creator proves how the creator has dispensed existence. At *C.G.* II, 38, Aquinas admits only a certain fittingness between God's goodness as the object of his will and the noneternity in God's created effects. And so likewise, for any one Thomistic philosophical explanation of evil, another explanation will always be possible. Settling on one possible explanation of evil as the true explanation will require religious faith in God's revelation concerning his designs for us.

BEING AS THE GOOD AND THE ERUPTION OF WILLING

One must begin with the various reactions of Rachel, Rieux, and the father. Rachel is full of *sorrow* over the loss of her child and cannot be consoled. Rieux finds a limited happiness, one that seems more like what we would call *joy*, in the waves on the sea, the fragrant brushwood, and human love. What the father described by Flew knows is *anger*. The father asks pointedly where is the aid of the loving God for his afflicted son? In Aquinas's philosophical psychology sorrow, joy, and anger are more profound than reactions of the sense appetites. People can be profoundly happy amid terrible physical deprivation and profoundly depressed when awash in material goods. As I will illustrate, for Aquinas these reactions are reactions of an intellectual appetite called the will and the will's primordial response of love to a prompt presented to it by the intellect. Hallmarks of Aquinas's psychology are the honesty and depth of its descriptions. Such a phenomenology seems to be just what is needed to address the reactions of the characters listed above.

At *ST* I, 20, 1c, Aquinas calls love the "first motion" of the will.[1] Yet this first motion does not possess the autonomy of a Kantian will. As Aquinas sees it, this love is a response to something. Love is a response to "the good universally: *bonum in communi*." The terminology for the object of love suggests intelligibility. Aquinas describes the universal good as an abstraction. He says that "love regards good universally, whether possessed or not." Just as one can consider the notion of animal as rational or not, so too the good can be considered apart from it differentiae of possessed or not possessed. Also, later in the *Summa Theologiae* the object of the will is the *ratio boni*: *ratio boni, quod est obiectum potentiae* (I-II, 8, 2c). But a *ratio* is an object of intellectual abstraction. For example in the *De Ente et Essentia* Aquinas describes a *ratio* like the "*ratio humanitatis*" in its absolute consideration "as abstract-

---

1. "Motion" has an improper sense that is common to acts of will, intellect, and sense, *In de Trin.*, 5, 4, ad 2m; at *In de Trin.*, 2, ad 7m, Aquinas assigns its study to the metaphysician (*divinum*), not the natural philosopher (*naturalum*). The motion studied by the natural philosopher or physicist is characterized by the replacement of one contrary in a subject with another contrary. See, *In III An.*, lect. 12.

ing, though not prescinding," from various features like white or black, one or many, existence in things or existence in the soul."[2] As Aquinas understands it, the will's first motion of love suffers an intellectual prompt, the *ratio boni*. This object of the will's first motion is what Aquinas also calls at I, 82, 1c the will's last end and happiness (*beatitudo*).

But as an *abstractum* does not the *ratio boni* leave items outside of itself as did the *ratio animalis* or the *ratio humanitatis*? As such is the *ratio boni* not pale and insipid? How, then, can one understand it as igniting something as ardent as love? In short, where is the final causality? Answering this last question requires one to understand a distinction between two types of *rationes*. Both types are products of what Aquinas in his *De Ente et Essentia* calls abstraction without precision. Characteristic of nonprecisive abstraction is that it does not exclude what it does not include. As such the *ratio* is still basically identical with the instances from which it was taken. Consequently, the identity relation of predication is respected. Whole is identified with whole, not part with whole.[3]

---

2. "Understood in this sense, a nature or essence can be considered in two ways. First, absolutely, according to its proper meaning [*secundum naturam et rationem propriam*] .... For example, to man as man belong 'rational,' 'animal,' and everything else included in his definition; but 'white' or 'black,' or any similar attribute not included in the notion of man [*de ratione humanitatis*] does not belong to man as a man. If someone should ask, then, whether a nature understood in this way can be called one or many, we should reply that it is neither, because both are outside the concept of humanity, and it can happen to both. If plurality belonged to its concept it could never be one, though it is one when present in Socrates. So, too, if oneness belonged to its concept, the nature of Socrates and of Plato would be identical, and it could not be multiplied in many individuals." Thomas Aquinas, *On Being and Essence*, translated by Armand Maurer (Toronto: The Pontifical Institute of Mediaeval Studies, 1968), 46. The mention of "abstraction without precision" is two paragraphs later. Such abstraction is delineated earlier in the work's second chapter.

3. In chapter 2 of his *On Being and Essence*, Aquinas also acknowledges precisive abstraction which does exclude what it does not include. As such the *abstractum* was only a part of the instance and could not be identified with the instance in predication. To illustrated precisive abstraction, Aquinas uses "body" understood as a part of the human in contrast to a genus in which humans, dogs, trees, rocks, etc. belong. In his "The Accidental and Essential Character of Being in the Doctrine of St. Thomas Aquinas," in *St. Thomas Aquinas on the Existence of God: the Collected Papers of Joseph Owens*, edited by John R. Catan (Al-

But a nonprecisive *ratio* can be "generic." Characteristic of the generic *ratio* is that the *ratio* contains the differences of instances implicitly and potentially, *implicite et potentialiter*. Even though the differences are not wholly outside (*penitus extra*) the *ratio*, the differences can be referred to as "extrinsic" (*quasi extranea*). The reason is that they are in the *ratio* only because of the capacity of the *ratio* to undergo division by them. Here the charge of pale and insipid has its appropriateness.

On the other hand, the *ratio* can be nongeneric, such as the notion of being (*ratio entis*); the notion of being does not behave exactly like a generic notion. An inability to appreciate this lack of equivalency is a fundamental misstep in one's philosophical life. Without drama Aquinas observes at *De Ver*. I, 1c and XXI, 1c that being includes the differences of particular things because everything is essentially a being. Implied here is the thought that real plurality of things would cease to exist if being failed to include the differences of things. As I noted, at *De Ver*. XXI, 1c, Aquinas says that the differences of a generic intelligibility remain in the intelligibility *implicitly and potentially*. This characterization implies that with the intelligibility of being the differences remain *implicitly* but *actually*.[4] So, though being cannot be identified with any existing thing, no thing can be disidentified with being. In other

---

bany: State University of New York Press, 1980), 84. Joseph Owens observes that at the time of Suarez this twofold sense of abstraction was lost, and subsequently philosophers identified abstraction with precisive abstraction. It could be further argued that this myopia fired the early nineteenth-century romantic revolt against reason as a fit instrument to handle reality. The revolt continues in twentieth-century existentialism and post-modernism. For the connection of romanticism and existentialism, see William Barrett, *Irrational Man: A Study in Existential Philosophy* (Garden City, N.Y.: Doubleday & Company, Inc.,1962), ch. 6, "The Flight from Laputa." For a Thomistic expression for this distaste of the conceptual intellect, see Pierre Rousselot, *The Intellectualism of St. Thomas*, translated by James E. O'Mahony (New York: Sheed and Ward, 1935), 309, 96–100. For a discussion of this critique of abstraction, see my "Does the Catholic Church Teach That There is No One True Philosophy?" *Angelicum*, 80 (2003): 422–24.

4. James Anderson's terminology from his *The Bond of Being: An Essay on Analogy and Existence* (New York: Greenwood Press, 1969), 256.

words, though a being is not equal to a daisy, horse, or mineral, each of these *in their unique differences* have to be equal to a being.

For Thomists this conversion phenomenon characterizes an analogical concept, or *ratio*, in contrast to a univocal concept. By "univocal concept" Thomists refer to what Aquinas called "generic." An example of a univocal *ratio* is the meaning of the word "triangle." For example, my awareness of this right-angle triangle, this isosceles triangle, and this equilateral triangle is more than an awareness of three figures. More accurately speaking, my awareness is of three figures with something in common. We mean to express this commonality by the word "triangle." The *ratio* of triangle lacks conversion. The proof lies in the reflection that the differences of the instances mentioned can all be found in nontriangular figures. The right angle that is the difference of the first figure can be found in a rectangle; the two equal sides of figure two can be in a quadrilateral, and so forth. In sum, if there were conversion, then the differences would carry the sameness wherever they appear. But having a right angle does not mean a triangle. Consequently, the univocal concept has been described as a sameness-apart-from-difference. In a sense, it does succeed in ripping itself apart from the real and evinces itself to be an impoverishment.

Analogical concepts, of which the *ratio entis* is one case, continue to embrace the differences of their instances even while abstracting from them. This assertion may sound beyond belief, but continue to reflect upon the above facts. If one's abstracting of being does not render the differences extrinsic to being, then the only way the differences can be placed aside is by compressing them within being. This thinking reveals the richness of being. Accordingly, at *De Ver.* I, 1c, the differences of being do not add to being from the outside but are said to "express" a mode of being. In the twentieth century a Thomist like Maritain can say: "Everything which divides [electrons and angels] from one another is the same being which I find in each of them—varied. I simply have to fix my attention on it to see that it is at once one and multiple." Other Thomists like Gerald Phelan and Joseph Owens describe the intelligibility of being as a sameness-in-difference.⁵ Sameness-in-difference they also call an analogous intelligibility, or an analogon; instances that harbor that analogon they call analogates.⁶ For my purpose I note that in keeping the differences of all things to itself, the notion of being as an analogon has an unparalleled richness. This richness will make understandable the denomination of being as the good.⁷

    5. Gerald B. Phelan, "St. Thomas and Analogy," in *G. B. Phelan: Selected Papers*, edited by Arthur G. Kirn (Toronto: Pontifical Institute of Mediaeval Studies, 1967), 114. Joseph Owens, "Analogy as a Thomistic Approach to Being," *Mediaeval Studies* 24 (1962): 308–9; also Joseph Owens, *An Elementary Christian Metaphysics* (Houston: Center for Thomistic Studies, 1985), 88, n. 14. Note that these Thomists describe the notion of being as a sameness in difference. This description does not say that sameness *is* the difference or that the difference *is* the sameness. To utter either of these would be to utter obvious contradictions. Rather, the Thomists claim that sameness was *in* the difference and that the difference was *in* the sameness. Neither of these claims is obviously a contradiction.

    6. On the terminology of analogon and analogate, see George P. Klubertanz, *St. Thomas on Analogy* (Chicago: Loyola University Press, 1960), 6–7.

    7. Brian Davies's discussion of goodness seems to lack this analogical character. In *The Reality of God and the Problem of Evil* (London: Continuum, 2006), 146, Davies explains that goodness simply means that something has succeeded in the way appropriate to it. In this interpretation the notion of goodness seems generic. One could say that animal, a generic notion, means that something has sensitivity in the way appropriate to it. Hence, it is difficult to see any intrinsic richness to goodness. In fact, Davies insists that there is not a "big picture" of goodness. His account of good "will not add up to a coherent description of anything. I take strawberries to be good in so far as they are sweet and juicy. I take parents to be good in so far as they look after their children .... I take good holiday places to have decent hotels .... But now imagine me saying that X is sweet, juicy, looks after its children..., has decent hotels .... You could make no sense of this." Ibid., 144–45. From my perspective on analogy, I take Davies's observation simply to reiterate my point that if an analogon is to be realized, then it will be realized within a difference. But this acknowledgement does not mean that we have to vacate the analogon to avoid absurdity. In fact we must not and cannot do it. Consider how we form any common meaning. We somehow get rid of the differences of the instances. One way of getting rid of the differences is by vacating them from the common meaning. But with the common meaning of goodness, the differences cannot shake off the commonality. They always bring along the sameness. For example, strawberry Y does not have to be sweet and juicy; but if Y is, then Y is a good strawberry like X. In comparison, if the difference of a right angle in triangle A is given to figure B, it is not necessary that B be a triangle. So, what do we do with the differences of goodness in order to form a commonality? The only remaining alternative is that we compress the differences within the commonality in order for the commonality to appear. But this situation admits that the commonality is a concrescence of perfection. The background is richer than the foreground.

So, Aquinas provides answers to the previous questions about the final causality of the *ratio boni* as a *ratio*. Not in every case does the intellect apprehend a commonality at the price of vacating the commonality of the differences of individual instances. Some commonalities are so meshed with the differences that the differences cannot be removed without taking the commonality with them. This conversion phenomenon leaves analogical commonalities with a density of perfection that can exert a fascination on the intellector. Hence, humans have some idea of what the Scholastics called the absolutely infinite in contrast to the relatively infinite. The relatively infinite lacks nothing in a particular line. For example, a ribbon without ends is an infinite amount in the line of ribbon. Yet it is still ribbon and as such lacking in many perfections. The absolutely infinite lacks no perfection, even no conceivable perfection and no degree thereof. The classical theist tradition has long used the absolutely infinite to characterize God. Hence, we have Anselm's that-than-which-no-greater-can-be-thought, the rationalists' actually infinite being, Kant's discussion of the *ens realissimum*, and Vatican I's one, true, living God infinite in intellect and will, and in every perfection. Charles Hartshorne, a Whiteheadian philosopher, has criticized the understanding of God as absolutely infinite on the ground that some perfections are mutually exclusive. For example, something cannot have at the same time the perfections of being both red and green all over. But before this linking of the infinite with God, Aquinas linked the infinite with the notion of being. As Aquinas says, being is that into which we resolve all of our concepts and being is added to not by bringing in something from the outside but by "expressing" a mode of being. In the notion of being, the intellect discerns an intelligible source from which stream all perfections. Hartshorne's objection applies to the perfections as expressed. He is surprisingly incognizant of the intelligible ground from whose depths the perfections arise.

BEING AND PHILOSOPHICAL PSYCHOLOGY

As mentioned, it makes sense to call being the good because of its intelligible richness. Aquinas says that if we can call some individual thing good because it has certain perfections, then we can call being *the* good because it has all conceivable perfections.[8] From linking being with the good Aquinas deduces many things, three of which follow. The first is the already mentioned volition consequent upon the intellect's presentation of the *ratio boni* to the will. There is no moral necessity here because there is no freedom. The will acts automatically. According to Aquinas, the will automatically desires its proper object. At I, 82, 1c, Aquinas insists that natural necessity (*necessitas naturalis*) is not repugnant to the will. For just as the intellect of necessity adheres to first principles, so too the will necessarily adheres to the last end, which is happiness (*ultimo fini, qui est beatitudo*). But here "happiness" is the *ratio boni*, for elsewhere the last end is the object of the will (*rationem finis, est obiectum voluntatis*), and the object of the will is the *ratio boni* (*ratio boni, quod est obiectum potentiae*, I-II, 8, 2c). Aquinas reiterates the point by saying that the will "tends naturally" (*naturaliter tendit*, I-II, 10, 1) to the *bonum in communi* which is its object and last end, just as the intellect knows naturally the first principles of demonstration. That the *ratio entis* understood as the *ratio boni* engenders willing is also expressed in this Thomistic argument for will in God:

From the fact that God is endowed with intellect it follows that He is endowed with will. For, since the understood good is the proper object of the will, the understood good is, as such, willed. Now that which is understood is by reference to one who understands. Hence, he who grasps the good by his intellect is, as such, endowed with will. But God grasps the good by His intellect. For, since the activity of His intellect is perfect, as appears from

---

8. "But everything is perfect so far as it is actual. Therefore it is clear that a thing is perfect in so far as it is a being." *ST* I, 5, 1c.

what has been said, he understands being together with the qualification of the good [*ens simul cum ratione boni*]. He is, therefore endowed with will.⁹

No empty or merely formal sense of the *ratio boni* could play these roles of igniting volition. Rather, it is the *ratio entis* that is playing the role of the *ratio boni*. At this moment, the will acts automatically and necessarily. According to Aquinas, the will automatically desires its proper object and this object is being, understood as the good. Being cannot but provoke a reaction in those that apprehend it. It spontaneously establishes a positive relation, an approval, within minds that apprehend it. If various analogates of the analogon of being have a transfixing power, then so too does the analogon.

The second implication of linking being with the good is the indeterminate disposing of the will before any individual thing that is only "a" good, not the good itself.

So good is the object of the will. Therefore if the will be offered an object which is good universally and from every point of view, the will tends to it of necessity, if it wills anything at all; since it cannot will the opposite. If, on the other hand, the will is offered an object that is not good from every point of view, it will not tend to it of necessity. And since the lack of any good whatever is a nongood, consequently, that good alone which is perfect and lacking in nothing is such a good that the will cannot not-will it: and this is happiness. But any other particular goods, insofar as they are lacking in some good, can be regarded as nongoods; and, from this point of view, they can be set aside or approved by the will, which can tend to one and the same thing from various points of view.¹⁰

Aquinas is not worried that this freedom, that is, the will's ability to set aside or approve, is an illusion or simply apparent. Rather, Aquinas knows that the will's indetermination is real and not illusory because Aquinas has built it up from the *ratio entis*, whose ob-

---

9. *C.G.* I, 72, *Ex hoc*; Thomas Aquinas, *Summa contra Gentiles*, vol. I, translated by Anton C. Pegis (Notre Dame, Ind.: University of Notre Dame Press, 1975), 239–40.

10. *ST* I-II, 10, 2c;, Anton C. Pegis, ed., *The Basic Writings of St. Thomas Aquinas*, vol. II (New York: Random House, 1945), 262.

jectivity is assured by its abstraction from the real beings perceived through the senses. Aquinas's direct realist epistemology regarding sensation has a crucial and basic role to play here.

The third implication is moral necessity, or oughtness. At *ST* I-II, 94, 2, Aquinas speaks of the first principle of practical reason: the good ought to be done and evil avoided. By "the good" the text means the *ratio boni*. Also, the first practical principle is self-evident, or *per se notum*. Aquinas describes what is predicated in such propositions as the meaning of the subject: *praedicatum est de ratione subiecti*. How are we to properly configure being as the good so that precisely moral obligation, not necessary volition or raw freedom, follows? My resolution of the issue is the realization that Aquinas is not speaking of being as the good pure and simple, but of being as the good when present in the human through the human's intellection of being.[11] Among all the instances of being as the good, the human, through intellection, has the good in an especially intense manner. Before such an instance we are free undoubtedly, but we are also morally constrained. In the human, the *ratio boni* burns more brightly than it does in other instances such as animals, plants, and minerals. Because of that truth, do not humans deserve a respect and a solicitude? In sum, the subject of the first practical principle should not be understood simply as the good but as the good intellected by the human.

A text from the *Summa contra Gentiles* provides confirmation for my process of elimination interpretation of the nature of the subject in the first practical principle. At Book III, chapter 112, Aquinas is discussing God's providence over rational creatures. Aquinas wants to make the point that in his governance, God provides for rational creatures for their own sake and not for the sake of something else. Providence for the sake of something else characterizes God's governance of plants and animals. Plants are for the sake of animals, and animals are for the sake of humans.

---

11. See John F. X. Knasas, *Being and Some Twentieth-Century Thomists* (New York: Fordham University Press, 2003), 261–72.

In chapter 112 Aquinas offers many arguments for God's governing humans for their own sake. One argument is striking for the connection made between a metaphysical understanding of the human and obligation.

> Furthermore, it is evident that all parts are ordered to the perfection of the whole, since a whole does not exist for the sake of its parts, but, rather, the parts are for the whole. Now, intellectual natures have a closer relationship to a whole than do other natures; indeed, each intellectual substance is, in a way, all things. For it may comprehend the entirety of being [*totius entis comprehensiva*] through its intellect; on the other hand, every other substance has only a particular share in being. Therefore, other substances may fittingly be providentially cared for by God for the sake of intellectual substances.[12]

Aquinas starts by noting that parts are for the sake of their wholes. But an intellectual substance is more like a whole than a part thereof, because the intellectual substance knows the whole of being (*totius entis*). Hence, in his governance, God provides for the sake of intellectors themselves. Notice Aquinas's deduction of obligation from a very metaphysical basis. God must or should treat the intellector in a particular way. In this case the reason for the obligation is the understanding of the intellectual substance as an intellector of being. But the intellector-of-being conception is closely related to the intellector-of-the-good conception because being is not just any whole, or entirety, but the entirety of perfection. Hence, it is not surprising that even a creaturely intellector of being would command respect. So *C.G.* III, 112, in my opinion, catches Aquinas doing what I claimed necessary to understand the subject of the first practical principle so that the subject contains the predicate of oughtness.

Aquinas's philosophical explanation of the initial phenomenon of obligation stands in opposition to David Hume's famous

---

12. *C.G.* III, 112, *Praeterea*; Thomas Aquinas, *Summa contra Gentiles*, III, 1, translated by Vernon J. Bourke (Notre Dame, Ind.: University of Notre Dame Press, 1975), 116–17.

distinction between fact and value. The eighteenth century British philosophical skeptic David Hume claimed: "Take an action allowed to be vicious: willful murder, for instance. Examine it in all lights, and see if you can find that matter of fact, or real existence, which you call vice. In which ever way you take it, you find only certain passions, motives, volitions and thoughts. There is no other matter of fact in the case."[13] In short, calling an act "evil" denotes nothing in the act, nothing objective. "Evil" denotes something in us, something subjective, viz., our emotion of revulsion. Of course, for Aquinas another matter of fact exists in the act of murder. The victim is an intellector of being as the good. In light of that fact, the moral viciousness of killing is patent in the act itself. In striking at the person, the murderer is striking at the good.

So the first rule of a moral life is to be respectful and solicitous of the human person. The moral life is a life of love. The human person is the lighthouse from which shines the good and to which we should direct our moral vessel. For example, the immorality of murder, theft, and lying is patent. In striking at the person, each of these actions strikes in an unseemly way at the good. Also, our awareness of ourselves as intellectors of being creates the injunction to do what respects our existence and to avoid what disrespects it, for example, abuse and suicide. Moreover, by its essentially unitive and procreative character the sexual embrace is unique among human activities. In one's sexual partner and also in the procreative teleology of the sexual embrace, one is handling the good and so sexual activity ought to be exercised in the context of committed monogamous relation, that is, of marriage. The fornicator and the adulterer unseemly discard that *ratio boni* given in the sexual embrace. The evil of contraception is likewise evident. By striking at the procreative powers contraception strikes unseemly at the *ratio boni* present in the person but also in

---

13. David Hume, *A Treatise of Human Nature*, bk. III, 1: T. H. Green and T. H. Grose, eds., *David Hume: The Philosophical Works*, vol. 2 (Darmstadt: Scientia Verlag Aalen, 1964), 245.

the offspring who is at least essentially, if not actually, present.[14] Great lovers take this norm of respect and solicitude of the human person with deep seriousness. Their most important thing is other people, or life in society. Nothing should be substituted for people and their well-being, not hobbies, studies, pleasure, money, fame, or the like. Pursuit of these things must always defer to the needs of persons.

Aquinas's conception of the human as an intellector of being also makes understandable the self-sacrifice involved in friendship. Following Aristotle, Aquinas roots friendship in self-love.[15] Self-love is not an egoistic predicament. What I find loveable in

---

14. Presence can be of two kinds, essential and actual. This distinction is illustrated handily enough in the case of the difference between a rock and a blind eye. Both do not see. Yet they are not equivalent. For at least in the blind eye as an eye, sight is essentially present. The rock does not have sight even essentially. Likewise, certain gestures just by themselves say something that may not in fact be the case. For example, an open extended hand is by its very nature a sign of friendship. It shows that no harm is intended. Contrast that gesture to an upraised fist. But the open extended hand may be offered by a conniving politician. So, friendship is essentially there in the handshake but not actually there. The conjugal embrace is another act that by itself says something. It is of its nature unitive. One is handling the other person, not just the other's body. Since the person is an intellector of being and being is the good, then the conjugal embrace in itself is a handling of the good. This fact of essence entails that the participants should not have sex in a casual and promiscuous fashion. Such behavior amounts to jettisoning the good itself. In short, the essentially unitive character of the act entails that it should also be actually unitive, i.e., marital. The conjugal embrace is also essentially procreative. Acknowledgement of the essential presence of procreation is behind the hesitancy to equate naturally infertile sex with unnatural forms of sexual activity. In the former case, procreation is at least essentially present, just as sight is in the blind eye, while in the latter cases procreation is both actually and essentially absent, just as sight is both actually and essentially absent from the rock. So, to deliberately take measures to render the conjugal embrace actually infertile is to strike at human life that is essentially present. Practitioners of natural family planning (NFP) never behave equivalently. Just as a near-sighted person should still try to see and is not acting against the essential presence of sight in his eye, so too practitioners of NFP are doing the best they can in the circumstances in which they find themselves. Just because one cannot act perfectly does not mean that one should not try to act at all. The naturally infertile couple at least realize procreation essentially if not actually.

15. See James McEvoy, "The Other as Oneself: Friendship and Love in the Thought of St. Thomas Aquinas," in *Thomas Aquinas: Approaches to Truth*, edited by James McEvoy and Michael Dunne (Dublin: Four Courts Press, 2002).

myself, viz., the notion of being, is found in others. Being offers itself to all intellectors. Hence, my fellow is another self. In this context, my loss should not be looked at simply as another's gain. To see the other as a friend is to see my loss for his sake as *our* gain. Love for self extended to others makes it possible to genuinely rejoice in their good fortune, even when that good fortune demands a sacrifice from us. Jealousy should have no place among people if they relate to each other as friends. And people should relate to others as friends if they view themselves as intellectors of being. The deep truth here is indicated by its contrary, rejection and its lacerating effect of isolation. Since being is so intensely present in our fellows, then their rejection of us can appear as being's rejection of us. And since being includes all, rejection can be experienced as total isolation. That is why though we may disagree, we should always remain friends.

AN ORDINARY KNOWLEDGE OF GOD AND METAPHYSICS

Later I will explain how this understanding of the dignity of the human person is compatible with Aquinas's treatment of evil, for example, at I, 48, 2. But presently what I want to emphasize is the "play" of being with respect to beings in the cases of freedom and obligation. Freedom with respect to beings results from the juxtaposition of beings with and against being. Obligation appears in human consciousness because of an intellectual integration of being with the human person. My point is that awareness of freedom and obligation depends upon a relation to the *ratio entis*, but for a full picture a further point ought to be noted. Though one may be conscious of freedom and some sense of obligation, one can be unaware of the intellection of being. In other words, like the human heart that functions automatically but with conscious effects, so too the intellect can automatically abstract the notion of being and grasp it as the good.

Aquinas's abstractionist epistemology explains how this can be. For example, in the *C.G.* III, 26, he explains that it is not strange that humans are motivated to act by sensual pleasures rather than intellectual ones because most humans lack intellectual experience. For this lack Aquinas appeals to his abstractionist epistemology. He says that external things are better known than intellectual things because human cognition begins from sensible things.[16] Later in the same work at IV, 52, he speaks of the "frailty of reason: *debilitas rationis*" and of the predominance of the phantasms. One would be wrong to interpret these remarks to mean that the workings of the intellect are totally absent or that these workings have no experienced effects. Even on the level of sensation, we know more than we are aware of. Sense has a focus that is narrower than its entire field. For example, my vision shows me a dozen objects, yet my awareness does not yet perceive that number. For Aquinas a similar relation can exist between sensation and intellection. Even though our attention is focused on sensible things, our intellection has gone on to grasp commonalities of which we are still unaware. How else does one explain that we abide by the noncontradiction principle, are inevitably dissatisfied by finite goods, and know that we are free with respect to anything in our experience? These phenomena show that the notion of being haunts the human mind. So much of Thomism involves making the implicit explicit, to borrow some language from transcendental Thomism.

What I now want to explain is how this same unconscious play of the *abstractum* of being can create confusion in our consciousness. Being can play tricks on its intellector. As just mentioned, not only can being hide itself in the process of revealing itself. Being can also become associated with things in such a way that these things become invested with a value out of all proportion to their true value. This point will go a long way to explain how one

---

16. "Nor do more persons seek the pleasure that is associated with knowing rather than the knowledge. Rather, there are more people who seek sensual pleasures than intellectual knowledge and its accompanying pleasure, because things that are external stand out as better known, since human knowledge starts from sensible objects." Aquinas, *Summa contra Gentiles*, vol. III, pt. 1, 109–10.

can be a victim to an exaggerated sense of human preciousness that makes the problem of evil intractable. In order to describe the genesis of this second trick, I want to comment on Aquinas's view about a general knowledge of God possessed by all.

Aquinas's distinction between what we know about ourselves versus what we realize about ourselves helps us to understand another primary precept mentioned by Aquinas at 94, 2: "Divine truth ought to be sought." Along with other primary precepts, Aquinas says that this one has universal truth and is *per se notum quoad nos*. But is it clear that God exists and, even if it is clear, is it clear that we ought to concern ourselves with knowing God? How does a primary precept about God arise in Aquinas's natural law?

Earlier in his *Contra Gentiles* III, 38, Aquinas describes an ordinary knowledge of God possessed by all mature human beings. Perhaps his description will answer my questions. This ordinary knowledge of God is *a posteriori* and appears to recount a primitive version of the teleological argument. It runs as follows:

> Man can immediately reach some sort of knowledge of God by natural reason. For, when men see that things in nature run according to a definite order, and that ordering does not occur without an orderer, they perceive in most cases that there is some orderer of the things that we see. But who or what kind of being, or whether there is but one orderer of nature, is not yet grasped immediately in this general consideration, ... Some people have believed that there is no other orderer of worldly things than the celestial bodies, and so they said that the celestial bodies are gods. Other people pushed it further, to the very elements and the things generated from them, thinking that motion and the natural functions which these elements have are not present in them as the effect of some other orderer, but that other things are ordered by them. Still other people, believing that human acts are not subject to any ordering, other than human, have said that men who order others are gods. And so, this knowledge of God is not enough for felicity.[17]

---

17. Ibid., 125–26.

Aquinas concedes that the argument has many shortcomings. For example, Aquinas notes that one does not yet grasp who or what is this orderer of if the orderer is one or many. On the strength of this argument, some identify the orderer with the heavenly bodies, the elements, or other human beings. But does not Aquinas's concession contradict his thesis that men know God? None of the characterizations of the orderer are remotely similar to the God of Aquinas's religious belief who is spiritual, unique, and nonhuman. Would it not have been clearer for Aquinas to say that men fail to attain a knowledge of God? In other words, when a physicist discovers a new particle, he does not exclaim "God." And if he did, we would think him strange. Hence, is not Aquinas odd to attribute man's knowledge of God to man's knowledge of the elements? In fact on another occasion, Aquinas is uncompromising, if not uncharacteristically harsh, in his dismissal of David of Dinant's identification of God with matter.[18]

Returning to the *Contra Gentiles*, it is important to realize that Aquinas does not say that men reach something "like" God. Aquinas's assertion is unqualified. Men reach God, even though they take what they reach and mistakenly identify it with nondivine instances. Consequently, when in the next chapter Aquinas introduces philosophical demonstrations to remove the errors of the mistaken identifications, Aquinas's philosophical procedure does not consist in moving on to a higher being than those mentioned. Rather, his procedure purifies, through removal of the errors, what the general reasoning had reached.[19] So, before this text on

---

18. "The third error is that of David of Dinant, who most stupidly taught that God was primary matter." *ST* I, 3, 8c; Pegis, *Basic Writings of Thomas Aquinas*, vol. I, 35.

19. "On the other hand, there is another sort of knowledge of God, higher than the foregoing, and we may acquire it through demonstration. A closer approach to a proper knowledge of Him is effected through this kind, for many things are set apart from Him, through demonstration, whose removal enables Him to be understood in distinction from other beings. In fact, demonstrations shows that God is immutable, eternal, incorporeal, altogether simple, one, and other such things which we have shown about God in Book One." Aquinas, *Summa contra Gentiles*, vol. III, Part 1, 127. For a description of "removal"

an ordinary knowledge of God can be used to support a universal knowledge of the primary precept obliging us to know divine truth, some explanation of how the conclusion of the reasoning can be so wrong and still be right is required. Here a return to Aquinas's abstractionist epistemology can be helpful.

According to Aquinas, the errors in man's ordinary knowledge of God are set aside by demonstration. The backward reference is important. Early in book one Aquinas reserves these points of demonstration in order to include them in the last part of philosophy to be learned, viz., metaphysics.[20] This assignment by Aquinas should mean that the ordinary knowledge of God is in some way metaphysical. Only as metaphysical could ordinary knowledge successfully reach God, albeit imperfectly, as Aquinas claims. But can one possibly regard ordinary individuals to be in possession of Aquinas's metaphysics?[21]

METAPHYSICS AS IMPLICIT KNOWLEDGE

The keynote in Aquinas's metaphysics is his understanding of the existence of a particluar thing. Unlike our common usage, in Aquinas's metaphysics "the existence of the thing" does not mean simply the fact of the thing. Aquinas regards existence as a distinct principle or act composed with the individual substance to render

---

as the negating capacity of the mind's second operation and how it is wielded to chisel out a confused knowledge of the divine quiddity, see my *Being and Some Twentieth-Century Thomists*, 236–44.

20. "In order to know the things that the reason can investigate concerning God, a knowledge of many things must already be possessed. For almost all of philosophy is directed towards the knowledge of God, and that is why metaphysics which deals with divine things, is the last part of philosophy to be learned." C.G. I, 4; Aquinas, *Summa contra Gentiles*, I, 67. In the chapter just previous naturally knowable truth about God includes the knowledge of his existence: "But there are some truths which the natural reason also is able to reach. Such that God exists, that He is one, and the like." Aquinas, *Summa contra Gentiles*, I, 63.

21. For the Thomistic texts behind the many points in my summary description of Aquinas's metaphysics, see Knasas, *Being and Some Twentieth-Century Thomists*, chapters 6 and 7.

the substance a being (*ens*), an existent. In fact at *C.G.* II, 54, the thing's existence is sufficiently distinct to allow comparison of its composition with a substance, with form's composition with matter within the substance. Aquinas employs the phrase "*actus essendi*," the act of being, and the Latin infinitive "*esse*" as a noun, or substantive, to express his unique act-sense of the thing's existence. It is not so much that Aquinas disagrees with the fact-sense of the thing's existence, but rather that Aquinas insists that the fact-sense be deepened to include the act in virtue of which the thing is a fact. A thing is a fact in virtue of its *actus essendi*. A being or an existent *qua* a being or an existent is a *habens esse*, a possessor of the act of being.

The relation of this act to the substance with which it is composed also bears mention. In respect to the substance rendered a being by composition with *esse*, *esse* is prior (*prius*), first (*primus*), most profound (*profundius*), and most intimate (*magis intimum*). *Esse* is the core around which the thing revolves. We are so accustomed to conceiving acts of a thing as items subsequent and posterior to the thing that the notion of an act basic and fundamental to its thing is strange. But if one is to correctly appreciate *esse*, usual ways of thinking must be suspended.

As an act *esse* is an *ipso facto* dependent item. No act as an act, even the *sui generis* act that is *esse*, is found by itself. Rather, an act is found as in and of a subject. However, there is no way to explain *esse* completely by the substance that is its subject. Substances that are complete explainers of an act are in some respect already in act. As a potency for its existential act, substance cannot position itself to completely explain its *esse*. The need for complete explanation in the case of *esse* drives the mind to conclude to a further being in which *esse* is not found as an act but as the very substance that is the further cause. Aquinas calls this further cause *esse subsistens* (subsistent existence), *esse tantum* (existence alone) and *esse purum* (pure existence). He also refers to it as *Deus* (God). Aquinas's stated reason is God's revelation to Moses in the book of Exodus that God's name is *Ego sum qui sum*: I am who am.[22] As subsistent *esse*, the first cause of *esse* embodies the key component in Aquinas's understanding of the notion of being, the *ratio entis*. Since the *ratio entis* is also the *ratio boni*, then the first cause is the preeminent epiphany of the good among all such epiphanies.

If the human commands respect and solicitude because the human as an intellector of being is an epiphany of the good, then *a fortiori* the first cause does likewise. In the light of Aquinas's metaphysics, to orient our moral compass to the divine instance is an obvious *per se notum* truth. This analysis also illustrates a

22. "This sublime truth Moses was taught by our Lord. When Moses asked our Lord: 'If the children of Israel say to me: what is His name? What shall I say to them?' The Lord replies: '*I am who am* .... Thou shalt say to the children of Israel: *He who is* hath sent me to you.' (Ex 3:13, 14). By this our Lord showed that His own proper name is He who is. Now, names have been devised to signify the natures or essences of things. It remains, then, that the divine being is God's essence or nature." *C.G.* I, 22, no. 10: Aquinas, *Summa contra Gentiles*, vol. I, 121. At this point one could bring up an objection mentioned by Anthony Kenny in his critique of Aquinas's *Prima Via* from motion in *C.G.* I, 13. In his *The Five Ways: St. Thomas Aquinas's Proofs of God's Existence* (New York: Schocken Books, 1969), 21–22, Kenny questions the ability of causal reasoning to determine the identity of the cause. His basis is that there is often a disjuncture between the nature of the effect and the nature of the cause. For example, though sometimes what is in the effect corresponds to what is in the cause, e.g., heat in the water corresponds to heat in the fire, that is not always the case, e.g., heat in the hands does not correspond to the rubbing of the hands. So it could be asked how Aquinas can be sure that *esse* is caused by *esse*. In reply, Kenny's observation causes a problem only where something can be the incidental effect of a proper line of causality. To stay with the hands, in the proper line of causality the effect is the locomotion of the hands and the cause is the stationary shoulders. Heat is thrown off as an incidental effect of this line of causality. But we have good reason to know that *esse* in things is not an incidental effect of some other line of causality. As there is only the existence neutral apart from *esse*, there can be no other line of causality. Hence, Aquinas's attempt to explain the attributive *esse* by more *esse*, but in a subsistent configuration, is not a wild-goose chase. One can answer likewise to the question of how God as spiritual can produce a material world. In Aquinas's metaphysics where the divine spirituality is subsistent *esse*, the spiritual can cause the material by causing the *esse* that actuates the material. Finally, Aquinas's claim of a likeness between cause and effect does not apply to death, as William Rowe suggests in his *The Cosmological Argument* (Princeton: Princeton University Press, 1975), 15. As will be explained in chapters 3 and 4, both natural and unnatural corruption is a "*per accidens*" effect of good in either one of two senses of "*per accidens*."

profound opening in human subjectivity for the life of grace and its culmination in beatitude.

But again, is it plausible to regard Aquinas's metaphysics as a natural and automatic achievement that exists below the level of conscious articulation so that most will have a knowledge of God, imperfect as it is? The answer depends upon our access to the data which contain Aquinas's key metaphysical notions. The setting up of things in various multiplicities is the standard procedure for the discernment of the thing's acts.[23] For example, because I find water both hot and cold, I come to discern the various temperatures as acts of the water that in itself is temperature neutral. Moreover, I come to understand each of the instances as a composition of the water plus some temperature. Likewise, because I can find Tom both pale and ruddy, I come to discern the complexions as acts of Tom who in himself is complexion neutral. But for Aquinas things are found not only in temperature and complexion multiplicities but also in existential multiplicities. Aquinas is an immediate realist in his understanding of sensation. Sensation provides not an image, a representation, a picture of the real thing but the real thing itself. Consequently, the hot water and the pale Tom do not just really exist, they also cognitionally exist in my sensation. The presentation of some thing in an existential multiplicity should drive the mind to understand the thing to be in itself existence neutral,[24] and to understand each instance as a composition of

23. The following is a nontechnical paraphrase of Aquinas's approach to the *actus essendi* of a thing by the twofold operation of the intellect, viz., conceptualization and judgment. For the twofold operation of the intellect presentation, see Knasas, *Being and Some Twentieth-Century Thomists*, 182–96. For a defense of *esse rei* as a distinct *actus* of its own and not second-order talk for something else in first-order, see ibid., 202–7; also my "Haldane's Analytic Thomism and Aquinas's *Actus Essendi*," in *Analytical Thomism: Traditions in Dialogue*, edited by Craig Paterson and Matthew S. Pugh (Burlington, Vt.: Ashgate Publishing Company, 2006), 233–52.

24. The "existence neutral" is my terminology for Aquinas's *De Ente et Essentia*, ch. 3, claim that the object of absolute consideration (*absoluta consideratio*) abstracts from every existence: "*abstrahit a quolibet esse.*" Again, see my *Being and Some Twentieth-Century Thomists*, 192–95. Joseph Owens summarizes the *De Ente* reasoning this way: "In the text

the said thing plus a real or cognitional existence in the sense of an act.

The answer to the above question reduces to an answer to this question. Is the existential multiplicity mentioned here available to the ordinary person? Certainly. No ordinary person doubts a real world in his sensation. No ordinary person questions the distinction between remembering his beloved in a memory versus being in the beloved's presence when in her arms. Even though modern philosophy has run away from the immediate presence of the real in sensation, ordinary people continue to live according to that marvelous truth. Furthermore, ordinary people have sufficient presence of mind that none lacks an awareness of their own sensation. Hence, they not only know real things, they know that they know real things. In other words, ordinary people not only sense real things, they also are aware that they sense real things. In short, there is every reason to think that the intellect not only discerns the notion of being, as I have claimed above, but that it also apprehends the notion of being in the sense of *habens esse*. The data is sufficiently available for the intellect to be led to the metaphysical distinction between a thing and its *esse*, even if our awareness is elsewhere.

But upon a grasp of the composition, cannot the intellect go on to grasp the conclusion that the *esse* is caused? One conscious outcrop of this activity is Leibniz's question of why there is something rather than nothing. As Heidegger points out at the very start of his *An Introduction to Metaphysics*, the question steals upon us in moments of despair, rejoicing, and boredom. Looked at Thomistically, Heidegger's remark makes sense. Common to these moods

---

the Avicennian position that nature as such is existent in neither sensible things nor the mind is followed closely enough, but the conclusion is drawn that the nature absolutely considered abstracts from any being whatsoever—*a quolibet esse*. No room seems left for a proper being of essence as such. This is quite in accord with St. Thomas's doctrine elsewhere, which regards every aspect of being as coming to the essence from without, and none whatsoever as belonging to it just in itself." "Common Nature: A Point of Comparison Between Thomistic and Scotistic Metaphysics," *Mediaeval Studies* 19 (1957), 6.

is the shutting down of our plans and designs so that we are left simply in the presence of things. But that hovering of things in our awareness bespeaks, as explained, an instability in existents that prompts Leibniz's question. Aquinas's metaphysics is as near as the sense realism of ordinary experience.

But if the metaphysics of *esse* is implicit, why are people so erroneous in their thinking about God? Answering this question goes a long way to grasping how the notion of being can play its mentioned second trick. Consider Aquinas's listing of identities for the orderers in this ordinary knowledge of God. All of these orderers are intensely related to the notion of being. I have spoken about the relation of the person to the notion of being. But even the contemplation of the heavens could impress the notion of being upon us. Because of their gargantuan dimensions, the notion of being would allow us to profile the heavens in our mind. But such an intense presence of the notion of being might lead one to confuse the heavens with the cause of being. As mentioned, the notion of being harbors causal implications. Causality goes with the notion of being. In an ordinary person these implications may not be sufficiently distinguished from the instance whose objectification can easily enlist the notion of being.

But if the physically great easily enlists the notion of being, so too does the physically small. Hence, at *C.G.* III, 38, Aquinas also mentions the identification of the divine with the elements. To contemplate the physically small, everything else must be removed from our awareness. That removal leaves the physically small alone with the notion of being. The heightened presence of being in the contemplation of minutiae could lead one to confuse the causal implications with the minutiae themselves.

In sum, God can be confused with both the great and the small because the presence of the notion of being, in which there are causal implications, can be employed for the contemplation of both the great and the small. It is no surprise that vacationers basically divide into those who like the mountains and those who like

Joy   41

the shore. One looks at the expanse of the sky, the other at vessels on the vast ocean. As the Thomist considers both observers, the Thomist believes that the genuine object of the contemplation is being and that their relaxation is some approximation of the happiness that would be achieved in knowing being itself.

BEING AND THE INTELLECTUAL EMOTIONS

As noted above when explaining the awareness of obligation, the human through intellection possesses an especially intense relation to being. That is an accurate observation. But now I want to speak of another relation to being that the human can suffer. This relation to being is like the relation to being undergone by entities either large or small. In the latter cases the relation to being is not quite accurate. Because of certain features of the data, we inappropriately aggrandize the importance of the relation of the data to being. If one does not realize what is going on, then the data can take on all the value of being itself. For example, consider the spontaneous reaction of adults to a young child or baby. Both the child and the baby are "so precious." Just as the consideration of minutiae entails vacating everything else from consciousness, so that the minutiae stand alone with being, so too does the fragility and helplessness of the child and baby vacate everything else from consciousness. Their perceived vulnerability is a reaction to their isolation. Unlike an adult, they have not yet effected relations that establish them in existence. But even though as yet they are isolated from everything else, they are not isolated from being. In fact, the association with being is intensified the greater the dissociation from other things. Here the experience of children as precious has everything to do with their association to being.

The above analysis illustrates that some of the most striking perceptions of human preciousness do not always derive from the correct source. The unwitting psychic association of the child or infant up and against being seems sufficient to generate in every day experience a modicum of respect for these small humans. In fact, for many it is a more persistent source of human dignity than Kantian reflections on the autonomy of the will and even Christian revelation on the direct relation of the person to God. This psychology may also be intermittently operative in Maritain's mind so that the vacillation in his philosophical estimate of the human as whole and as part is traced to its true source. Nevertheless, the "wildness" of this psychology, that is, its applicability to any thing, belies it as truly locating the basis of human dignity. That true source of dignity for all humans, Thomistically speaking, is the intimate relation of the rational soul to the *ratio entis*.

As just admitted, one can multiply phenomena of deep joy and sadness brought about through a psychic association with being. I have already mentioned Camus's list of the ordinary things in which the tired populace takes joy after the plague. Consider also the experience of viewing old photographs. Even if the subjects bear no relation to the viewer and even if the subjects are ordinary, at certain moments the pictures can take on a poignancy. Out of all possible moments we, the viewers, are involved in that moment. Just as the contemplation of physical minutiae enlists the aid of being, so too does the contemplation of temporal minutiae. Moreover, because we know that we are looking at a moment in the past, then the poignancy includes a note of sadness. Why? By its association with what is past, being suffers an eclipse. This psychology of an association with the *abstractum* of being, in my opinion, is the explanation of an experience related to me by a grade school friend. The friend would contemplate himself standing at the opposite side of the school yard and then enjoy making it real by walking to that side. What was the fun in this apparently trite exercise? I think that the exercise drew its joy from the fact that out of all possibilities, my friend was picking out that one. In his mind his choices left the one possibility alone with being, and so allowed it to draw some of the preciousness of being.

The point I wish to make is that knowing the correct relation of being to a thing is crucial for understanding the reactions of our will and ultimately for understanding Aquinas's thoughts on evil. Is the thing a true epiphany of being as is the human intellector, the creator, spousal union, and society (and still distinctions are necessary here), or is the thing merely cognitively associated with being? In other words, with an epiphany of being, the nature of the thing involves being. There is an intrinsic intensity of the *ratio entis*. On the other hand, the thing's relation to being can be more superficial. Certain accidents like physical or temporal size can prompt us to use the notion of being in our consciousness of the thing. I will argue that knowing when the latter is taking place is crucial for understanding many of Aquinas's remarks on why evil exists. For the merely associative play of being always leads to an inaccurate estimate of things. It always invests things with a worth out of all proportion to the truth. As noted, since the association of a thing with being introduces the causal considerations of being, then the thing can take on a divine appearance. A thing's preciousness can become so exaggerated that nothing will console us at its loss. Hence, Aquinas will argue that happiness is not to be found in the motions of the will. Joy and delight are not to be trusted. Aquinas explains, "Now, in their relation to the will act, true happiness does not differ from false happiness. In fact, the will, when it desires, loves or enjoys, is related in just the same way to its object, whatever it may be that is presented to it as a highest good, whether truly or falsely. Of course, whether the object so presented is truly the highest good, or is false, this distinction is made on the part of the intellect."[25] The intellect's discerning work consists in differentiating an epiphany of being from a mere, albeit intense, association with being. This effect is what Aquinas's explanations of evil achieve. We are not left prey to our psychology. Such are, I believe, the quandaries of sorrow, joy, and anger suffered by Rachel, Rieux, and the father. Rachel's sorrow cannot be consoled because a whole, what she thinks is a universe, has suffered an

---

25. C.G. III, 26; Aquinas, *Summa contra Gentiles*, vol. III, 105.

eclipse. Despite the pestilence and the disavowal of God, Camus's joy in nature cannot be forsaken because of the play of being in the considerations of the discrete fragrant brushwood, the waves on the sea, and the expansive sky. Finally, Flew's anger cannot be abated because Flew cannot understand why God cannot share Flew's confusion of a part with the whole, the child with being.

3

Quandoque Evils

Aquinas's psychology means that, as philosophers, we must be on guard against unwarrantedly aggrandizing ourselves. If the philosopher is a Catholic, then through the Catholic faith the philosopher will know that the human is an adopted child of God. But the Catholic faith also tells the believing philosopher that this adoptive status is a supernaturally elevated status achieved through God's free offer of grace. Moreover, a Catholic theologian like Aquinas will explain why humans suffer, viz., *à la* Maritain, because of original sin and also will explain why even baptized humans continue to suffer, viz., to follow in the footsteps of Christ. But the question is whether the philosopher as a philosopher has decisive evidence for such an exalted view of the human. I will argue that the philosopher does not. The philosophical psychology of the human as an intellector of being, while decisive for dignity in a human ethics, does not mean that the human is a whole unto itself. The problem is the analogical nature of the intellection of being. As analogical the intellectual perception of being is a sameness-in-difference. That view of being means that in the human mind being does not seat itself perfectly. Hence, Aquinas will say at *C.G.* III, 112, that the intellector of being has "a closer relationship to a whole than do other natures," is "a principal part of a whole" and at *ST* I, 29, 3c, is "the most perfect in all nature." In other words, for all of its dignity as an intellector, the human, naturally speaking, is part of the natural whole. That truth will strike many, as it once did Maritain, as an "utter anomaly." But apart from religious revelation speaking more intimately about the creator's *de facto* designs for the human and apart from the play of being in cognitionally entertaining objects like the great or the small, it is unclear what basis remains for the protest of Maritain's Rachel. What a Thomistic philosopher could rejoin is that philosophy cannot know if this "principal part" understanding is the definitive word on the existence of evil. For as Aquinas points out at *ST* I, 12, 4, ad 3m, the intellection of being and the intellection of its core constituent, the *ratio essendi*, establish in human nature at least the remote disposition to supernatural elevation. In other words, what theologians call the beatific vision is a philosophically grasped possibility. What the philosopher cannot determine is whether the creator deems to actualize this possibility.

AQUINAS'S RATIONALE FOR THE CORRUPTIBLE ORDER

In this chapter I want to begin a presentation of a Thomistic philosophical answer to the question of why humans suffer. I will return to Maritian's embarrassing Thomistic text, *ST* I, 48, 2. Perhaps somewhat sobered in the estimate of the human, one can better appreciate its reasoning. Among the various points established will be a rare distinction among evils. For instance, when Aquinas mentions evil as an objection to God's existence, as he does in an objection preparatory to listing his famous "Five Ways to God" at *ST* I, 2, 3, surprisingly it is not every and any evil that Aquinas has in mind but only those evils "permitted" by God for some good and that happen "sometimes." These evils are unnatural corruptions in which the lower acts against the higher, for example, an earthquake or a hurricane destroying a city, a lion or a shark mauling a human. Other corruptions are "natural" defects. Aquinas does not consider them an embarrassment to God. Rather, God wills, or intends, *per accidens*, these natural defects for some legitimate good. Death as such, for example, is not an utter anomaly for the human. For even understood as an intellector of being, the human remains a part of nature, although a principal part. In other words, implicit in Aquinas's evil texts is an ambiguous sense of "evil." This ambiguity is not the standard ambiguity of natural and moral evil.[1] Aquinas's ambiguity affects what the standard discussion of evil calls natural evil, viz., evils that humans can suffer not as a result of human agency—for example, earthquakes, hurricanes, pestilences. Aquinas divides natural evils into natural and unnatural corruptions. Natural corruptions are so natural that they constitute no theistic problem. It is not always clear which of these two are involved in any Thomistic text on evil. When a failure to appreciate that ambiguity is combined with the prompts cited above to regard the human as a whole, then a distorted view of Aquinas is produced.

Requoted, 48, 2c, reads as follows:

The perfection of the universe requires that there should be inequality in things, so that every grade of goodness may be realized. Now, one grade of goodness is that of the good which cannot fail. Another grade of goodness is that of the good which can fail in goodness. These grades of goodness are to be found in being itself [*in ipso esse*]; for there are some things which cannot lose their being [*suum esse*], as incorruptible things, while there are some which can lose it, as corruptible things. As, therefore, the perfection of the universe requires that there should be not only incorruptible beings, so the perfection of the universe requires that there should be some which can fail in goodness and which sometimes [*interdum*] do fail. Now it is in this that evil consists, in the fact that a thing fails in goodness. Hence it

---

1. Bruce Reichenbach, *Evil and a Good God* (New York: Fordham University Press, 1982), xi, distinguishes between moral and natural evils in terms of calamities brought about by responsible human agency or not. For Aquinas moral evil is more profound. It is sin, which is an interior act of will. Hence, moral evil can occur even if it is never actualized in the visible world.

is clear that evil is to be found in things in the way that corruption also is found; for corruption itself is an evil.[2]

It is important to understand the evils Aquinas is considering. Aquinas says that evil consists in a failure in goodness and that this failure happens occasionally (*interdum*) among corruptible things. While restating his case in the reply to the third objection, Aquinas uses "*quandoque*" interchangeably with "*interdum*." Hence, Aquinas is understanding "evils" as the occasional foul ups that can occur among corruptible things.[3] Elsewhere it is Aquinas's opinion that nature attains its ends for the most part or in the majority of cases. And so it does not appear that Aquinas is considering as evil the regular and persistent cycles of generation and corruption that occur in nature. Rather, he is speaking of tragedies like the lion killing or mauling the child or adult, the typhoons that obliterate cities, the pestilences that ravage populations. In sum, these are cases in which the lower acts against the higher. I will continue to refer to these evils as "*quandoque* evils."

To begin his explanation for *quandoque* evils, Aquinas says: "the perfection of the universe requires that there should be inequality in things, so that every grade of goodness be realized." For the connection between perfection and inequality, 48, 2c, references 47, 2c. There Aquinas explains that inequality of things goes along with a formal distinction between things. He says:

Now, formal distinction always requires inequality, because, as the Philosopher says, the forms of things are like numbers in which species vary by the addition or subtraction of unity. Hence in natural things species seem to be arranged in a hierarchy: as the mixed things are more perfect than the elements, and plants than minerals, and animals than plants, and men than other animals; and in each of these one species is more perfect than

---

2. Thomas Aquinas, *Summa Theologiae* I, 48, 2c; Anton C. Pegis, ed., *The Basic Writings of St. Thomas Aquinas*, vol. I (New York: Random House, 1945), 467.

3. That contingent things "can fail to happen, in a few cases" is used by Aquinas in his first argument at *C.G.* III, 74, to argue that divine providence includes chance events which "happen rarely."

others. Therefore, just as the divine wisdom is the cause of the distinction of things for the sake of the perfection of the universe, so is it the cause of inequality. For the universe would not be perfect if only one grade of goodness were found in things.[4]

God is the cause of inequality because he is the cause of different forms whose very differences involve inequality. So Aquinas observes that a horse is not just different from a man but it is also unequal because the man has the perfection of a horse, viz., life and sensation, but also reason. Likewise a horse is not just different from a mineral; the horse is also unequal because the horse not only exists but also lives and senses. These differences of inequalities mean that the forms of things are also unequal and so lend a basis for the comparison of form to number. Just as form cannot undergo the addition or subtraction of a perfection without a change of form, so too a number cannot undergo addition or subtraction without a change of the number.

So far then Aquinas has said that the inequality of things results from the formal distinction between things. Why is a formal distinction required for the perfection of the universe? 47, 1, answers this question.

Hence we must say that the distinction and multitude of things is from the intention of the first cause, who is God. For He brought things into being in order that His goodness might be communicated to creatures, and be represented by them. And because His goodness could not be adequately represented by one creature alone, He produced many and diverse creatures, so that what was wanting to one in the representation of the divine goodness might be supplied by another. For goodness, which in God is simple and uniform, in creatures is manifold and divided; and hence the whole universe together participates the divine goodness more perfectly, and represents it better, than any given single creature.[5]

Because no one creature can represent the divine goodness, which God intends in his creative activity, then creation takes the form of a

---

4. Pegis, *Basic Writings of Thomas Aquinas*, vol. I, 461.
5. Ibid., 459.

multitude of different creatures. Behind this reasoning is Aquinas's metaphysics in which *esse* as subsistent is infinite and unique, a one and only. This metaphysical truth requires that if *esse* is found anywhere else, then *esse* must be found in a nonsubsistent way, that is, with something else, and finitized by the thing it is with. Thus, any creature is necessarily a limited and finite being.

In sum, since no one creature can adequately manifest the divine perfection, creation takes the form of a multiplicity of things; but because multiplicity means inequality, the created multitude takes the further form of a gradation. Hearing Aquinas's reasoning so far, some may want to raise an objection of inconsistency. Since as Aquinas admitted, the higher creatures contain the perfection of the lower, then would it not suffice to represent the divine goodness by creating just the higher creatures? In other words, it seems that there is no metaphysical necessity to have the lower portions of creation. But a text exists in the *Summa* that enables us to understand the need for a plurality of both higher and lower creatures. The text is 76, 3, and it explains in more detail how the lower is contained by the higher.

> For this reason Aristotle compares the species of things to numbers, which differ in species by the addition or subtraction of unity. He also compares the various souls to the species of figures, one which contains another, as a pentagon contains and exceeds a tetragon. Thus the intellectual soul contains virtually whatever belongs to the sensitive soul of brute animals, and to the nutritive soul of plants. Therefore, just as a surface which is of a pentagonal shape is not tetragonal by one shape, and pentagonal by another—since a tetragonal shape would be superfluous, as being contained in the pentagonal—so neither is Socrates a man by one soul, and an animal by another; but by one and the same soul he is both animal and man.[6]

Here Aquinas is arguing for one soul in man. This is a classic Thomistic position compared to the Bonaventurian. But the comparison of forms to numbers connects the text to the earlier texts on natural corruption. In that respect 76, 3, contains an enlighten-

6. Ibid., 706.

ing remark that the higher form contains the lower just as a pentagon contains a tetragon. The pentagon contains the tetragon "virtually." What "virtual" means is best understood by thinking the example through. In a pentagon we have a tetragon but not actually until two angles are intersected by a line. So virtual containment seems to mean potential or implicit containment. Now this is important for understanding why a single higher creature would not *represent* the divine goodness just as well as a plurality of higher plus lower. The higher alone is inadequate representation of the lower because the higher contains the lower only virtually and so less strikingly. Note that the tetragon "pops out" only with the division of the pentagon. So even though in terms of perfection the higher contains the lower, in terms of *representing* the divine perfection, which is, as mentioned, God's point in creating, the higher alone lacks something.

Returning to 48, 2, Aquinas speaks about a gradation among creatures in respect to their *esse*. Once created, some creatures cannot lose their *esse*, others can. Since for Aquinas the most basic commonality is the *ratio entis* and, as mentioned, its basic description is *habens esse*, then the present gradation is the most basic within being (*ens*) itself. Moreover, God acts in light of himself, understood as subsistent *esse* which, as just noted, cannot be communicated except as a *sui generis actus* of a thing. Hence, Aquinas insists that for the perfection of a created ensemble, the gradation of corruptible and incorruptible beings must be present. So, any created universe must at least include these two grades. A caveat is important. Aquinas is not Leibniz. According to Leibniz, God is constrained to produce the best possible world. Such a world requires that there be no gaps between things arranged hierarchically. A gap would immediately bring up the idea of a better world in which that gap is occupied. Leibniz enshrined this conclusion of no gaps in the principle of continuity.[7] Despite Aquinas's talk of

---

7. "However, this hypothesis of leaps cannot be refuted except by the principle of order with the aid of the Supreme reason, which does everything in the most perfect way." Gott-

the created world requiring gradation, Aquinas cannot affirm Leibniz's principle. The source of Aquinas's disagreement goes back to his metaphysics. Because *esse* in a subsistent configuration is infinite and hence unique, then *esse* anywhere else will be *esse* in a nonsubsistent configuration. Nonsubsistent *esse* will mean *esse* with something else and finitized by it. Any ensemble of creatures will be an ensemble limited in perfection, and as so limited, it will have gaps allowing the thought of other and more perfect worlds.[8]

It does Leibniz no good to observe that since the effect must resemble its cause and the first cause is infinite, then the effect must reflect that infinity. In Aquinas's metaphysics a finite universe can reflect the divine infinity in two ways. The first way is in the finite's manner of coming to exist. As created, the finite comes from no material cause. Such a mode of coming to exist reflects the creator's infinite power.[9] Second, by its apprehension of the notion

---

fried Wilhelm Leibniz, Third Letter to DeVolder in *Gottfried Wilhelm Leibniz: Philosophical Papers and Letters*, vol. II, translated and edited by Leroy E. Loemker (Dordrecht, Holland: D. Reidel Publishing Company, 1976), 521.

8. *ST* I, 25, 6. Also see Charles Journet, *The Meaning of Evil*, translated by Michael Barry (New York: P. J. Kennedy & Sons, 1963), 109–18. David Ray Griffin, *God, Power, and Evil: A Process Theodicy* (Philadelphia: The Westminster Press, 1976), 90–94 agrees with Journet's Thomistic reasoning, but Griffin denies the conclusion's relevance for the evil problem. The metaphysical necessity for creation to be finite is not the necessity for creation to include natural and moral evils. Griffin cites Journet as admitting that God could have created a world without natural and moral evils. Though later I will disagree with Journet, here I will defend him. I believe that Griffin misses the following points. First, a created world without natural and moral evils is a world with supernatural gifts and so is a world God is not obliged to create. Second, Journet, p. 42, explicitly disagrees with the "Leibnizian" view that the finite is evil. Third, at *ST* I, 25, 6 (cited by Griffin), Aquinas himself understands "better" worlds in terms of humans more virtuous and wise. So the better world discussion is relevant for the evil problem. Fourth, though neither Journet, nor Aquinas, identifies the finite with evil, they connect it with evil. As my next section explains, the generable and corruptible order by its own nature must include evils ordinarily understood and mentioned by Griffin, for example, deformed babies, dogs with rabies, personages like Hitler. For Aquinas God is obliged to create what is a reflection of his goodness, and even worlds with evil do that. Reichenbach, *Evil and a Good God*, 128, sounds this Thomistic note when he concludes, "In speaking of God's creative activity, the theist need only affirm with the writer of Genesis that what God created was good."

9. "The power of the maker is reckoned not only from the substance of the thing made, but also from the mode of its being made; for a greater heat heats not only more, but also

of being, any created intellect reflects the infinity of the creator. Of course, since this apprehension is analogical, then it will admit of degrees according to the lesser or greater perfection of the difference in which the sameness of being is apprehended. Nevertheless, no created difference is so impoverished that it fails to acquaint the intellect with being. In sum, Aquinas's demand of grades seems to be a demand for very generic ones and does not extend to a demand for the subdivisions within the generic grades.

THE CORRUPTIBLE ORDER AND *QUANDOQUE* EVILS

Granting Aquinas's thinking so far, it still remains to explain how the gradation of corruptible to incorruptible entails *quandoque* evils. At 48, 2c, Aquinas simply asserts that the corruptible sometimes fails. A helpful start is to notice an example of an evil that happens *quandoque* and *interdum*. *De Ver.* 5 is one of Aquinas's discussions of divine providence and like all of his discussions of providence, *De Ver.* 5 includes remarks on evil. At *De Ver.* 5, 4, he discusses whether the motions of bodies are subject to providence. Aquinas begins his response by stating the familiar distinction of incorruptible and corruptible beings but extrapolates this distinction to mean that some things unfailingly keep their direction to their ultimate end while others sometimes (*quandoque*) diverge from their ultimate end. As an example of the latter, Aquinas cites the human generative powers whose action occasionally (*interdum*) results in natural monstrosities (*monstra*). This example of a *quandoque* evil is helpful because Aquinas has some explicit remarks about the occasions of monsters, and these provide a look at what lies behind all *quandoque* evils.

In his *De Malo* 1, 3c, Aquinas famously argues that the first cause of evil is something good. He says that this thesis appears easily in natural things (*in rebus naturalibus de facili apparet*).

---

more quickly. Therefore, although to create a finite effect does not reveal an infinite power, yet to create it from nothing does reveal an infinite power." *ST* I, 45, 5, ad 3m; Pegis, *Basic Writings of Thomas Aquinas*, vol. I, 441.

54   *Quandoque* Evils

[The fire] does not principally and *per se* intend the not to be of the water, but principally intends to induce the form of fire in the matter to which is joined from necessity the not to be of the water; and so it is *per accidens* that fire makes the water not to be. Of that evil which is the monstrosity of parts [*monstruositas partus*], the cause is the deficient power in the seed. But if the cause of this defect which is the evil of the seed is asked for, one will come to some good which is the cause of evil *per accidens*, and not insofar as it is deficient. For of this defect which is in the seed, the cause is some altering principle, which induces a contrary quality to the quality which is required for the good disposition of the seed. The power of the one altering is more perfect, and so it induces more that contrary quality, and consequently the defect of the seed follows. Whence the evil of the seed is not caused from good insofar as it is deficient but it is caused from the good insofar as it is perfect but *per accidens*.

Later in chapter 4, I will discuss an ambiguity in the meaning of "*per accidens*." But for now, Aquinas appears to say that processes, which attain their ends for the most part, are susceptible to ambush by other things good in themselves. This collision of opposed lines of causality, a collision that results in failures, is understandable to us who view the universe as a scattering of matter streaming from an initial explosion. But in Aquinas's cosmology the universe is a much more orderly affair that makes an explanation of *quandoque* evils imperative, especially for a universe created by a good God. Following Aristotle's natural philosophy, Aquinas placed a celestial source for terrestrial processes of generation. A nonunivocal cause is required for the full explanation of the various substantial forms found in matter. The need for this cause is brought out as follows. As determinations of matter, these forms are dependent. But they are not completely dependent either upon the matter or upon another individual of like species. They are not completely dependent upon the matter because as determined by the form, the matter is in potency to it. Material forms are not completely dependent upon another like individual, for example, the baby upon the parents, because as a supposedly complete explainer of the form in matter, that individual would also have to explain its own form and so cause itself—an absurdity. So the complete explanation of form in matter entails a reference to a universal cause that is unlike the individuals dealt with. Accordingly Aquinas says at *ST* I, 13, 5, ad 1m:

> In actions the non-univocal agent must precede the univocal agent. For the non-univocal agent is the universal cause of the whole species, as the sun is the cause of the generation of all men. But the univocal agent is not the universal efficient cause of the whole species (otherwise it would be the cause of itself, since it is contained in the species), but is a particular cause of this individual which it places under the species by way of participation. Therefore the universal cause of the whole species is not a univocal agent: and the universal cause comes before the particular cause.[10]

What is the universal cause? At *C.G.* III, 23, Aquinas mentions four possibilities. The universal cause could be a nonhylomorphic body like the celestial spheres, or an angel, or God himself, or all the

---

10. Pegis, *Basic Writings of Thomas Aquinas*, vol. I, 120. Also, *C.G.* II, 21. John Quinn, "The Third Way to God: A New Approach," *The Thomist* 42 (1978), argues for the current validity of the argument for a first physical cause despite an inability to empirically cash in the argument's conclusion: "The disintegration of its original concrete itequments, however, does not essentially affect the need for a universal physical cause. It may indeed savor of the genetic fallacy to insist that the philosophically viewed structures of equivocal causation be discarded along with now dead associated notions that it is only linked to by historical accident. The concept of a universal physical cause remains intact amid the fluctuations of experimental science, ... We cannot look to the specialized sciences, as Aquinas did, to pinpoint its residence, its specific nature, and its proper attributes," 66–67. But in this distinction between philosophical conclusion and its instantiation, Quinn appears to be following Aristotle. Aristotle identified the heavens with the immobile movers of the *Physics* only on the basis of past human observation of their regular cyclic motion: "The mere evidence of the senses is enough to convince us of this, at least with human certainty. For in the whole range of time past, so far as our inherited records reach, no change appears to have taken place either in the whole scheme of the outermost heaven or in any of its proper parts." Aristotle, *De Caelo* I, 3, 270b 11–16; Richard McKeon, ed., *The Basic Works of Aristotle* (New York: Random House, 1970), 403. Not surprisingly Aristotle can remark at *Topics* I, 11 104b 14–18; McKeon, *Aristotle*, 197: "Others also in regard to which we have no argument because they are so vast, and we find it difficult to give our reasons, e.g., the question whether the universe is eternal or no: for into questions of that kind too it is possible to inquire." Aquinas, at *ST* I, 46, 1, cites the *Topics* text not to assert a question about instantiation but to assert in Aristotle a doubt about the probity of the *Physics* VIII proof that there is no eternal world of creatures.

previous three. The fourth option is Aquinas's position. Terrestrial things generate other members of their species in virtue of the sun, but the sun moves by a celestial sphere moved by an angel moved by God. As can be seen, Aquinas has quite a robust understanding of nature.[11] What needs to be noticed is that as reached in natural philosophy as a necessary condition for generation, the nonunivocal heavenly causes are movers. As causes within the genre of movers, the heavens will cause only by presupposing something else for which they do not account. In other words, their causality goes out to meet something whose disposition is independent of their causality.[12] Such a mode of causality guarantees indispositions in the presupposed material that will impact adversely upon the causality of the higher cause. Despite the presence of a celestial first physical cause in Aquinas's cosmology, there still remains, given the motive framework, something like free radicals, that allow terrestrial events to be contingent, or able to fail, and sometimes with catastrophic results, for example, the late frost that wipes out the fruit blossoms.[13]

---

11. Unlike Bruce Reichenbach (who will be discussed in "Bruce Reichenbach: Developing Plantinga and Swinburne" in chapter 7), Aquinas does not view the natural world as discrete things operating by natural laws. Rather, as I noted in n. 10, natural bodies are contained within the causality of a larger thing and are susceptible to the larger thing's causal influences.

12. "Those dispositions that resist the force of the celestial bodies are caused in the original creation, not by a heavenly body, but by God's operation, which has made fire to be hot, water to be cold, and so forth. Consequently, we should not reduce all impediments of this kind to the celestial bodies." *De Ver.* 5, 9, ad 2m. Also, "But since it acts by moving, and since every agent of this kind requires a matter which is properly determined or disposed, then in the case of natural beings it can happen that the power of a celestial body fails to produce its effect because the matter is not disposed; and this will be accidental." *In VI Meta.*, lect. 3, no. 1211; John P. Rowan, trans., *Commentary on the Metaphysics of Aristotle* (Notre Dame, Ind.: Dumb Ox Books, 1995), 416.

13. "Indeed, the fact that plant bears fruit is a fact contingent on a proximate cause, which is the germinative power which can be impeded and can fail, even though the remote cause, the sun, be a cause acting from necessity. So, since there are many things among proximate causes that may be defective, not all effects subject to providence will be necessary, but a good many are contingent." *C.G.* III, 72. Thomas Aquinas, *Summa contra Gentiles*, vol. III, part 1, translated by Vernon J. Bourke (Notre Dame, Ind.: Notre Dame Press, 1975), 242. Note that the contingent, what is *able* to fail, is not identical to a *quandoque* evil, viz., an actual failure.

In sum, one possible explanation for why we suffer *quandoque* evils is because we are parts of a material universe that though it has great arrangement, still lacks perfect arrangement. By its nature a material cosmos is inherently messy. By what it is, it will possess ragged edges. The reason for a lingering imperfect arrangement is that the chief causal factors in the material universe are movers and so do not completely account for their effects. They act on something presupposed and must make the best they can with it. A material universe by its nature will contain free radicals that can ambush teleologies in that universe. Hence, though the sun in the springtime intends the blossoming of the fruit trees, that teleology is cut short by a late frost. Even though the omnipotent God intends the blossoming, God can intend that it take place through creaturely causes like the sun.

BRACKETING *QUANDOQUE* EVILS BETWEEN GOODS

So one explanation for *quandoque* evils is that they are the permitted but not willed effects of a corruptible order which God does will to have a created universe that evinces the divine perfection and goodness in being. This order of corruptible being that is a possible explanation of the *quandoque* evil is antecedent to or before the *quandoque* evil. So far it is not by looking ahead to future goods that Aquinas explains evil but by looking back to goods already existing. Aquinas sums up this line of thought by quoting Dionysius in his reply to the third objection of 48, 2. The line from *On the Divine Names* IV, 3, is: "It belongs to Providence, not to destroy, but to save nature." But important to note is that Aquinas's reply appears to go on to open a second line of explanation of why *quandoque* evil exists in things. The second line is taken from St. Augustine who remarked in his *Enchiridion*, XI: "God is so powerful that He can even make good out of evil." The metaphysics that is in play does not allow Aquinas to leave his treatment of *quandoque* evils just with a reference to antecedent goods, although such a reference seems to provide an integral plausible answer.

58   *Quandoque* Evils

For Aquinas God also orders *quandoque* evils to some good. In other words, Aquinas brackets *quandoque* evils between antecedent and consequent goods.

Aquinas had stated this thesis in his *Sentences* commentary at the start of his theological career, as is clear from two texts. First:

> Evil *per se* does not confer perfection on the universe: for that which *per se* confers perfection on some whole is either a constituent part of the whole or a cause *per se* of some perfection in the whole. But evil is not a part of the universe because it lacks the nature of a substance and of an accident, but is a privation only, as Dionysius says; neither does it *per se* cause something good. But *per accidens* it contributes to the perfection of the universe insomuch as it is joined to something that is about the perfection of the universe. This is able to be either through something antecedent to the evil or something following the evil. Something antecedent just as a nature that sometimes is deficient and sometimes is not, as the free will of man; and without such a nature from the defect of which evil happens, there would not be a universe perfect in all grades of goodness. Something consequent is that good which is occasioned from the evil, which is the beauty resulting in the good from a comparison to evil, or some perfection to which the evil materially has itself, just as the persecution to the sufferers, or to other infinite modes; because *per accidens* causes are infinite.[14]

I explained how Aquinas relates *quandoque* evils to an antecedent good. Now, what is this relation of *quandoque* evil to a consequent good? In the above text Aquinas describes the consequent relation of these evils to good as one of *per accidens* material causality. Understanding this causality is important for understanding that Aquinas is not speaking of *quandoque* evils within the context of a means to end relationship. The standard example of a *per accidens* cause is the doctor who builds. The doctor is a *per accidens* cause because it just so happens that the doctor is a builder. In other words, it is not necessary that the doctor be a builder. Now this

---

14. *In I Sent.* d. 46, q. 1, a. 3c; Thomas Aquinas, *Scriptum super Libros Sententiarum Magistri Petri Lombardi Episcopi Parisensis*, edited by Pierre Mandonnet (Paris: P. Lethielleux, 1929) I, 1056.

example is a case of a *per accidens* efficient cause. But the example is helpful to construct analogously an example of a *per accidens* cause in the line of material causality. For instance, just as the doctor is an accidental cause of the building because the doctor does not have to be a builder, so too persecution is an accidental cause of patience because patience just so happens to be joined to the persecution. There is no requirement within the persecution that patience be joined to it. Elsewhere Aquinas mentions that the manifestation of the glory of the martyrs is outside the intention of the persecutions. So for persecution to be a material cause for patience is not for the persecution to be orientated to the patience as a means to an end. Instead of a means Aquinas calls the evil an occasion for the consequent good.

The above analogy also helps to understand Aquinas's claim that accidental causes are infinite. Insofar as the doctor can be associated with many other *per se* causes, for example, teachers, musicians, artists, then the effects of the accidental cause are unending. Likewise, as a material cause persecution is open to conjunction with many other things and so has an infinity about it.

In the very next article Aquinas describes the relation of God's will to these evils that are joined either to an antecedent good or to a consequent good.

> Since the will of God is the cause of all good things and of all of them having been willed, in this way something is willed by God just as it has itself to that which is good [*se habet aliquid ad hoc quod sit volitum a Deo, sicut se habet ad hoc quod sit bonum*]. Since evil to be made is according to itself not good, as was said, it will not be willed *per se* by God. But the good joined to the evil is good and willed by God. Namely the antecedent good which is the condition of nature able to defect which God institutes and conserves in such a condition; whence it is said that God does not will evil to be made but wills to permit [*permittere*] evil to be made. Also, God wills the consequent good from which evil is ordered. From which it follows that he wills to order [*ordinare*] made evil, not that he wills it to be made.[15]

---

15. Aquinas, *Scriptum super Libros*, 1059.

That God does not will these evils as such but only wills to permit and to order them indicates that Aquinas is speaking of the second sense of *evil*. Though, in my opinion, Aquinas could have left his explanation of evil with the antecedent goods, Aquinas insists that God also orders the evils that God permits. For example,

> A defective act which results occasionally in the generation of natural monstrosities is, of course, directed by God to some useful purpose; but to this defective act itself nothing else was directed. It happened merely on account of the failure of some cause. With regard to the first-named act of generation, the providence is one of approval; with regard to the second, it is one of permission. These two kinds of providence are discussed by Damascene.[16]

The basis for Aquinas's confidence that permitted evils are also ordered to consequent goods is indicated in the text from the famous article on the *Quinque Viae*: "As Augustine says: 'Since God is the highest good, God would not allow any evil to exist in His works, unless His omnipotence and goodness were such as to bring good even out of this evil.' This is part of the infinite goodness of God, that He should allow [*permittat*] evil to exist, and out of it produce [*eliciat*] good."[17]

Aquinas's confidence that permitted evils are divinely ordered to consequent goods is based in his metaphysical knowledge of the infinite perfection of God. As infinite, God has the wherewithal to match any permitted evil with a redeeming good so that no evil is left pointless. None of this means, however, that we know in detail what this redeeming good is. Our ignorance here is characterized in the following way:

> Even though it may seem to us that all things happen equally to the good and to the evil since we are ignorant of the reasons for God's providence in allotting these things, there is no doubt that in all these good and evil things happening to the good or to the evil there is operative a well worked

---

16. *De Ver.* V, 4c;.Thomas Aquinas, *The Disputed Questions on Truth*, vol. I, translated by Robert W. Mulligan (Chicago: Regnery, 1952), 219.
17. *ST* I, 2, 3, ad 1m; Pegis, *Basic Writings of Thomas Aquinas, vol.* I, 23.

out plan by which God's providence directs all things. It is because we do not know His reasons that we think many things happen without order or plan. We are like a man who enters a carpenter shop and thinks that there is a useless multiplication of tools because he does not know how each one is used; but one who knows the trade will see that this number of tools exists for a very good reason.[18]

Aquinas's sandwiching of *quandoque* evils between antecedent and consequent goods is a beneficial complexity. As Aquinas noted and we know personally, often we cannot frame the consequent good to which the permitted evil is divinely ordered. Finding solace will take the form of a reference back to the antecedent good. For example, newscasters have been known to subtly taunt victims of natural catastrophes by asking if they still had faith in a good God. One interviewee deflected the question by asking what kind of a being the interviewer thought we were that we should be exempt from these kinds of occurrences. There is a deep Thomistic wisdom in that reply that penetrates through the association with the notion of being that can skew our contemplation of some things.

A CAVEAT IN UNDERSTANDING THE SUBJECT OF THE CONSEQUENT GOOD

One should not be so quick to assume that the consequent good will befall the individual sufferer of the *quandoque* evil. In the contemplation of the Thomistic philosopher that may be God's providence, but then again it may not be. Yet fellow Thomists may want to disagree with me. These Thomists might cite *C.G.* III, 112, in which Aquinas insists that God provides for the intellectual creature for its own sake. Hence, in the case of humans at least, the suffered *quandoque* evils must rebound to some consequent good for the individual who suffers the *quandoque* evil. My reader will recall that in his *The Person and the Common Good*, Maritain cited 112 in behalf of his thesis that the human is not just a part

---

18. *De Ver.* V, 5, ad 6m; Aquinas, *Disputed Questions on Truth*, vol. I, 224.

of a whole but a whole, even a universe, unto itself. In fairness, though, Maritain appears to take the thesis theologically. As I noted earlier, Maritain interprets the thesis that intellectual beings are provided for their own sakes to mean that God wills and loves them for their own sake, before loving and willing them for the order and perfection of the universe of nature and creation. But Maritain concedes such a perspective only "if we pass to the supernatural order." Maritain gives no reason for taking 112 theologically. He just assumes that since the divine providence governs intellectual substances for their own sake, then Aquinas must be speaking about the special Christian order in which we are adopted children of God. Yet a look at the arguments of 112 shows genuinely philosophical middle terms. Hence, does 112 constitute a challenge to the above explanation of *quandoque* evils, in which humans are still regarded as parts of the cosmos and so could have the redeeming good fall not on themselves but on their fellows?

Not at all. A look at its seven arguments reveals that the thinking has never left the context of *ST* I, 48, 2. In sum, 112 never describes the human as a whole or, to use Maritain's expression, as a universe unto itself. The first two arguments deal with the intellectual creature as "master of its own acts." As the second argument makes clear, this description means that the intellectual creature is free. However, this freedom is not the intellectually ungrounded freedom of Kant's autonomous will or the "authentic" existence of the twentieth-century existential philosophers Heidegger and Sartre. In their cases choice has no intellectual prompt. Hence, what is good is simply what we have decided to be good. In Aquinas, as explained in chapter 2, the moral good is objective and is presented by the intellect to the will to be embraced. The freedom of the intellectual creature consists in its ability to embrace or to reject this intellectually presented good. In other words, my freedom does not mean that I form the moral law; I am not a self-legislator. Instead my freedom consists in my ability to conform or not to conform to the moral law. I am a self-determiner.

In his first argument Aquinas says that the freedom of self-determination suffices to conclude that the intellectual creature must be treated with respect and solicitude. God will not deal with us in a way that enlists us in a project for which we do not give our consent. In sum, there is no divine manipulation, as there often is in human affairs. This lack of divine manipulation of rational creatures is what Aquinas means when Aquinas says that God governs rational creatures for their own sakes. Instead of a behind the scenes manipulation of the rational creature, God respects the rational creature's capacity for self-determination. God's respect means that God will govern the creature through an intellectual presenting of the good to the creature.

This first argument does not exclude rational creatures from suffering *quandoque* evils. The openness of the first argument to that idea is apparent if one remembers, as explained in my last chapter, that the human will's freedom is rooted in the *abstractum* of being as the good. This *a posteriori* epistemology anchors the human in the material world and so leaves the human vulnerable to its slings and arrows, even when they are outrageous. The autonomy of the Kantian self and the Sartrean *pour-soi* is absent in the Thomistic understanding of the human who wills. In sum, nothing in this first argument excludes the possibility that humans suffer *quandoque* evils for the good of the cosmos, including a level of free creatures.

In the second argument Aquinas notes that in every kind of governance provision is made for the free man, not for slaves. Since, as noted, the free man is a self-determiner, then the provision of governors is to enable the free man to see the good and to choose it. Even though the free man is placed on a high rung of the social ladder, this rung is not so high that the free man ceases to be a part of the material cosmos. The above mentioned epistemology is still true.[19]

19. As a comment, Aquinas's second argument has both good and bad sides. The good side is that in its political extrapolation the state is ultimately for the person, not the person for the state. Any totalitarianism is excised from Aquinas's politics. The bad side is that the second argument seems to admit the existence of slaves that Aquinas describes as for the

In the third argument Aquinas says that since God acts with himself as a final cause, or point of attraction, then those creatures that can attain a likeness to God through some knowledge and love of God are the principal end of creation. Now only the intellectual natures are such creatures. Hence, they are governed for their own sakes and not for the sake of something else. As Aquinas's example of the soldiers who by their efforts attain victory indicates, the third argument is talking about the natural capacity of the intellectual creature to know and to love the creator. Chapter 2's discussion of our implicit knowledge of God described the main lines of Aquinas's understanding of this attainment in us. Hence, in argument three Aquinas is not speaking about the supernatural end of the beatific vision. The attainment of a vision, a direct knowledge, of the creator is beyond our capacities to realize and requires the assistance of the creator itself. The argument's restriction to knowledge and love of the creator that can be attained by our own efforts again presents the human with an epistemology that locates the human within the cosmos. That God governs such a rational creature for its own sake does not entail that the rational creature is exempt from *quandoque* evils.

The fourth and fifth arguments take advantage of implications in the concepts of whole and part. These arguments are the strongest indications that 112 has not left the context of 48, 2. The fourth argument begins by claiming that principal parts of a whole are willed for themselves. But intellectual natures are the principal parts of the whole that is the created universe because intellectual natures come closest to a divine likeness, as mentioned in the third argument. Hence, they are willed by God for their own sakes. Here the intellectual nature is explicitly branded "a princi-

---

sake of the free man. A way out of the problem would be to say that Aquinas is just reporting about slavery, not sanctioning it. Of course making that move would mean that for consistency Aquinas's remarks about free men would also be just a report and require some kind of philosophical validation. Hence, I believe that this second argument is not probative without falling back on the first argument.

pal part." The created intellect does not elevate the creature to the status of a whole. As far as I know, Aquinas never speaks of the rational creature as a whole.

The fifth argument comes nearest to that way of speaking but remains faithful to the "principal part" characterization. Aquinas says that intellectual creatures have "a closer relationship to a whole" than other things. Intellectual natures have this closer relation because they intellect the whole of being [*totius entis*]. Hence, unlike parts of a whole, intellectual natures are governed for their own sakes and not for the sake of another. For the special divine governance or providence over rational creatures, it suffices that the rational creature come closer than other beings to the whole of wholes that is being (the *ratio entis*). Though not mentioned here, I believe that the reason such creatures only come close to being but fail to achieve identification is that the intellection of being is, as Aquinas says elsewhere and as I explained earlier, analogical. Grasped as a sameness-in-difference, the notion of being does not perfectly seat itself in the created intellect. Hence, for all of its exalted status as an intellector of being, the human is still a part of the whole that is the cosmos, albeit the principal part.[20]

The sixth argument observes that the way a thing acts through the course of nature gives us some idea of what the originator of nature, the creator, intends. Now we see intellectual natures using others for themselves. Hence, God governs things for the sake of the intellectual. Obviously the argument does not go beyond "the course of nature" in which the intellectual nature is a part. In such a scenario the intellectual nature for all of its height and dignity is a possible victim of *quandoque* evils.

Finally, the seventh argument begins with the thought that

---

20. Hence, I do not find Aquinas making Maritain's argument that as free the person is a universe unto himself. For Aquinas, freedom is not autonomous but is related to the intellection of being. Up against being things appear as goods not the good. Hence, we can will things but we do not have to. But, as just noted, the intellection of being brings the rational creature only closer to being itself a whole.

what we desire for its own sake, we always desire. On the other hand, what we desire for something else is not always desired. It is desired only as long as the something else is not attained. So, an everlasting creature is taken as an indication of a thing being desired for itself by the creator. Now intellectual creatures as incorruptible "come closest to existing always." Hence, we can conclude that they are governed for their own sakes. Notice that for all their incorruptibility, Aquinas says that intellectual creatures only approximate existing always. Why the distinction? Is not to be incorruptible to be existing always? Some idea of what Aquinas has in mind may be indicated in a thesis of the most famous of the Gilsonian "existential" Thomists of the last century. Joseph Owens makes a distinction between incorruptibility, that is, continued existence, versus immortality, that is, continued operation. He argues that philosophically Aquinas can give a strict demonstration of the former but not the latter. In other words, though we can prove that the soul can exist separate from the body we cannot prove that it will operate. Since the human intellect for its operation naturally requires sense images and these require the body, then the separated soul has no way to exercise its intellectual power. Such operation is possible only in virtue of the supernatural assistance of the creator, but no philosophical way exists to prove that the creator will furnish that assistance.[21] Owens's thinking

21. "Life in a separated soul will consist in intellection or what follows upon intellection. Without intellection, then, there will be no life. But human intellection, as naturally knowable, requires the sensible images of the imagination. It cannot take place outside of them. Separated from the body, however, the soul does not have any merely natural means of thinking these images. The independence in regard to matter found in reflexively observable intellection is the basis for demonstrating that the soul will continue to exist perpetually even apart from matter. It is not a basis for demonstrating that the soul will think apart from images, at least in an Aristotelian context." Joseph Owens, "Soul as Agent in Aquinas," *The New Scholasticism* 48 (1974), 65. Owens also remarks, "But the immediate data of awareness, as assessed by Aristotle in *De Anima*, III, 4 (429b 4–10) and *Meta.*, XII, 9 (1074b 35–36), ground the conclusion that as far as unaided natural reason is concerned even self-knowledge on the part of the soul takes place objectively through material images." Ibid., n. 31. Aquinas's claim of no substance without activity is grounded in a "theological context of congruence and present providence." Ibid., 72. On this context, see chapter 4, "Natural

would explain why Aquinas says that an intellectual nature only comes "closest" to existing always and would justify continuing to look at the human in this seventh argument as only a part, although the principal part, of the material order of creation.

Hence, a study of the arguments of 112 shows that Aquinas's thinking has not left the framework of 48, 2. The natural dignity of the human as rational does not consist in rendering it a whole but in rendering it the principal part of a whole. As a part, however, the human, like any other part, is victim to *quandoque* evils as explained above. As a part that is principal, the human can expect that providence orders *quandoque* evils to some human good, another's if not one's own. But most damaging for my fictional Thomist "newscaster" is the end of Chapter 112. In paragraph 10, Aquinas says, "However, we do not understand this statement, that intellectual substances are ordered for their own sake by divine providence, to mean that they are not more ultimately referred to God and to the perfection of the universe." This admission that the previous arguments do not exclude a reference of the rational creature to the perfection of the universe also shows that Aquinas's thinking has not left the context of 48, 2.

It is important to understand my interpretation of chapter 112. In sum, since Aquinas never characterizes the human as a whole but as always less than that, then the conclusions of the seven arguments are not strictly demonstrated. Rather, the philosophical considerations of the human that serve as the middle terms of the arguments entail the conclusions only with a certain fittingness or appropriateness. In fact the conclusion of argument five is introduced by "*convenienter*." Also, because the conclusions are not

---

Corruption as Non-Definitive." At *ST* I, 89, 1, ad 3m, Aquinas does attribute knowledge in the separated soul to grace. Owens again presents this position in "Towards a Philosophy of Medieval Studies," *The Etienne Gilson Series 9* (Toronto: Pontifical Institute of Mediaeval Studies, 1986), 11–13. On the other hand, in "The Natural Meaning of Death in the *Summa Theologiae*," *Proceedings of the American Catholic Philosophical Association* 52 (1978), 87–95, Mary Rousseau argues that the separated soul would naturally operate but at such an imperfect level that its life here and now would be better.

strictly entailed, Aquinas can say, as I noted, that the human is still ordered to the perfection of the universe. Of course the philosopher can imagine a number of possibilities for human destiny. But I want to insist upon a baseline consisting of what is strictly entailed by human nature. In a word, what is strictly entailed, though not to the exclusion of supernatural possibilities, is a this-worldly life in which the creator's providence orders other things to the good of the human species and humans are ordered at least to the good of others if not to their own.[22]

Aquinas's view of the human as a principal part establishes an important baseline in his discussions of evil. For Aquinas, God could eliminate all *quandoque* evils. In fact God did. In the state of innocence in which Adam and Eve were created, God preserved our first parents from all physical harm.[23] Also, I suppose that God could continually create more matter in the universe so that its taking up into the divinely governed higher species would not bring the universe to a grinding halt. God could even continually create food in the bellies of beasts so that they would not devour other animals or humans. But if one remembers Aquinas's baseline, then one will understand that all of these scenarios are supernatural scenarios and so are not things that in our natural condition we are in any position to demand of God or to fault God if they are unrealized. An imaginative philosopher working with Thomistic ideas could discern the possibility that the creator loves us as wholes unto ourselves, as the "apples of God's eye." In other words, this philosopher could see the possibility of God relating to us as the father driven to distraction in Flew's earlier mentioned example.[24]

---

22. Interestingly, at the end of the response at *De Ver.* 5, 3, Aquinas does allow one to say that things are provided for their own sake if they are provided for their species.

23. *De Ver.* 24, 9c and *ST* I. 97, 1c.

24. Actually, Aquinas's view of a loving father stays within the context of the children as parts of the whole. In *De Ver.* 5. 3c, Aquinas remarks that God's providence is like the providence by which a father of a family rules his household, in which the common good has primacy over the good of the individual. Hence, the father must pay more attention to what is good for the family than to what is good for the individual. To be noted is that for hu-

But the philosopher would not be able to establish that this possibility is also a fact, for this heavenly concern is over and above what is owing to us as principal parts of a whole. Far from being an embarrassment as Flew implies, the distinction between a natural and a supernatural state is necessary and legitimate "doublethink." Nor does God's infinite love and mercy obliterate the distinction. As mentioned above, that love and mercy would have already been exemplified in bringing the creature in its natural state, viz., as a principal part, from nonbeing to being. Witnessing these divine qualities would not require a further and supernatural state.

THE EFFECT OF HUMAN PROVIDENCE UPON THE FREQUENCY OF *QUANDOQUE* EVILS

A final point about *quandoque* evils concerns Aquinas's claim about their limited frequency as is implied in the very word "*quandoque*." A reader could understandably object that the smashing of the higher by the lower is a much more frequent occurrence. For example, we all die but few die peacefully in their beds surrounded by loved ones after a long life. Also, the attack of a lion on the human may be infrequent, but pestilence and disease seem to be regular. In the light of these facts, what can Aquinas mean when he says that nature attains its end for the most part but sometimes (*quandoque*) monsters result?

It is important to realize that Aquinas's remarks are made in reference to the natural world without the intrusion of human providence. If human providence is brought into consideration, then the chances for foul ups are greatly increased. Aquinas first mentions

---

man dignity it suffices that the human be a "principal" part, not a whole or a universe unto itself, as Maritain says. Hence, after arguing for capital punishment on the basis that the human is a part of the social whole, Aquinas says (*ST* II-II, 64) that the ruler should not kill the innocent for the good of the whole because the innocent are the principal part of that good. That the human achieves the status of a principal part because of the human's intellection of being is explained by Aquinas at *C.G.* III, 112. See above at n. 20. On how sin can compromise one's status as an intellector of being, see John F. X. Knasas, *Being and Some Twentieth-Century Thomists* (New York: Fordham University Press, 2003), 271, n. 32.

these two considerations in his *Sentences* commentary. While discussing whether God's providence applies to all things, Aquinas brings up this objection: "Everything that is provided for attains the end in the majority, unless the providence is errant. But evil, which is a departure from the end, is found in many cases. Therefore, the universe is not ruled by providence."[25] In his long reply Aquinas immediately distinguishes between the way evil is in natural things (*in rebus naturalibus*) and the way evil is in voluntary things (*in voluntariis*). In the former case it remains true that evil exists in fewer cases (*in paucioribus*). Aquinas gives two reasons. Appealing to the cosmology of the time, Aquinas notes that evil only happens on the earth which is miniscule in size compared to the rest of the cosmos, a consideration that may still be true as I noted when discussing John Quinn's claim for the probity of the argument for a first physical cause.[26] In addition, and with our attention on terrestrial things, Aquinas makes his claim that natural causes obtain their effects for the most part and that they are deficient only in a few cases (*in majori parte, et deficient in minori*).

Turning to voluntary things, Aquinas first mentions the angels and notes that evil exists also in a few cases because the number of angels that remained firm is greater than the number of both angels and men who fell. But turning attention to humans, Aquinas concedes that good seems to be only in a few cases. For first is the corruption of human nature from original sin, an evil that God foresaw but did not prohibit. Aquinas insists that God did not issue a prohibition so that human nature would remain in its liberty, without which the reason for human nature would be lost. How liberty is the reason for human nature should be clear from my above discussion of *C.G.* III, 112, viz., providence provides for the free man. Another soon to be presented text will cement this connection of "a reason for human nature" with *C.G.* III, 112.

25. *In I Sent.* d. 39, q. 2, a. 2, 4 obj; Aquinas, *Scriptum super Libros Sententiarum*, 929–30.
26. *Supra*, n. 10.

Quandoque Evils 71

Second, there is the consideration of the human nature just in itself (*natura humana in se considerata*). Citing Aristotle, Aquinas notes the comparison of the human intellect to prime matter which is only in potency. The human intellect is not yet perfected by the second acts that are the virtues which will perfect its activity, for the most part, in this life. Hence, being equally disposed to all, the human is turned to evil in many things. The inherently messy human advance to virtue will be more elaborated at *C.G.* IV, 52. The point now is to notice the restriction of the infrequency of evil to the natural world, and the admission that such infrequency is no longer the case when human willers are introduced. Given that the human intellectual advance is hard-won, many regularly occurring evils can be understood as self-inflicted through ignorance and vice. For example, a tribal people leave the disease of the jungle for the health of the coast only to be wiped out by a tidal wave. Even after the dangers of living on the coast are known, a people can be too lazy to take precautions and again suffer calamity.

Soon after in *De Veritate* V, 5, Aquinas repeats the distinction between evils in natural things versus evils in human affairs. But Aquinas now mentions human providence as the reason for human nature. He says, "But human acts can be defective because of human providence. For this reason, we find more failures and deordinations in human acts than we do in the acts of natural things. Yet, the fact that man has providence over his own acts is part of his nobility. Consequently, the number of his failures does not keep man from holding a higher place under God's providence."[27] As messy

---

27. *De Ver.* V, 5, ad 2m; Aquinas, *Disputed Questions on Truth*, vol. I, 224. Some might ask why Aquinas does not mention Satan as a cause of evils in this world. Satan, philosophically understood as a superior yet still finite intelligence who has chosen against the creator, is metaphysically a graspable possibility. Satan's evil choice would also explain why Satan is intent upon directing all things to himself. (See *ST* I, 65, 3) Yet how likely, for Aquinas, would the fact of this possibility be? It could be argued that just as Aquinas downplayed Satan as a direct cause of all sins, since human nature suffices for this direct cause (*ST* I, 114, 3, and *C.G.* IV, 52), so too the natural system of movers with the participation of humans fallible in knowledge and in will suffices to explain many calamities. Another remark could be made from Aquinas's conclusion that the number of angels that remained firm was far greater

as human providence is, it is providence. This self-directedness is not only a good but a good that gives the human a nobility among things. Man's dignity is clearly elaborated in the previously studied arguments of *C.G.* III, 112, in which Aquinas argues that God governs the rational creature for its own sake.²⁸

Finally, *C.G.* IV, 52, can be viewed as elaborating the proliferation of *quandoque* evils, thanks to the human intellect being potential like matter. Evils can be considered to be so regular that they can be called "natural defects." Speaking of the frailty of reason (*debilitas rationis*), Aquinas says:

> For all that, one could say that defects of this kind, both bodily and spiritual, are not penalties, but natural defects necessarily consequent upon matter. For, necessarily, the human body, composed of contraries, must be corruptible; and the sensible appetite must be moved to sense pleasures, and these are occasionally contrary to reason. And, since the possible intellect is in potency to all intelligibles, possessing none of them actually, but by nature acquiring them from the senses, one must arrive at knowledge of the truth with difficulty, and due to the phantasms one with ease deviates from the truth.²⁹

Aquinas repeats the description of the human intellect as potential so that knowledge is hard-won, abstractive intellection is occluded by phantasms, and a body necessary for sensation will cause drives that are often at odds with virtue. Such are Aquinas's remarks following an absolute consideration of human nature. For all the dignity associated with the human as an intellector of being, that same intellection is precarious enough to leave humans in the "darkest shadows of ignorance (*maximis ignorantiae tene-*

---

than the number who fell. (*ST* I, 63, 9) Hence, it appears unlikely that the creator would have allowed sinful angels to run riot over the rest of creation without opposition from the good angels.

28. I am following Weisheipl's dating of the *De Veritate* (1256–59) and the *Summa contra Gentiles* (1259–64). See James Weisheipl, *Friar Thomas D'Aquino: His Life, Thought, and Work* (Garden City, N.Y.: Doubleday & Company, Inc., 1974), 362 and 359 respectively.

29. Thomas Aquinas, *Summa contra Gentiles, vol. IV, translated by* Charles O'Neil (Notre Dame, Ind.: University of Notre Dame Press, 1975), 218.

bris)."³⁰ This guarantees tragedies and leaves our beastly appetites not entirely overcome.

The following text from the *Summa Theologiae* summarizes the natural situation quite well. It is interesting in two respects. First, Aquinas uses the term *"malum"* without qualification even though he is evidently speaking of *quandoque* evil. Natural corruption, the corruption that God wills for the sake of the whole, is not felt to be a problem. Aquinas appears to assume that the reader understands this. Second, Aquinas is evidently unconcerned that the amount of good over evil in human affairs, naturally considered, be greater.

Hence, to say that evil is in the majority of cases is absolutely false. For things which are generated and corrupted, in which alone there can be natural evil, are a very small part of the whole universe. Then again, defects in nature are found in every species only in a small number of cases. In man alone does evil manifest itself in the majority of cases. For the good of man as regards the senses of the body is not the good of man as man, but the good according to the reason. More men, however, follow the sense rather than the reason.³¹

The few cases in which human natural perfection is realized suffice to make human nature a fitting object of divine providence.

30. "If the only way open to us .for the knowledge of God were solely that of the reason, the human race would remain in the blackest shadows of ignorance. For then the knowledge of God, which especially renders men perfect and good, would come to be possessed only by a few, and these few would require a great deal of time in order to reach it." *C.G.* I, 4, *Remaneret*; Thomas Aquinas, *Summa contra Gentiles*, vol. I, translated by Anton C. Pegis (Notre Dame, Ind.: University of Notre Dame Press, 1975), 67–68.

31. *ST* I, 49, 3, ad 5m; Pegis, *Basic Writings of Thomas Aquinas*, vol. I, 479.

4

Natural Corruptions

For those of us lucky enough to live in prosperous post–World War II America, *quandoque* evils have been beaten to a minimum. Certainly there are the crosses of backbiting, slander, and politics, but few of these are serious enough to prevent the happiness of finding work and raising a family. Rather, the evil that looms large in consciousness and whose presence no social prosperity eradicates is our eventual demise. No doubt interwoven into the contemplation of our demise is the notion of being. And this presence of being casts thoughts of our death as a phantom that haunts our later years. At *C.G.* IV, 52, Aquinas characterizes death as the "greatest bodily penalty" suffered because of original sin. Yet Aquinas is surprisingly very matter-of-fact in his discussion of death. As has been noted and will be explained further, death in old age is not a *quandoque* evil. Instead Aquinas calls death "a natural defect." In fact, such death is so natural that it is no sure sign of original sin. Also, it is not so evil that God fails to will it. What is little noticed among commentators on Aquinas is that behind *quandoque* evils is a view of nature in which regular corruption is the order of the day.

In other words, *quandoque* evils are spinoffs of a natural world in which corruptible parts have their time of growth and maturity, but then of inevitable decay. As the standard example of a major premise in logic says: man is mortal. Corruption in old age is in a sense a good, not an evil. As has been remarked, it is a sign that one has lived a full life. That Aquinas can regard such death as a natural defect may explain why Aquinas's treatments of evil focus on the *quandoque* evils. It would also explain Aquinas's observation that if *quandoque* evils were not permitted, then there would be no killing of the ass or stag and so no life of the lion. In other words, the occasional devouring of the human by the lion is an evil permitted for the functioning of the food chain through which species are kept in existence. Noteworthy is that Aquinas says that the nutritive use of the lower by the higher is good.[1] I wish to present Aquinas's views on death, not as a *quandoque* evil, but as a natural corruption.

DEATH AS A NATURAL CORRUPTION

To deal with this new issue, we must turn to *ST* I-II, 85, 6c, with its parallel text at *De Malo* 5, 5c. In the first Aquinas reasons:

> Universal nature is the active power in some universal principle of nature, as in some celestial bodies; or in some other superior substances, according to which God also by some is called *natura naturans*. This power intends the good and the conservation of the universe, to which is demanded the alternation of generation and corruption in things. And according to this the corruptions and defects of things are natural, not indeed according to the inclination of the form, which is a principle of being and perfection, but according to the inclination of matter, which is attributed proportionately to such a form according to the distribution of the universal agent. And although every form intends to always exist insomuch as it is able, yet no form of a corruptible thing is able to assure its perpetuity, outside the rational soul, because it is not wholly subject to corporeal matter, just as

---

1. "Et ideo quamvis hominem in sua dignitate manentem occidere sit secundum se malum, tamen hominem peccatorem occidere potest esse bonum, sicut occidere bestiam." *ST* II-II, 64, 2, ad 3m; Ottawa ed., 1757a.

other forms: rather it has a proper immaterial operation as was explained in the *prima pars*. Whence from the part of its form incorruption is more natural to man than to other corruptible things. But because he has matter composed from contraries, corruptibility follows in the whole. And according to this, man is naturally corruptible according to the nature of matter left to itself but not according to the nature of the form.

There are many points to make from this selection; but for our purposes I want to mention only the following. First, what is this universal nature or efficient cause that intends the good and conservation of the universe? What Aquinas is speaking about is the nonunivocal cause necessary for the full explanation of the various substantial forms found in matter. As I have already noted, the need for this cause is brought out as follows. As determinations of matter, these forms are dependent. But they are not completely dependent either upon matter or upon another individual of like species. They are not completely dependent upon matter because as determined by the form, matter is in potency to it. Material forms are not completely dependent upon another like individual, for example, the baby upon the parents, because as a supposedly complete explainer of the form in matter, that individual would also have to explain its own form and so cause itself—an absurdity. So the complete explanation of form in matter entails a reference to a universal cause unlike the individuals dealt with. Accordingly Aquinas says: "But the univocal agent is not the universal efficient cause of the whole species (otherwise it would be the cause of itself, since it is contained in the species), but is a particular cause of this individual which it places under the species by way of participation. Therefore the universal cause of the whole species is not a univocal agent: and the universal cause comes before the particular cause."[2]

What is the universal cause? At *C.G.* III, 23, Aquinas mentions

---

2. *ST* I, 13, 5, ad 1m; Anton C. Pegis, ed., *The Basic Writings of St. Thomas Aquinas*, vol. I (New York: Random House, 1945), 120. See also *C.G.* II, 21, 5.

four possibilities. The universal cause could be a nonhylomorphic body like the celestial spheres, an angel, God himself, or all three. The fourth option is Aquinas's position that terrestrial things generate other members of their species in virtue of the sun, but the sun moves by a celestial sphere moved by an angel moved by God.[3]

Second, as Aquinas said at 85, 6, the universal efficient cause intends the good, and conservation of the universe of which is demanded the alteration of generation and corruption. According to the text corruption follows the "inclination" of matter. What is this inclination? Aquinas describes it as the proportional attribution of matter to form according to the distribution of the universal cause. In other words, there is a movement of matter to various forms caused by the universal cause. Why? This text does not go any further, and I know of no other text that does. The reader is left to his own resources but I have surmised the following. Again, this inclination of matter that is its distribution to various forms is somehow tied to the good and conservation of the universe. The material universe demands a cycling of matter through its various parts if the universe is not to destroy itself through the proliferation of its higher members and the exhaustion of its lower members. In other words, higher species while living off of lower species also generate other members of their species. If there is no corruption of the higher, then there will result a loss of the various kinds of things in and through which the universe reflects the divine perfection. To rectify this disorder, the universal cause periodically sees that matter is redistributed to the lower species. This redistribution, however, means the corruption of the higher. Hence, to the question, "Why do good persons grow old and die?" Aquinas could answer that the overpopulation of good persons is not a good thing. It is in

---

3. As can be seen, Aquinas has quite a robust understanding of nature. The cosmos is not discrete things operating by natural laws. Rather, things are contained within the causality of a larger thing and are susceptible to the larger thing's causal influences. For the case that the natural philosophy argument for a first physical cause still holds today, see the reference to John Quinn in chapter 3, n. 10.

the reordering of this disorder that the universal cause intends the death of men.

Could God avoid death in his creation by creating beings that lack the capacity to reproduce and so not cause the overpopulation problem? I think Aquinas would admit it as a possibility, but not as something God is somehow required to do. For a creation with beings able to procreate will also reflect his goodness. Aquinas repeatedly insists that part of the perfection of a cause is to share causality with its effects.[4] In that case, however, a limited existence for creatures is necessary to preserve the order and perfection of the universe, namely, to avoid the overpopulation problem and its attendant effects. Again, nothing the philosopher knows about the dignity of a rational animal would make death an "utter anomaly." The same thinking would apply to God producing a group of humans that all promise to take a vow of celibacy. As I will explain in chapter 6, Aquinas understands God as able to cause the free acts of creatures, so the case of vowed celibacy is a possible created effect. Moreover, God could supernaturally conserve creatures in existence just as God intended to free Adam from death. But again, another creative option remains, the one in which creatures exercise their procreative powers which are kept within bounds by mortality. In fact, this creative scenario is more probable (hence, Aquinas's denomination of death as a "natural defect") given that the celibacy case involves supernatural factors.

Third, the above interpretation of how God wills natural corruptions for the sake of the order of the universe drives home the truth that man is mortal and definitely injects a tragic compo-

---

4. "Indeed, it is part of the fullness of perfection to be able to communicate to another being the perfection which one possesses. Therefore, this position [that creatures are not causes] detracts from the divine power." *C.G.* III, 69; Thomas Aquinas, *Summa contra Gentiles, vol. III, translated by* Vernon J. Bourke (Notre Dame, Ind.: University of Notre Dame Press, 1975), pt. 1, 230. "For [God] governs things inferior by superior, not because of any defect in His power, but by reason of the abundance of His goodness; so that the dignity of causality is imparted even to creatures." *ST* I, 22, 3; Pegis, *Basic Writings of Thomas Aquinas*, vol. I, 235.

nent into human existence. This first possibility for the meaning of death is a call to ourseves to resolutely accept death and to do good without counting the cost. At this point one could discuss some similarities between Aquinas and Heidegger. Also, I do not think it can be said that we can demand or expect God to avoid this human tragedy by continually creating new matter so that matter's redistribution to the lower species, and hence corruption of the higher members, is rendered unnecessary. There is nothing inherently untoward in a universe created to reflect the perfection of the creator functioning in the way described above. Just as each passing frame of the film produces the movie, so each passing individual of a species produces the continued representation of some one of the creator's perfections. So, as far as the philosopher can see, the creator is not under any constraint to continually create new matter to afford the continued existence of the lower species as old matter is taken up into the higher species.

NATURAL CORRUPTION AS NONDEFINITIVE

Is, then, the elaboration of death as a natural corruption philosophy's last word about death? To the contrary, the reply to the objection mentioned in the previous section indicates that there are supernatural options for the creator that make circumspect any claim by the philosopher to have the last word about the meaning of death. At *De Malo* 5, 5c, Aquinas again argues that death and other defects are natural to man. But they are not so natural that a supernatural override of material conditions is tantamount to an absurdity or a contradiction to human nature as seen in the following excerpts:

> Whence if in nature there could be found some body composed from elements which was incorruptible, without doubt such a body would be fitting to the soul according to nature; just as if unbreakable and non-rusting iron were able to be found, it would be a most fitting matter for the saw, and the builder would request such; but because such is not able to be found, the builder takes what he finds, namely iron as hard and break-

able. And similarly because nature is not able to find a body composed from elements which according to the nature of matter is incorruptible, a corruptible organic body is naturally adapted to an incorruptible soul. But because God, who is the institutor of man, is able to prohibit by his omnipotence that this necessity of matter not come forth into act, by God's power it was brought about for man before sin that he be preserved from death until when man rendered himself unworthy of such a blessing by sinning; just as the maker would take iron from which he works, if he were able, which would never break.

So therefore, death and corruption are natural to man according to the necessity of matter; but according to the nature of form immortality would be fitting to him; to which nevertheless the present principles of nature do not suffice, but a certain natural aptitude to it belongs to man according to the soul; however, its completion is from a supernatural power [*ex supernaturali virtute*].

Aquinas is explaining that because the abstractive intellect naturally requires a sense organ composed of matter subject to contrariety of form, man is inserted into the cosmic redistribution of matter that dooms him to exist only for a time. But the creator can override, supernaturally, this necessity of matter. In fact in an allusion to the doctrine of original sin, Aquinas says that the creator did first create man in this state of supernatural override and that man lost it through transgression.[5] So the meaning of death might be, not that it is a natural defect, but that it is a punishment. That the creator could have initially brought man to be immortal is a philosophically discernable possibility in Aquinas's metaphysics. But is the fact of such an initiation philosophically knowable? Aquinas says that God causes man to be immortal "just as the maker would take iron from which he works, if he were able,

---

5. Aquinas explains the immortality of the first humans this way: "A thing may be incorruptible on the part of its efficient cause, and it is in this sense that man would have been incorruptible and immortal in the state of innocence.... For man's body was indissoluble, not by reason of any intrinsic vigor of immortality, but by reason of a supernatural force [*vis quaedam supernaturaliter divinitus data*] given by God to the soul, whereby it was enabled to preserve the body from all corruption so long as it itself remained subject to God." *ST* I, 97, 1c. In ad 1m, this force is called "a gift of grace: *donum gratiae*."

which would never break." The analogy suggests that God does what he can do just as the builder would do if he could. The divine override of corruption is explicitly called "supernatural." But the supernatural is grace, and grace is not owing to nature and so not deducible from nature. At *De Ver.* 6, 2c, grace depends upon God's gratuity and not upon his justice.[6] So the supernatural character of God's assistance suggests that Aquinas is speaking from a theologically informed context when he makes the above analogy.

The same point of a philosophically known possibility versus a theologically known fact comes out in an important discussion of the knowability of original sin at *C.G.* IV, 52.

For all that, one could say that defects of this kind, both bodily and spiritual, are not penalties, but natural defects necessarily consequent upon matter. For, necessarily, the human body, composed of contraries, must be corruptible; and the sensible appetite must be moved to sense pleasures, and these are occasionally contrary to reason. And, since the possible intellect is in potency to all intelligibles, possessing none of them actually, but by nature acquiring them from the senses, one must arrive at knowledge of the truth with difficulty, and due to the phantasms one with ease deviates from the truth. But for all that, let one weigh matters rightly, and he will be able to judge with probability enough, granted a divine providence which for every perfection has contrived a proportionate perfectible, that God united a superior to an inferior nature for this purpose: that the superior rule the inferior, and that, if some obstacle to this dominion should happen from a failure of nature, it would be removed by His special and supernatural benefaction. And the result would be, since the rational soul is of a higher nature than the body, belief that the rational soul was united to the body under such a condition that in the body there can be nothing contrary to the soul by which the body lives; and, in like fashion, if reason in man is united to the sensual appetite and other sensitive powers,

---

6. "But if there is anything which is not necessary for that which God wills, then that thing comes from God, not as something due, but simply as a result of His generosity. Now, the perfection of grace and glory are goods of this kind, because nature can exist without them inasmuch as they surpass the limits of natural powers." *De Ver.* VI, 2c; Thomas Aquinas, *The Disputed Questions on Truth*, vol. I, translated by Robert W. Mulligan, SJ (Chicago: Regnery, 1952), 265.

that the reason be not impeded by the sensible powers, but be master over them.... Of course, although defects of this kind may seem natural to man in an absolute consideration of human nature on its inferior side, nonetheless, taking into consideration divine providence and the dignity of human nature on it superior side, it can be proved with enough probability that defects of this kind are penalties. And one can gather thus that the human race was originally infected with sin.[7]

The divine providence that contrives a proportionate perfectible, so that current disorder is a probable basis for judging a fault on man's part, seems to be a theologically known providence. Aquinas says that this divine providence furnishes a "special and supernatural benefaction." Later in the chapter, Aquinas characterizes this special and supernatural benefaction as a gratuitous gift: "Clearly, then, from what has been said, the vice of origin in which the original sin is caused comes from the failure of a principle, namely, the gratuitious gift [gratuiti doni] which human nature at its institution had had bestowed upon it."[8] Also, in its absolute consideration, human nature has the above defects as natural. They are implied by human nature itself. The philosophical study of human nature would not seem to discern the fact of the supernatural. Finally, elsewhere Aquinas presents this providence as known by revelation. In *ST* I, 95, 1c, Aquinas again covers the above subjections, but his starting point is the text of Ecclesiastes 7: 30: God made man right. Aquinas says that the subjections are not from nature since they do not remain after sin. Rather, they are a supernatural endowment of grace.

This same context of a theologically known divine providence provides the context for understanding a later Thomistic argument for the resurrection. In *Contra Gentiles* IV, 79, Aquinas says,

Moreover, to establish that there will be a resurrection of the flesh there is an evident supporting argument which is based on the points made earlier.

---

7. Thomas Aquinas, *Summa contra Gentiles*, vol. IV, translated by Charles J. O'Neil (Notre Dame: Notre Dame Press, 1975), 217–18.

8. Ibid., 221.

For we showed in Book II that the souls of men are immortal. They persist, then, after their bodies, released from their bodies. It is also clear from what was said in Book II that the soul is naturally united to the body, for in its essence it is the form of the body. It is, then, contrary to the nature of the soul to be without the body. But nothing which is contrary to nature can be perpetual. Perpetually, then, the soul will not be without the body. Since, then, it persists perpetually, it must once again be united to the body; and this is to rise again. Therefore, the immortality of the souls seems to demand a future resurrection of bodies.[9]

Some Thomists consider this text to be a philosophical demonstration of the resurrection. Montague Brown claims that the argument shows "beyond a doubt" that God "... cannot create a human being whose natural unity does not require final resurrection of the body."[10] Brown also says that a resurrection of the body is "naturally due the human being by creation."[11] Brown acknowledges that a resurrection will be a supernatural event but denies that that admission makes the resurrection something not due and natural considering the nature of the soul as form of the body. He explains: "Although the efficient principle will be supernatural, this does not discount the naturalness of the resurrection, any more than the fact that the efficient cause of the soul is supernatural (the rational soul is created) requires us to deny the naturalness of human generation."[12] What aids Brown's thesis is the apparent philosophical character of the major premise of Aquinas's argument, viz., what is against nature cannot be perpetual. The derivation of the major premise from the pagan Aristotle's *De Caelo* 2, 269b 7–10, only cements this impression.

Nevertheless, as Aquinas's recap at the start of chapter 81 indicates, there is an ambiguity, unsuspected by Brown, in Aquinas's use of the term "natural." To solve certain problems about the

9. Ibid., 299.
10. Montague Brown, "Aquinas on the Resurrection of the Body," *The Thomist* 56 (1992), 186.
11. Ibid., 204.
12. Ibid., 186.

resurrection, Aquinas says that we have to recall something from chapter 52's discussion of original sin that God: "When He established human nature, [God] granted the human body something over and above that which was its due in its natural principles: a kind of incorruptibility, namely, by which it was suitably adapted to its form, with the result that, as the life of the soul is perpetual, so the body could live perpetually by the soul."[13] This incorruptibility is not simply above what is due the body but is the same thing that was earlier called a gratuitous gift to human nature.

Aquinas next says that this incorruptibility is not natural in its active principle but is "somehow natural" in its order, the end of which is the human soul. But importantly, the subsequent paragraph makes clear that Aquinas is speaking of the human soul as already within a special and more intimate divine providence: "When the soul, then, outside the order of its nature, was turned away from God, that disposition was lost which had been divinely bestowed on the soul's body to make it proportionally responsive to the soul: and death followed. Death, therefore, is something added as an accident, so to say, to man through sin, if one considers the establishment of human nature."[14] The "establishment of human nature" refers to chapter 52's divine providence, which for every perfection provides a proportionate perfectible and whose effects are gratuitous gifts. So, when Aquinas says "the unnatural is not perpetual," the nature about which he is speaking is a nature considered within a special and undue divine providence.[15] Precisely within a context of an especially solicitous divine providence over the human soul, no resurrection appears as *contra* the nature of the human soul. The mentioned reference to Aristotle's

13. Aquinas, *Summa contra Gentiles*, vol. IV, 302
14. Ibid.
15. "The vice of origin in which the original sin is caused comes from the failure of a principle, namely, the gratuitous gift [*gratuiti doni*] which human nature at its institution had had bestowed upon it. To be sure, this gift was in a sense natural: not natural as caused by the principles of the nature, but natural because it was given to man to be propagated along with his nature." *C.G.* IV, 52; Aquinas, *Summa contra Gentiles*, vol. IV, 221.

De Caelo would simply be a theological extrapolation from ungraced nature to graced nature.[16]

Philosophically speaking, the separated soul logically entails as something due a *previous* bodily existence in a world in which the soul perfected, with difficulty, an analogical knowledge of the creator from the sensitive data of a body *ipso facto* corruptible. The fact, as distinct from the possibility, of a resurrection is seen as something due only on the theological assumption of an initial supernatural state in which the creator contrived for every perfection a proportionate perfectible. Importantly for my concerns of a philosophical explanation of evil, the philosophically known possibility of original sin and hence of the resurrection again shows that the philosopher has no explanation because the philosopher sees too many possible explanations.

At this point it is worth mentioning Aquinas's commentary on Job.[17] It is valuable for a number of reasons. First, the Job commentary seems to confirm the theological character of the truth of the resurrection. In the commentary, a future resurrection is a key theme for Job in handling his adversities. But Aquinas never refers to the resurrection as a truth demonstrated in philosophy. Rather, Aquinas describes the resurrection as a work of "grace" for the "hope" of which "plausible reasons" are forthcoming.[18] Also, the position of Job's interlocutors that God's providence is confined to this life is not described as a philosophical error but an error against the "truth of faith."[19] On the other hand, Job foresaw the resurrection through a "spirit of faith."[20] The lack of philosophical grounds is also clear from the basis for the hope of resurrection.

---

16. The other arguments of chapter 79 appear to be theological. In the preceding paragraphs to our text, Aquinas argues scripturally. In the subsequent paragraphs the arguments are based upon "the ultimate happiness" of the beatific vision, the fact of which philosophy cannot know.

17. Aquinas, *The Literal Exposition on Job: A Scriptural Commentary concerning Providence*, translated by Anthony Damico (Atlanta: Scholars Press, 1989).

18. Ibid., 229.   19. Ibid., 471 and 214.
20. Ibid., 269.

Aquinas interprets Job as appealing to the incorruptibility of the human soul. Properties of man indicating this incorruptibility are free will's capacity for infinite actions and the capacity for intellectual knowledge.[21] But as I pointed out in reply to Brown, resurrection follows incorruptibility only on the supposition of a specific form of divine providence.

Second, the commentary on Job is interesting in another respect. As mentioned my thesis is that the problem of evil has no philosophical answer because there are too many philosophically discernable possibilities. As such, the philosopher's conclusion is similar to Aquinas's conclusion regarding the world's creation in time or from eternity. On the latter topic Aquinas says that demonstrative arguments do not exist for one or the other alternative. Hence, Aquinas concludes that the philosopher does not know how creation has taken place. In the Job commentary, Aquinas has God castigating both Job and his interlocutors for claiming a certitude that neither has. Job's error is to think that he can prove the resurrection when in fact it is a truth of faith. The interlocutors, as mentioned, erroneously limit God's providence to only this life.

But since human wisdom is not sufficient to comprehend the truth of divine providence, it was necessary that the debate just mentioned be determined by divine authority. But since Job had the right opinion about divine providence but had been so immoderate in his manner of speaking that scandal was produced from it in the hearts of the others when they thought that he was not showing due reverence to God, the Lord, therefore, just like the determiner of a debate, criticized Job's friends because they did not have the right opinion, Job himself because of his inordinate manner of speaking, and Elihu for his unsuitable decision.[22]

---

21. Ibid., 230–31.
22. Ibid., 415. In the interpretive essay that prefaces Damico's translation, Martin D. Yaffe remarks: "The debate eventually culminates in the revelation of Job's sinfulness in attempting to convert his friends to a full understanding of the cause of his suffering merely by arguing with them. Thomas's exposition is accordingly designed to show not only the merit of Aristotelian philosophy for understanding divine providence in a Christian setting, but also its limitations." Ibid., 28–29. See also, 44–45 on the disjunction in Aquinas's text

AMBIGUITY OF "*PRAETER INTENTIONEM*" AND "*PER ACCIDENS*"

My previous chapter noted that the relation of God to *quandoque* evils was one of permission. Given that *quandoque* evils are cases of the lower acting adversely on the higher, it is clear that *quandoque* evils strike against the divinely intended perfection of the universe. Such evils would not be willed or intended by God; hence, Aquinas's description of them as "permitted." What about the relation of God to natural corruptions? In contrast to *quandoque* evils, which are only permitted, natural corruptions, one could surmise, are in some sense willed or intended by God. In the above quote of *ST* I-II, 85, 6c, Aquinas said that the universal cause intends the good and conservation of the universe to which is demanded the alteration of generation and corruption. Does the conservation of the universe demand the willful alteration of generation and corruption? In the previous lines, Aquinas has contrasted the particular nature with this universal nature. He described the particular nature as intending being (*esse*) and its conservation. Hence, a reader might surmise that the universal nature intends nonbeing also.

An earlier text from the *Prima Pars* would appear to confirm the inference that God has some willful relation to evil when the kind of evil is natural corruption. The text is I, 19, 9c, and is devoted to the question of whether God wills evil.

> Since the good and the appetible are the same in nature, as was said before, and since evil is opposed to good, it is impossible that any evil, as such, should be sought for by the appetite, either natural, or animal, or by the intellectual appetite which is the will. Nevertheless evil may be sought accidentally [*per accidens*], so far as it accompanies a good, as appears in

---

at chapter 14, verse 15; ibid., 229. For a contemporary and popular Jewish reading of the book of Job that views God as all-good but finite in power, see Harold S. Kushner, *When Bad Things Happen to Good People* (New York: Avon Books, 1981), chapter 2: "The Story of a Man Named Job."

each of the appetites. For a natural agent does not intend privation or corruption; he intends the form to which is yet annexed the privation of some other form, and the generation of one thing, which yet implies the corruption of another. For when a lion kills a stag, his object is food, which yet is accompanied by the killing of the animal. Similarly the fornicator has merely pleasure for his object, which is yet accompanied by the deformity of sin.

Now the evil that accompanies one good is the privation of another good. Never therefore would evil be sought after, not even accidentally, unless the good that accompanies the evil were more desired than the good of which the evil is the privation. Now God wills no good more than He wills His own goodness; yet He wills one good more than another. Hence He in no way wills the evil of sin, which is the privation of right order toward the divine good. The evil of natural defect, or of punishment, He does will, by willing the good to which such evils are attached. Thus, in willing justice He wills punishment; and in willing the preservation of the order of nature He wills some things to be naturally corrupted.[23]

I want to make three comments. First, note the division of the *responsio*. The *responsio* consists of two main parts. The first main part is a general discussion of the relation between appetite and evil. The second main part applies this discussion to the relation of God's will to evils of natural defect, sin, and punishment. Obviously, the very organization of the material indicates that the first of the two parts is what is logically crucial.

Second, in the first main part Aquinas says that evil as such is not intended by any appetite. Rather, evil is sought accidentally insofar as it accompanies a good. He then provides a number of examples. It is very important to understand what Aquinas means when he says here that evil is accidentally sought, for sometimes what he says can be confused with not willing the evil at all or with not willing the effect in any way. In such cases evil is a purely unintended spin off of what one is intending. For example, the surgeon who removes the cancerous uterus and accidentally causes

---

23. Pegis, *Basic Writings of Thomas Aquinas*, vol. I, 209–10.

sterilization, or the traveler who takes the plane trip knowing that he will become airsick, or the person who goes to the dentist for a filling knowing that he will suffer pain. In all these cases the evils are not intended, or willed. They may be known and anticipated, but their inclusion within one's knowledge does not place them within the scope of what one wills. The evils simply accompany what is willed or intended. That these evils can be outside of the intention is confirmed by the fact that even if they failed to occur, the ends would still be achieved. For instance, I would still get to my destination if I did not get sick.

This kind of situation is acknowledged by Aquinas in his argument for the individual exercising self-defense at *ST* II-II, 64, 7. At the beginning of the response, Aquinas says that it is possible that one action can have two effects, only one of which is intended.[24] Private individuals in no way can morally include in their willing the death of an assailant. Only by acting under the authority of the person in charge of the common good can a private individual intend the assailant's death. Noteworthy is the self-defense article's use of the terms *"praeter intentionem"* and *"per accidens"* to describe the moral relation of the individual to the assailant's death. Unfortunately, this usage sets a textual trap for any reader who may be reading 19, 9, in the light of 64, 7.

What I want to emphasize is that at 19, 9, Aquinas is not speaking about such a situation as 64, 7. What he does mean at 19, 9, is clear from *C.G.* III, 6. He says first concerning humans:

> Though evil be apart from intention [*praeter intentionem*], it is nonetheless voluntary, ... though not essentially but accidentally so [*per accidens*]. For intention is directed to an ultimate end which a person wills for its own sake, but the will may also be directed to that which a person wills for the sake of something else, even if he would not will it simply for itself. In the example of the man who throws his merchandise into the sea in order to

---

24. "Dicendum quod nihil prohibit unius actus esse duos effectus, quorum alter solum sit in intentione, alius vero sit praeter intentionem." Ottawa ed., 1762b 37–40.

save himself, he does not intend the throwing away of the merchandise but his own safety; yet he wills the throwing not for itself but for the sake of the safety. Likewise, a person wills to do a disorderly action for the sake of some sensory good to be attained; he does not intend the disorder, nor does he will it simply for itself, but for the sake of this result [*non intendens inordinationem, neque volens eam simpliciter, sed propter hoc*]. And so, evil consequences and sins are called voluntary in this way, just as is the casting of merchandise into the sea.[25]

As the examples of the merchant and the sensual person indicate, evil is both "willed" and "intended." Hence, despite similar terminology to 64, 7, this *Contra Gentiles* passage has no connection to 64, 7. But, evil is not intended or willed simply for itself, or directly; some good is directly intended. This is a profound fact of human psychology. We can only will what appears as good. As the opening line of 19, 9c, said, the good and the appetible are the same in nature. In chapter 2, I presented this psychological dynamic when I explained Aquinas on the genesis of willing. Furthermore, because of a relation that an evil can have to the intended good, the evil can take on the appearance of good and so also be intended or willed. For example, in itself the loss of the goods in the sea is an evil, yet in the relation to one's survival the loss appears as good and so can be willed along with willing the good of one's survival. Likewise, sex with someone not one's wife is an evil, yet in relation to one's pleasure the illicit sex can appear as good and so be willed along with the willing of the pleasure. Note again that while the evils are willed or intended they are not willed in themselves but as they are related to goods that can be willed. So the merchant does not will the loss as loss but the loss as life saving. Evidently, what is *per accidens* and *praeter intentionem* can be what is willed or intended, though not willed or intended only but on account of some good. Again, this is a different use of these phrases than at 64, 7, in which "*praeter intentionem*" means not intended in any

---

25. Aquinas, *Summa contra Gentiles*, vol. III–I, 47.

sense, viz., neither simply nor indirectly. Finally, the moral neutrality of the analysis is striking. The point that evil is willed or intended but willed or intended accidentally is true both of moral situations, for example, the merchant jettisoning the goods into the sea, and immoral situations, for example, the fornicator willing the illicit sex.

In the next paragraph of *C.G.* III, 6, Aquinas says that this model for intending evil holds on the sub-human level.

Indeed, the change of corruption is never found without the change of generation; neither, as a consequence, is the end of corruption found without the end of generation. So, nature does not intend the end of corruption as separated from the end of generation, but both at once. It is not the unqualified intention of nature [*de intentione naturae absoluta*] that water should not exist, but that there should be air, and while a thing is so existing it is not water. So, nature directly intends [*intendit natura secundum se*] that this existing thing be air; it does not intend that this thing should not exist as water, except as a concomitant of the fact that it is to be air. Thus, privations are not intended by nature in themselves [*secundum se intentae*], but only accidentally [*secundum accidens*]; forms, however, are intended in themselves.[26]

First, nature intends. "Intends" has obviously shifted its meaning. In the previous paragraph Aquinas employed the word for action to a good with an awareness of it as good. In other words, intending was willing. As the example of the air makes plain, nature does not act for a good with an awareness of the good. Nature simply acts for a good, or for an end. Elsewhere, Aquinas explains why he maintains this ordination of nature: "For if the agent were not determinate to some particular effect, it would not do one thing rather than another; consequently in order that it produce a determinate effect, it must of necessity, be determined to some certain one, which has the nature of an end."(*ST* I-II, 1, 2c) So for our present purposes, we should be taking "nature intends" simply for ac-

---

26. Ibid., 47.

tion to an end, or for directed action. Second, nature intends evil, for example, corruption, as evil is united with a good, for example, generation. That is, nature intends evil but indirectly or accidentally. Third, again the analysis is morally neutral, for nature does not commit moral evil.

The last paragraph continues the discussion of intending evil on the subhuman level. However, the paragraph introduces some concepts that will have wider application.

It is clear, then, from the foregoing that what is evil in an unqualified sense [*simpliciter malum*] is completely apart from intention [*omnino est praeter intentionem*] in the workings of nature, as in the birth of monsters; on the other hand, that which is not evil in the unqualified sense, but evil in relation to some definite thing, is not directly intended by nature but only accidentally [*non est intentum a natura secundum se, sed secundum accidens*].[27]

Aquinas mentions a new item that he describes as evil in an unqualified sense and which he illustrates in the birth of monsters. Also, this type of evil is not intended at all. As not intended at all, this type of corruption would seem to be only "permitted." At *De Ver.* 5, 4c, Aquinas again brings up the case of monsters and has them falling under God's providence of "permission."[28] As only permitted, these corruptions would contrast to the "natural corruptions" intended *per accidens* back in 19, 9. My point is that Aquinas seems to distinguish kinds of corruptions on the subhuman level. There are natural corruptions that are intended *secundum accidens* and there are "unnatural" corruptions that are intended not at all but only permitted. The linking of permission talk, as well as the linking of *quandoque* and *interdum* talk, with this second kind of evil

---

27. Ibid., 48.
28. "A defective act which results occasionally in the generation of natural monstrosities is, of course, directed by God to some useful purpose; but to this defective act itself nothing else was directed. It happened merely on account of the failure of some cause. With regard to the first-named act of generation, the providence is one of approval; with regard to the second, it is one of permission." Aquinas, *Disputed Questions on Truth*, vol. I, 219.

will be an important hermeneutical device to determine the type of evil about which Aquinas is speaking. Unfortunately, in his discussions of evil Aquinas does not always do the reader the courtesy of indicating the kind of evil under discussion.

In sum, to accidentally intend evil is to intend it. It is not simply to know evil but to leave evil outside of what one wills. Also, the willing of the evil is possible because the evil can be related to some good and so take on the appearance of good. So we will the evil not as evil but as related to some good.

Finally, third and returning to 19, 9, Aquinas completes the general framework by noting that doers of evil desire more the good to which the evil is attached than the good of which the evil is the privation. Again, the analysis is still morally neutral as can be seen from the previous examples of Aquinas's claim. The merchant desires (and rightly so) the preservation of his life over the profit from the merchandise. The fornicator, an example at *C.G.* III, 6 and repeated at 19, 9, desires (and unrightly so) pleasure over continued rectitude with the moral norm for sexual activity. With the framework complete, Aquinas now turns to God. He says that God does will the evils of punishment and natural corruption insofar as he does will the goods of justice and the perfection of the universe. Yet the evil of sin God wills in no way. The reason is that sin requires an order to a nondivine good and God cannot deny himself.[29] I have already elaborated how the universal cause intends natural corruption for the good that is the perfection of the universe. Now I want to elaborate how, for Aquinas, God wills *per accidens* the evil of punishment. After that I will be in a position to address some Thomists who reinterpret *per accidens* intention as permission.

---

29. For an elaboration of the immoral act as a turning from God, see chapter 7, "Avoidance of Culpability."

GOD AND THE EVIL OF PUNISHMENT (*POENA*)

Aquinas explicates God's willing of punishment by a comparison to the just judge. The just judge intends punishment like the fire that intends the corruption of the air. Aquinas says:

> It is not necessary that the good thing that is the accidental cause of evil be a deficient good. So God is the cause of the evil of punishment: for in punishing God does not intend the evil of him who is punished, but God intends to impress on things the order of his justice to which follows the evil of him who is punished, just as to the form of fire there follows the privation of the form of the water.[30]

We have seen how in natural things the corruption is intended. The corruption is not intended unqualifiedly but it is intended. So the judge would not intend for itself the deprivation of liberty or of life but for the order of justice. The comparison of the just judge to the fire is furthered by another text in which Aquinas brings out an indisposition to the form of justice in the sinner so that the imposition of the form of justice entails an evil in the sinner.

Punishment happens from a defect of matter; which is evident so. The just judge intends to place in his subjects the order of justice. That order is not able to be received in the sinner except insofar as the sinner is punished through some defect; and so although that defect by reason of which the punishment is called evil is not intended by the judge, but the order of justice is intended, nevertheless, the just judge is called the author of punishment, insofar as the punishment is ordered as he says.[31]

Like the air that cannot receive without loss to itself the fire, so too the sinner cannot receive without a loss to the sinner the justice.

---

30. "non oportet quod bonum quod est causa mali per accidens, sit bonum deficiens. Sic autem Deus est causa mali poenae: non enim in puniendo intendit malum eius quod punitur, sed ordinem suae iustitiae imprimere rebus, ad quod sequitur malum eius quod punitur, sicut ad formam ignis sequitur privatio formae aquae." *De Malo*, q. 1, a. 3, ad 10m; P. Bazzi and P. M. Pession, eds., *Questiones Disputatae de Malo. In Quaestiones Disputatae*, vol. 2, (Turin and Rome: Marietti, 1965), 456.

31. "poena incidit ex defectu materiae; quod sic patet. Ordinem justitiae justus judex

But the fire intends in a qualified manner the corruption of the air, that is, insofar as that is good for the generation of the fire. So too the just judge intends the punishment, not unqualifiedly, but as it is ordered to the order of justice.

That the punishment is in some way intended by the judge is also indicated by the above-mentioned *ST* II-II, 64, 7, discussion of self-defense. There the private citizen must in no way intend the death of the assailant. The death must be *praeter intentionem* in the sense of being in no way intended. For the citizen to intend the death of the assailant is to wrongly usurp what belongs to those in charge of the common good and their executors. Obviously, these latter can intend the death of the sinner when that appears as good in relation to the common good. But the judge is included among those in charge of the common good. Hence, the judge can and does intend the evil of punishment in the qualified way explained in *C.G.* III, 6.

Finally, obviously God would will, or intend, the evil of punishment in the same manner as the just judge. So that is what Aquinas seems to mean when he says that God wills the evil of punishment in willing the good of justice.

OTHER INTERPRETATIONS: CHARLES CARDINAL JOURNET AND PATRICK LEE

I have been arguing that something evil can be willed insofar as it can take on the appearance of good by a relation to something good. So, in other circumstances, the loss of the merchandise always appears as evil. But in the circumstances of the storm, the loss appears as good insofar as the loss saves the merchant's life. Aquinas's technical way of expressing this point is variously ex-

---

in suis subditis ponere intendit. Ille ordo non potest in peccante recipi nisi secundum quod per defectum aliquem punitur; et ideo quamvis defectus ille ratione cujus poena malum dicitur, a judice intentus non sit, sed ordo justitiae: tamen justus judex poenae auctor dicitur." *In II Sent.* d. 37, q. 3, a. 2, ad 2m; Thomas Aquinas, *Scriptum super Libros Sententiarum Magistri Petri Lombardi Episcopi Parisensis*, vol. II, edited by Pierre Mandonnet (Paris: P. Lethielleux, 1929), 959–60.

pressed. The loss is willed *per accidens*, intended *secundum quod*, intended *propter hoc*, not intended *secundum se*, not intended *absolute*. So when Aquinas says that evil is *praeter intentionem*, Aquinas does not mean necessarily that evil is completely outside of intention. He means only that it is completely outside of what is intended absolutely or according to itself. However, if the evil is an evil *simpliciter*, then the evil is *praeter intentionem* in the sense of not intended at all. Permission talk will be a textual indication of this latter case.

My conclusion so far does not have Aquinas espousing that any end morally justifies the means. Aquinas's examples of the adulterer or fornicator follow the above psychology for intending evil but both are sins for Aquinas. As noted in chapter 2, fixed coordinates for our moral compass exist. These coordinates correspond to situations that are heightened presentations, or epiphanies, of being. As an intellector of being, the human person is such a situation. Actions disrespectful of the person are actions disrespectful of the good because of the person's intellection of being. So, the adulterer acts immorally insofar as the adultery amounts to jettisoning "the good" donated to him by his spouse in the marital embrace. One does not treat the good that disrespectfully.

As should also be clear, in my interpretation of Aquinas, God himself does will, as distinct from merely permits, some kinds of evils. The evils that God wills, *pace per accidens* and *praeter intentionem*, are the evils of natural corruption and punishment. Such willings do not make God morally deficient because God's willing of these evils is in relation to morally legitimate goods for a creator. In contrast *quandoque* evils and the evil of sin are in no way willed by God. The reason is that they involve a break with morally legitimate goods. As an attack of the lower on the higher, *quandoque* evils aim to wreck the perfection of the universe to which the creator is committed. Also, by disrespecting an epiphany of being, sin *qua* sin amounts to a turning away from being which as subsistent *esse* the creator is by its nature.

Yet, other Thomists insist that the relation of God to every kind of evil, even to natural corruption and punishment, is on the model of what I have called *quandoque* evils. In other words, God wills evils in no way; God's relation to all evils is simply permission. Aquinas's talk about willing evil *per accidens* and evil being *praeter intentionem* is retranslated into permission talk according to which evil is not at all willed. One such Thomist is Charles Cardinal Journet, an ardent disciple of Jacques Maritain. Journet's thinking is expressed in the following remarks from his *The Meaning of Evil*. He elaborates his model for God's relation to all evil by explaining God's relation to the evil of punishment. He says,

> In absolutely no way at all is God the cause of the evil of guilt, but he is the cause of the evil of punishment in exactly the same way as he is of the evil in the universe. It is the order of the universe that God wills; punishment, which he does not will or intend—and God should not be thought of as a torturer—is the injury self-inflicted by those who rebel against an order which, being divine, could never be upset by a creature. God only "wills" it in this quite indirect way, reluctantly, *praeter intentionem*. Jesus wept at the tomb of Lazarus and over the coming ruin of Jerusalem. About the evil of punishment as well as physical evil it can be said, to ward off any misunderstanding, not that God "causes" it or "wills" it, but that he permits it.[32]

The two cases of Jesus weeping are meant to illustrate that God intends neither death nor corruption nor punishment. Journet claims that in "exactly the same way" as God is the cause of corruption God is the cause of punishment. He elaborates this claim by describing how God is a cause of punishment. The sinner's punishment is self-inflicted. By sinning the sinner places himself contrary to the order God places in creation and so suffers the nasty consequences. The sinner is doing an about-face in the parade of creatures marching to God. Hence, the sinner suffers punishment

---

32. Charles Journet, *The Meaning of Evil*, translated by Michael Barry (New York: P. J. Kenedy & Sons, 1963), 75.

without God having to intend the punishment. Likewise, as God the just judge intends the order of justice, God the creator intends the order of the universe. The preservation of the order of the universe requires redistributing matter from the higher to the lower species. That redistribution entails the corruption of the higher and the generation of the lower. Similarly, the intended redistribution of bricks from one edifice to another means the unintended destruction of the first edifice. Journet concludes that the proper way to speak of God's relation to punishment and to evil in the universe is to speak of permission not volition.[33]

No doubt cases do exist in which the evil is an unintended effect of what is intended. I mentioned some cases when describing one of two senses of *"praeter intentionem."* But to make this model universal so that the "willing" of any evil is only permission seems to greatly simplify a very complex situation. Judges protect the order of justice, but they do that by ordering executions or imprisonments. These evils for the sinner are intended as a means to the end of justice. Here the judge is not intending simply the order of justice. Execution and imprisonment are also intended insofar as they appear as good in respect to the good of justice. Likewise, before there is a redistribution of the bricks, there is the demolition. In relation to the planned edifice, the demolition appears as a sufficiently distinct good to be an object of willing. As it happens, I recall the nun in my seventh grade literature class assigning us to memorize William Blake's *The Tiger* but telling us not to think about the poem too much. Obviously her reason was related to the

---

33. Journet summarizes his view: "God neither *creates* nor *causes* evil. He does not *will* evil. To think that he seeks, desires or intends privation for its own sake would be an absurdity. In *nature* he wills and intends the renovation, not the destruction which goes with it. He wills and intends not the evil of punishment, but the order and good with which disorder and rebellion clash. The evil in nature and evil of punishment, which are not willed for their own sakes or intended, and which are only willed by reason of the good which they include, can be said to be willed *accidentally*, or more simply, *permitted*." Meaning of Evil, 75. The last line summarizes Journet's interpretative strategy, viz., to understand *per accidens* willing as permitting. This move means that *per accidens* willing is not willing at all.

fact that before the phenomenon of nutrition, there is the slaughtering. And the tiger's "fearful symmetry" is geared to effect that bloodletting. Hence, the "framer" of that fearful symmetry, God, is cruel.

In response, I would begin by saying that some Thomists have a simplistic understanding of Aquinas's reiterated Aristotelian maxim—the corruption of one thing is the generation of another. True, a substantial change happens in a moment, and at that moment corruption is one side of a coin whose other side is generation. But that instant can be preceded by a destructive process that on the sentient level is excruciating. Aquinas would not shirk from the conclusion that the tiger is partly designed to produce the ripping and tearing of that process. Aquinas is well aware that obtaining food means intending to kill. At *C.G.* III, 112, Aquinas acknowledges that the killing is "an act of cruelty" (*aliquid crudelitatis*). In fact, the violence involved is one of Aquinas's reasons against random killing of animals. Random killing may dispose humans to be violent to each other.[34] But what Aquinas affirms is that in respect to the needs of the higher, because more perfect, existent, the killing of animals is "good."[35] Hence, Aquinas says that "man uses [brute animals] without any injustice, either by killing them or by employing them in any other way." The killing is not something only "permitted" but clearly an intended means to an end and morally so.

In his already referenced *The Meaning of Evil*, Journet cites various Thomistic texts but seems to have a persistent problem in understanding that Aquinas does not seem to be speaking about

---

34. "Indeed, if any statements are found in Sacred Scripture prohibiting the commission of an act of cruelty against brute animals ... this is said either to turn the mind of man away from cruelty which might be used on other men, lest a person through practicing cruelty on brutes might go on to do the same to men." *C.G.* III, 112; Aquinas, *Summa contra Gentiles*, vol. III, part 1, 119. Actually, Aquinas's argument at *ST* II-II, 64, 1c, is quite restrictive. He mentions killing of animals for food use. Surprisingly there is no mention of using animals for clothing, presumably because clothing can be produced without killing animals. Hence, one could conclude that Aquinas would be open to vegetarian arguments, provided human nutritional needs can be met.

35. Above n. 1.

all evils but only about *quandoque* evils. On page 80 Journet cites *In I Sent*, d. 39, q. 2, a. 2, in which Aquinas says that evil is known and governed but not intended by God. The concern of the article is whether God's providence is of all things. In the response of the article, Aquinas says that the evils that God only knows and governs without intending are of two kinds. The second kind of evil mentioned is defects of the will, viz., immoral choices or sins. All Thomists admit that God does not in any sense intend these evils. I have already noted the very clear expression of this thesis in *ST* I, 19, 9. The first kind of evil mentioned is evil of nature (*malum naturae*). Aquinas connects this evil to a grade of nature that is able to be impeded and made defective. Aquinas identifies this grade with generable and corruptible things. Hence, evils of nature appear to be identical to the *quandoque* evils mentioned later at *ST* I, 48, 2.[36]

Aquinas's reply to the fourth objection in our *In I Sent* d. 39, q.2, a.2 text corroborates this impression. In the fourth reply Aquinas again divides evils into the two types, defects of will or evils of nature, and then goes on to argue that natural evils occur only in a few instances (*in paucioribus*). Aquinas provides two reasons, the second of which is relevant for my purposes. First, appealing to his Ptolemaic cosmology, evils of nature are confined to earth, which is small compared to the cosmos.[37] Second, and pertinent to my argument, natural causes are deficient only in a minority of cases and from this failure evil happens. Aquinas clearly seems to be speaking of instances like the monsters mentioned in *De Ver.* V. 4c, which we saw were also *quandoque* evils.

In *The Meaning of Evil*, 82, Journet cites *In I Sent.*, d. 46, q. 1, a. 4, ad 2m and a. 2. These texts have Aquinas saying that God neither wills evils to be, for God would then be responsible for evil, nor does God will evils not to be, for then God's will would be inef-

---

36. See "Aquinas's Rationale for the Corruptible Order" in chapter 3.
37. For a description of this cosmology, see Thomas Kuhn, *The Copernican Revolution: Planetary Astronomy in the Development of Western Thought* (Cambridge, Mass.: Harvard University Press, 1956), ch. 1.

Natural Corruptions   101

fectual. Hence, the only thing left to say is that God wills to permit evils. Again, Journet understands God's permission here to be in respect to all kinds of evils. But as the response makes clear, the evils that God wills to permit to be made (*vult permittere mala fieri*) are not all kinds of evils but only *quandoque* evils. In the response Aquinas says that God wills antecedent and consequent goods that are joined to evil. The antecedent good is a condition of nature that is able to become defective, which God institutes and conserves in such a condition. In the preceding third article, which is devoted to the topic of whether evil belongs to the perfection of the universe, Aquinas describes this antecedent good as "some time defecting" (*quandoque deficit*) and as necessary for the universe's perfection in every grade of goodness (*sine tali natura, ex cujus defectu incidit malum, non esset universum perfectum in omnibus gradibus bonitates*). These remarks indicate that the evils that God wills to permit to be made are not all evils but *quandoque* evils. Again, Aquinas is speaking of evils like the birth of monsters and the attack of the lower upon the higher that happen occasionally in a universe that without supernatural assistance cannot be perfectly ordered. Aquinas is saying nothing about natural corruptions like death in old age or after reaching maturity. My remarks apply to Aquinas's discussion at *In I Sent.*, of d. 46, q. 1, a. 2, whether it is good that evil be made. Properly speaking, it is good that evil be an "occasion" of a good elicited by God. But in article three the evils that "occasion" these divinely ordered goods are *quandoque* evils, as I have noted.

Also, in *The Meaning of* Evil, 82, Journet cites three texts from the *Summa Theologiae*. For Journet, an argument that is common to all three texts is that "... before even distinguishing between types of evil, St. Thomas teaches in general that God, while not willing evil, permits it." In contrast to Journet, I claim that in the *Summa* texts Aquinas is speaking of a specific type of evil, *quandoque* evil. The first text is Aquinas's third reply at I, 19, 9. To the objection that God either wills evils to be or wills them not to be, but not the second and so the first, Aquinas replies that properly speaking God wills to permit evils to be. In order to comment, I want to note that the *Summa* text is identical to the just mentioned *In I Sent.*, d, 46. q, 1, a. 4, ad 2m. But the *Sentences* text is clearly not speaking about all evils but only of *quandoque* evils. Also, 19, 9, itself indicates a specific kind of evil as the focus of the third reply. In the article's response Aquinas says that God does will the evils of natural corruption and punishment, though only in the light of morally legitimate goods, while God in no way wills the evil of sin. Journet's interpretation of Aquinas's third reply would have Aquinas contradicting himself in the article's response. In other words, the third reply says no evils are willed but all are only permitted; the response says some evils are willed, viz., natural corruptions and punishments, and others are permitted, viz., sin. To avoid this contradiction a reader, in my opinion, should understand the third reply to be speaking about the evil of sin or something like sin. At the minimum, the contradiction generated by Journet's interpretation should cause the reader to keep an open mind with the hope that further reading will resolve the issue. As I will soon note, further reading is instructive.

Journet is sensitive to this appearance of contradiction. His solution is illustrative of the desperate situation in which he finds himself. After arguing that all talk of willing *per accidens* is really not willing at all but permitting, Journet acknowledges that Aquinas seems to reserve permission talk for the evil of sin. We saw this to be the case at 19, 9, and at the very end of *C.G.* III, 6, in which Aquinas mentions unqualified evils, for example, the birth of monsters, as completely apart from intention. Journet remarks, "[I]t has just been said that God *permits* the evil in nature and the evil of punishment. But it is already apparent that he must be said to permit the evil of sin in a different, and much more mysterious, way."[38] If "permits" means not willed at all, what sense of permission remains for sin? For Aquinas, God cannot relate to evil in na-

---

38. Journet, *The Meaning of Evil*, 78.

ture and to punishment in the same way as he relates to the evil of sin. But if Journet makes the relation to the first two a relation of permission, then it seems he has lost the contrast. Sin will be permitted also. Journet's talk of a different and more mysterious way of permission for the evil of sin appears to be just special pleading.

A study of Journet's other *prima pars* texts confirms the linkage of permission talk, not with all evils, but with particular kinds, viz., *quandoque* evils and the evil of sin. At q. 22, a. 2, ad 2m, Aquinas argues that everything is subject to divine providence. The second objection argues that a wise provider excludes any evil, as far as he can, from those under his care. But since many evils exist, then either God is not omnipotent or else God does not have care for all. In his reply Aquinas insists that the wise provider of which the objection speaks is a particular one. A universal provider permits some defect in some particular (*permittit aliquem defectum in aliquo particulari*) so that the good of the whole is unhindered. Aquinas says: "It pertains to its providence that it permit some defects to be in some particular things, that the perfect good of the universe is not impeded."³⁹ Even though "*quandoque*" and "*interdum*" are absent from the text, the permitted evils are characterized as few and that is consistent with *quandoque* evils. More importantly, the language and thinking of Aquinas's second reply is echoed by Journet's last *prima pars* text, q. 48, a. 2, ad 3m. In chapter 3, I already analyzed 48, 2. Aquinas's text was my original locus for the delineation of permitted evils as *quandoque* evils.

In sum, Aquinas does speak of God permitting evil. But Journet is wrong to make this thesis universal. Some evils are permitted, some are willed. The former are *quandoque* evils and sin; the latter are natural corruptions. A source of Journet's confusion is Aquinas's terminology of *praeter intentionem* and *per accidens* when speaking of willing evil. But a careful reading of *C.G.* III, 6, in the

---

39. "Cum igitur Deus sit universalis provisor totius entis, ad ipsius providentiam pertinet ut permittat quosdam defectus esse in aliquibus particularibus rebus, ne impediatur bonum universi perfectum."

light of Aquinas's psychology of willing shows that these phrases should not be taken to mean that evil is not willed at all and only permitted. Rather, though evil is not willed in itself, evil is willed when it appears as good in relation to a desired good. If the desired good is moral, then the willing of the evil is moral. The desired good is moral if it is respectful of the person understood as an intellector of being.

Hence, there are two crucial ambiguities in Aquinas's text. The first ambiguity concerns the term "evil." Evil can stand for a natural corruption or for a *quandoque* evil. The former is willed by God insofar as God wills the perfection of the universe. The latter smashes that teleology insofar as the latter attacks the higher. *Quandoque* evils are unfortunate side effects of a corruptible order in which the agents are only movers and so presuppose something that they do not set up. This presupposition will contain factors that will infrequently ambush the agent's causality so that a *quandoque* evil results. The divine will both permits these evils and orders them to some good. When Aquinas discusses evil as an objection to God's existence and providence, the evil that he seems to have in mind is *quandoque* evil.

The second ambiguity concerns the phrase "outside, or beyond intention: *praeter intentionem*." The phrase can stand either for something not willed at all, or in no respect, such as in double effect reasoning, or for something willed only in relation to some intended good, such as in the example of jettisoning the cargo in the storm. *Quandoque* evils are for God *praeter intentionem* in the first sense; natural corruptions are *praeter intentionem* in the second sense.

Another and more recent Thomist who takes the same line as Journet concerning the relation of God's will to evils is Patrick Lee. In an article devoted to the existence of moral absolutes in Aquinas's natural law ethics, Lee asserts that God is totally innocent of evil and does no evil whatsoever.[40] Like Journet, Lee interprets

---

40. Patrick Lee, "Permanence of the Ten Commandments: St. Thomas and His Modern Commentators," *Theological Studies* 42 (1981): 422–43.

Aquinas's saying that God does not intend evils *per se* to mean that God does not intend these evils at all. Accordingly, "God intends only the goodness communicated."[41] In my analysis of the article, Lee provides two reasons for his assertion. To begin, no Thomist argues that evil is *per se* intended. That claim would contradict Aquinas's psychology of willing in which being, as the good, calls forth volition. But a Thomist like myself argues that evil can be willed when evil appears as good in relation to some good. For example, adultery appears as good as productive of pleasure; the jettisoning of the precious cargo appears as good in relation to saving one's life in a storm-tossed ship. Hence, Lee first argues that God cannot will evil in this *per accidens* sense because "God does not intend means of any kind, whether good or evil."

It is true that in respect to himself as all-perfect, God has no need for anything, and so strictly speaking nothing is a means for God. As Lee notes, creatures are a communication and participation in God's goodness, not a means to it.[42] One could also add that God's willing a means would place an unacceptable discursion and/or complexity in God's eternal and simple willing. But in respect to his creatures, God does will one thing to be a means to another. I have already mentioned God's willing of natural corruption for the continuance of species and hence for the perfection of the universe and God's willing of punishment for the order of justice. One could add God's ordering of the lower to the higher and so God's sanctioning of the killing of the lower to be used as food for the higher. "For animals are ordered to man's use in the natural course of things, according to divine providence. Consequently, man uses them without any injustice, either by killing them or by employing them in any other way."[43] In sum, some evils are necessary conditions for other creaturely goods and these evils God wills.[44]

---

41. Ibid., 436. 42. Ibid., 434–35.
43. C.G. III, 112; Aquinas, *Summa contra Gentiles*, vol. III–II, 119.
44. God does this by a willing of himself that is not different for the willing's includ-

Second, like Journet, Lee mentions the thesis that generation and corruption are distinct aspects of the same physical effect.[45] I have already mentioned that this thesis is simplistic. The thesis does not address the destruction that is the necessary condition for the critical moment in which we have both generation and corruption.

Of course, on behalf of his interpretation that God intends only the goodness communicated, Lee also cites Aquinas's texts. Some of them I have already mentioned above, viz., *In II Sent.* d. 37, q. 3, a. 1, ad 2m, at my n. 23 and *De Malo* q. 1, a. 3, ad 10m at my n. 22. I find Lee saying nothing to counter my interpretation of these passages. New texts cited by Lee do require comment. First, again from the *Sentences* commentary II, d. 32, q. 2, a. 1, Lee references Aquinas's explanation about how God causes punishment.[46] Lee mentions only one way while the text describes two. There is not one way in which God causes punishment. On the one hand, God causes punishment as an agent inflicts a contrary. Aquinas sees nothing untoward in God doing this since every punishment is just. On the other hand, God can cause punishment not as an agent but by sim-

---

ing creatures or not including them. On Aquinas's understanding of God's willing, see my "*Contra* Spinoza: Aquinas on God's Free Will," *American Catholic Philosophical Quarterly* 76 (2002), 417–29.

45. Lee, "Permanence of the Ten Commandments," 436.

46. "But not in the same way is God the cause of all punishment. For some punishment is through the infliction of some destroying and corrupting contrary; and such punishment is from God the agent, from whom every action, insofar as it is ordered, and subsequent passion, takes a beginning. Every punishment, since it is just, is ordered. Some punishment exists which consists simply in removal or defect, just as the subtraction of grace, and others of this kind. And these punishments are from God, not as from some agent, but more as by not causing [*a non influente*] such perfection; because in him is to cause [*influere*], and of both the cause is his will. Hence, if the *fomes* insofar as they are a punishment are considered, one does not speak of some inflicted punishment, because the supernatural principles do not suppose something positive in man but the *fomes* pertain to that genus of punishments which consist simply in defect. For from this the *fomes* or concupiscence incline inordinately, because there is subtracted the chain of original justice holding the inferior powers in the obedience of reason. And according to this God is said to be the cause of this kind of punishment insofar as he does not confer on a born man what he gave to the first created man."

ply removing the supernatural assistance by which the agitation of our lower human nature, called *fomes*, is curtailed in the state of original justice. It is this second way of punishing that appears to fit Lee's model, in which God does not have to intend the punishment in any way at all. Here God intends simply the removal of the supernatural support that protected our higher nature from the assault of our lower. The resulting conflicted situation is an automatic, but unintended, result of that removal.

By way of comment, I have two remarks. First, Lee fails to mention the first way God causes punishment, viz., God punishes as an agent inflicting a contrary quality. There is no problem with God acting in this way because the punishment is just. It is noteworthy that Aquinas describes the agent's action as an infliction (*inflictio*). Elsewhere at *C.G.* III, 146, Aquinas says that the punishments of the judge are inflicted (*infligantur*), and we know that, unlike the private citizen, the judge inflicts these punishments intentionally. In fact 146 repeats the capital punishment argument. So the inflictor, divine or human, seems to apply will to the punishment. Examples of such actions might include incarceration instead of freedom, pain instead of pleasure, death instead of life. In light of justice each first member of these pairs appears as good and so can be willed, albeit indirectly.

My second comment is to question whether God's second way of punishing fits Lee's model. At first glance, it appears so. For a just end God would intend only the removal of supernatural assistance and the punishment described as the conflict between our lower and higher natures would automatically result. But the problem is that Aquinas says that God wills both punishments: *utriusque sua voluntas causa est*. So though in the second way of causing punishment, the punishment could be left unintended, it is not. God intends both the removal and the punishment. Likewise, I would say, though a private citizen could intend to defend himself without intending to kill the assailant, the scope of his willing could go on to include the killing for purposes of revenge, for example. So what could be left unintended does not have to be. In the case of the second type of the way God causes punishment, the punishment is willed.

So nothing in the *In Sententiae* text verifies Lee's thesis that for Aquinas God causes punishment without intending it. Lee's next text is *C.G.* II, 41. The text argues that evil is caused accidentally. Here "accidentally" seems to mean "not willed at all" because the text uses the accidental discovery of treasure as an example. The text concludes that such is the way in which evil results in the effects of the first principle of all things. Aquinas goes on to say that in this way God causes those evils among men which are called penal. Aquinas does not elaborate but quotes St. Gregory: "[God] is said to create evils when He uses created things, which in themselves are good, to punish us for our evil doings." Later at III, 145, Aquinas appears to elaborate:

> Besides, if a man makes inordinate use of a means to the end, he may not only be deprived of the end, but may also incur some other injury. This is exemplified in the inordinate eating of food, which not only fails to maintain strength, but also leads to sickness. Now, the man who puts his end among created things does not use them as he should, namely, by relating them to his ultimate end. So, he should not only be punished by losing happiness, but also by experiencing some injury from them.[47]

Pain results from the sinner using created goods inordinately. For example, food is for nourishment. Over and beyond that it causes sickness. Such a result is simply automatic. Likewise, the digging farmer is intent on planting. Yet if he keeps on digging he will find the treasure. So too, the glutton is intent on pleasure. Yet if he continues eating, he will discover sickness. Accordingly, what Aquinas appears to be saying back in *C.G.* II, 41, is that God has so designed the world that good things are a brake on our pursuit of evil. In effect, the sinner is walking against the traffic flow of creation toward good and so naturally and automatically suffers injury.

47. Aquinas, *Summa contra Gentiles*, vol. III–II, 219.

Again, Lee uses this text for the thesis that God in no way wills the evil of punishment. The problem, in my opinion, is that *"praeter intentionem"* qualifies creatures not the creator. Like the treasure is to the farmer, evil is *praeter intentionem* "among the things that God has created." The text says nothing about the relation of God's willing to these evils that the wicked suffer. Or perhaps, the text says a little something. The Gregory quote mentions God using creatures to punish evil doers. And as mentioned, it appears that God has designed things that way. But if *C.G.* II, 41 is basically neutral for purposes of Lee's thesis, other texts are clearer. As pointed out, both *ST* I, 19, 9, and *In I Sent.* d. 32, q. 2, a. 1, have Aquinas saying that God wills punishment. Finally, there is this argument. I have noted that Aquinas says that the evil of sin is something that is permitted within divine providence. Furthermore, permitted evils are ordered by God to some good. But why cannot that good be, along with the patience of the martyrs, the good of punishment as it reflects God's justice? Aquinas acknowledges such a case of divine ordering: "For example, when a man sins, God orders the sin to the sinner's good, so that after his fall, upon rising again, he may be a more humble person; or it is ordered at least to a good which is brought about in him by divine justice when he is punished for his sins."[48] I submit that "ordering" means "willed."

The last of Lee's texts is *ST* I, 49, 2. Aquinas asks if God is the cause of evil. Aquinas's reply lists the threefold division of evil from I, 19, 9, viz., corruption, sin or fault, and punishment. Aquinas's conclusion at 49, 2, is identical to that at 19, 9. By causing the order of the universe and of justice, God causes *per accidens* the evils of corruption and penalty. God does not cause the evil of sin. The sense of *per accidens* is indicated by Aquinas saying that God does not will death for its own sake. As I have noted, this is not the same sense of *"per accidens"* when the phrase is used by Journet and Lee. In sum, nothing of 49, 2, goes beyond my interpretation of 19, 9.

48. *De Ver.* 5, 5c; Aquinas, *Disputed Questions on Truth*, vol. I, 223.

ABRAHAM AND ISAAC

My thesis that God wills some evils in the course of willing some goods enables one to understand Aquinas's quite literal discussions of the Abraham and Isaac incident. In commanding Abraham to sacrifice Isaac, God is caught intending an evil, viz., the death of a young innocent. Aquinas's offered rationale is that the death of nature is the just penalty both for the innocent and the guilty because of the sin of our first parents: "All men alike, both the guilty and innocent, die the death of nature; which death of nature is inflicted by the power of God because of original sin, according to 1 Kings 2:6: *The Lord killeth and maketh alive.* Consequently, by the command of God, death can be inflicted on any man, guilty or innocent, without any injustice whatever."[49] Aquinas's reference to the death of nature is interesting. It seems to be a reference back to his explanation of how God wills the evil of natural corruption insofar as God wills the perfection of the universe. As I explained above while commenting upon I-II, 85, 6, for the universe to reflect the divine perfection through different kinds of things, each thing has its appointed time of existence and then its matter is recycled to others. This recycling of matter avoids the higher kinds of things, appropriating the matter of the lower and so destroying the diversity of things necessary for the universe to reflect the divine perfection.

This context for Aquinas's remarks on Abraham and Isaac raises some questions. First, if death is a natural defect consequent upon matter, then how can Aquinas speak of it as a punishment? The tension between these two characterizations of death is reflected in an objection to Aquinas's 85, 6, view that death is a natural defect: "That which is natural cannot be called either a punishment or an evil, since what is natural to a thing is suitable to it. But death and such defects are the punishment of original sin,

---

49. *ST* I-II, 94, 5, ad 2m; Pegis, *Basic Writings of Thomas Aquinas*, vol. II, 780.

... Therefore they are not natural to man."[50] Aquinas replies that a natural defect can be a punishment considering the perspective of the initial establishment of humans: "But God, to Whom every nature is subject, in forming man supplied the defect of nature, and by the gift of original justice gave the body a certain incorruptibility, ... It is in this sense that it is said that God made not death, and that death is the punishment of sin."[51] The removal of gifts once possessed is also painful. Simply ask any child who suffers the loss of Christmas or birthday gifts by a disciplining parent. So in a context of religious revelation, Aquinas's estimate of death is that it is both a natural defect and a punishment. In both cases evil is willed by God.

When I explained Aquinas's thesis of death as a natural defect, however, I noted that the death of an organism that had reach maturity was the subject of discussion. Death before maturity was a *quandoque* evil and not willed by God but only permitted by God. Since Isaac is a child, a second question follows. How can Aquinas take advantage of his explanation of death as a natural defect to explain the death of a child? I think the answer is that a child's death is a *quandoque* evil and is only permitted by God in the *natural* order of the universe. But, as far as the philosopher knows, the order of the universe may be wider than natural, as it was for Abraham and his people. God was not just the creator but the creator who freely revealed himself and spoke to Abraham in human history. In that more special setting and plan, God wills the death of Isaac for some perfection just as in the natural order death after the reaching of maturity is ordered for the perfection of the universe.

Aquinas's understanding of the Abraham and Isaac incident takes the full brunt of Maritain's Rachel and Camus's Rioux whom I described at the end of chapter 1. When given this explanation

---

50. *ST* I-II, 85, 6, 2 obj; Pegis, *Basic Writings of Thomas Aquinas*, vol. II, 703.
51. *ST* I-II, 85, 6c; Pegis, *Basic Writings of Thomas Aquinas*, vol II, 704.

of a child's death both Rachel and Rioux recoil in horror. Maritain remarks: "Tell [Rachel] this thing was necessary in order that every degree of being should be filled and she will answer that she cares not one whit for the machine of the world,—let them give her back her child." Likewise, Rioux: "No, Father [Paneloux], I've a very different idea of love. And until my dying day I shall refuse to love a scheme of things in which children are put to torture."

As noble as these reactions are, they are false. As I noted, Aquinas says the motions of the will are not to be trusted.[52] Superficial features of things, for example, diminutiveness, can draw being to things so that things appear as more precious then they are. In chapter 2's discussion of joy, I argued that we have all been subject to this confusion. I believe that this confusion is behind the reactions of Rachel and Rioux. For in truth, even the intellection of being, which gives the human a dignity crucial for ethics, still renders the human only a part of the created order. Intellection does not so intensely draw the analogon of being to the human that the human becomes the analogon. In Aquinas's metaphysics only the creator is a being that is being. In relation to God the creator, everything else is a part. This relation is a privilege of perfection. Hence, humans are always entangled in "a scheme of things." It is a confused but understandable and regrettable hubris to think otherwise. The result of Aquinas's open-eyed metaphysics is that a good always exists in virtue of which the creator can dispense death to any of us.

A third question looms. If God can command the slaying of Isaac to exemplify the faith of Abraham and the slaying of the Canaanites to exemplify God's love of and fidelity for his chosen people, what other acts can God command? Sexual abuse, rape, torture? The Christian God of Aquinas's metaphysics appears to be as wild and as unpredictable as some have depicted the God of Islam, according to Pope Benedict XVI's 2006 Regensburg address.[53]

---

52. See "Being and the Intellectual Emotions" in chapter 2.

53. "The decisive statement in this argument against violent conversion is this: not to act in accordance with reason is contrary to God's nature. The editor, Theodore Khoury,

Yet in the 1970s this line of Aquinas's thought was exploited by Catholic moralists to suggest the morality of contraceptive and homosexual acts if God ordered them. In his magisterial "Moral Absolutes and Thomas Aquinas," John G. Milhaven extensively investigates the nature of Aquinas's thinking not only in the Abraham and Isaac incident but also the incidents of God ordering Hosea to marry an adulterous woman, the polygamy of the patriarchs, and the Israelites taking the possessions of the Egyptians on the way to the promised land. Milhaven characterizes Aquinas's thinking this way:

> What emerges progressively from the analysis was that the moral center of gravity for Thomas did not lie in the act itself and its physical effect, though these were relevant factors. As long as the acts contributed to some good purpose, the crucial question to decide the legitimacy of a given means was the authority of the person acting: not what was to be done, but who would do it. Abortion and premarital sexual intercourse would be absolutely wrong if the agent had only normal human authority. But God could, by a special initiative, authorize a man to perform the same acts.[54]

With Aquinas's method of thinking settled, the interesting issue for Milhaven is "the question whether or not God has shared with man the authority and dominion to take certain means when, perhaps by way of exception, they serve the greater good."[55] Toward answering this question Milhaven affirms that twentieth-century man knows something that Aquinas did not because Western man was yet to learn it: "The extent of man's fantastic power over nature and human life and the extent of his inescapable moral autonomy. And might not the modern vision of the greater dominion and authority that God has shared with men have led Thomas by

---

observes: For the emperor, as a Byzantine shaped by Greek philosophy, this statement is self-evident. But for Muslim teaching, God is absolutely transcendent. His will is not bound up with any of our categories, even that of rationality." Pope Benedict XVI, "Regensburg: University Address, 12 September 2006." EWTN website, papal documents, www.vatican.va.

54. John G. Milhaven, "Moral Absolutes and Thomas Aquinas," in *Absolutes in Moral Theology*, edited by Charles E. Curran (Washington, D.C.: Corpus Books, 1968), 181–82.

55. Ibid., 183.

his own principles to rethink his conclusions on negative moral absolutes?"[56] I will argue that the possibility of a transfer of power from God to man is wishful thinking because God never had this authority and dominion in the first place. As we have already seen in both this chapter and in chapter 3, God's authority stems from his goodness as from a final cause and his goodness establishes boundaries for what God can do. In that way also I will reply to my third question.

Key passages for Milhaven's supposed discovery of the above mentioned framework are *In I Sent* d.47, q.1, a.4, and *De Malo* 3, 1, ad 17m. In the first Aquinas speaks, rather abstractly, of a twofold order to the good. He says,

For the good in things arises from a twofold order: of which the first and principle order is of all things to the ultimate end, which is God; the second order is of one thing to another thing: and the first order is the cause of the second, because the second order is on account of the first. For from this that things are ordered to each other, mutually helping themselves, so they are ordered fittingly to the ultimate end. Whence it is necessary that having subtracted the goodness which is from the order of one thing to the ultimate end, nothing of goodness is able to remain. But having subtracted the goodness which is the order of one thing to another thing, there is able to remain nevertheless that goodness which is from the order of the thing to the ultimate end: because the first does not depend from the second, just as the second from the first.[57]

Aquinas proceeds to apply this general framework to human acts. He says,

---

56. Ibid., 185.

57. "Bonum enim in rebus surgit ex duplici ordine: quorum primus et principalis ordo est rerum omnium ad finem ultimum, qui Deus est; secundus ordo est unius rei ad aliam rem: et primus ordo est causa secundi, quia secundus ordo est propter primum. Ex hoc enim quod res sunt ordinatae ad invicem, juvant se mutuo, ut ad finem ultimum debite ordinentur. Unde oportet quod subtracta bonitate quae est ex ordine unius rei ad finem ultimum nihil bonitatis remanere posit. Sed subtracta bonitate quae est ex ordine unius rei ad rem aliam, nihilominus potest remanere illa bonitos quae est ex ordine rei ad finem ultimum; quia primum non dependet ex secundo, sicut secundum ex primo." Aquinas, *Scriptum super Libros Sententiarum*, vol. II, 1072.

I say therefore, that certain sins name a deordination of one thing to another thing, just as homicide, fraternal hatred, disobedience to superiors, and the like. Whence if such things are able to retain that goodness which is from the order to the ultimate end, then they would be able to be good and in them the will would be able to act. But this would not be able to be except by divine power, through which order in things is instituted. For just as it is not able to be done, except through the miraculous operation of the divine power, that what receives being from the first agent, by some mediating second cause, has being when the second cause is destroyed or subtracted, as happens when an accident is without a subject, just as in the sacrament of the altar: so also it is able to be done, only through the miraculous power of the divine, that what is apt to receive goodness from the order to the ultimate end by the mediating order to some thing has goodness, the order which was to that thing having been subtracted; whence, that act which is to kill the innocent or to resist a superior is not able to be good nor to be done well except by divine authority or command.[58]

Milhaven's gloss is:

Just as God, and God alone, can work a miracle and make something exist without using the secondary causality of creatures which normally does it, so he and he alone can make something good without that order to a particular creature which normally would give the thing its goodness. Where the order to the creature was the natural way by which the thing in question was ordered to its last end and received its goodness, now God gives it goodness directly, by giving it, through his command, a direct ordering to its last end.[59]

---

58. "Dico ergo, quod quaedam peccata nominant deordinationem unius rei ad rem aliam, sicut homicidium, odium fraternum, inobedientiam ad praelatum, et hujusmodi. Unde sit alia bonitatem illam retinere possent quae est ex ordine ad finem ultimum, proculdubio bona essent, et in ea voluntas ferri posset. Sed hoc non posset esse nisi virtute divina, per quam ordo in rebus institutus est. Sicut enim non potest fieri, nisi per miraculosam operationem virtutis divinae, ut quod recipit esse a primo agente, mediante aliqua causa secunda, habeat esse destructa vel subtracta causa secunda, ut hoc quod accidens sit sine subjecto, sicut in sacramento altaris: ita etiam non potest fieri, nisi per miraculum virtutis divinae, ut id quod natum est recipere bonitatem ex ordine ad finem ultimum mediante ordine ad rem illam, habeat bonitatem, subtracto ordine qui erat ad rem illam; unde ille actus qui est occidere inocentem, vel resistere praelato, non potest esse bonus nec bene fieri, nisi auctoritate vel praecepto divino." Ibid., 1073.

59. Milhaven, "Moral Absolutes," 163.

Again, for Milhaven, Aquinas's logic implies that owing to his goodness God can order, or command, "any" physical means to a good end. Hence, Milhaven wonders if God could command acts of sodomy and contraception.

Another text in which Aquinas gives an analogous case of a creature's twofold ordering to goodness provides helpful commentary. Referencing a remark of Aristotle in the tenth chapter of Book XII of the *Metaphysics*, Aquinas remarks in *De Veritate* V, 3c:

> In an army we find two orders, one by which the parts of the army are related to each other, and a second by which the army is directed to an external good, namely, the good of its leader. That order by which the parts of the army are related to each other exists for the sake of the order by which the entire army is subordinated to its leader. Consequently, if the subordination to the leader did not exist, the ordering of the parts of the army to each other would not exist.[60]

With the example of the leader of the army in mind, it becomes clearer how God's ordering of some actions to himself can render them good even though considered in themselves the actions are evil. To achieve victory, the leader orders the squire and the smith to serve the knight and his horse for purpose of the knight's fighting well and achieving victory. The entire order of the army to the leader's goal of victory establishes the goodness or rectitude of the suborder of squire and smith to knight. Yet because of the fortunes of war, the leader may command that the squire and smith be ordered to victory in another way, for example, as foot soldiers. So, by the order of the leader, both the squire and the smith have rectitude and goodness apart from the normal secondary cause of that rectitude and goodness. God is like the leader and creatures are like the members of the army.

With that clarification of Aquinas's thinking, I return to Milhaven's claim the Aquinas's framework allows God to will *any* physical means for a good end of his choosing. Accordingly, Milhaven is

---

60. Aquinas, *Disputed Questions on Truth*, vol. I, 214.

suggesting that just as God can command Abraham to kill Isaac for some good purpose, so too God could command Abraham to sodomize Isaac for some good purpose. The latter suggestion would be along these lines: Sex is good when ordered to procreation. Procreation is the mediating secondary cause conferring goodness on sex. Hence, God can order sex apart from procreation and make it good. Milhaven's absolute claim that God can order any physical means for a good end is crucial. Is it correct? I think not. Milhaven is missing a metaphysical context for Aquinas's thinking. That context blocks the implications that Milhaven wishes to draw.

We already know that God cannot will any physical means for a good end of his choosing. If God is to create a world that reflects his goodness, then in respect to his goodness God creates a world within certain boundaries and with certain natural conditions. For instance, the created world must contain both the corruptible and incorruptible. For the well-being of the corruptible order, God, or an agent that he appoints, wills natural defects, for example, death. Death assures that matter is not appropriated by the higher corruptible species to the detriment of the lower. Such an appropriation would destroy the multitude of species through which the divine goodness is reflected. But if there were only corruption, again the divine reflection in things would be destroyed. To remedy that problem, the corruptible world contains bodies than can generate others like themselves. The sexual act, in this case, the emission of semen, has this generation as its purpose. With that purpose, the sexual act is recognized to serve the good of the species. Aquinas says,

> Now, though the male semen is superfluous [*superfluum*] in regard to the preservation of the individual, it is nevertheless necessary in regard to the propagation of the species. Other superfluous things, things, such as excrement, urine, sweat, and such things, are not at all necessary; hence, their emission contributes to man's good. Now, this is not what is sought in the case of the semen, but, rather, to emit it for the purpose of generation, to which purpose the sexual act [*coitus*] is directed.[61]

61. *C.G.* III, 122; Aquinas, *Summa contra Gentiles*, vol. III–II, 143.

As ordered to generation the sexual act is ordered to the propagation of the species, which in turn contributes to the universe's reflection of the divine goodness. This proximity of sex to the good of the universe makes sex sacrosanct in God's providence. Just as God creates a universe within boundaries, so too God creates the conditions that realize and conserve those parameters. One of those conditions is sex. Through its procreative purpose sex contributes to the preservation of a species. So, in commanding nonprocreative sex, God would be acting against his own goodness. God's commanding nonprocreative sex would be just as incongruous as the leader of the army ordering some to commit treason. Unlike Milhaven for whom procreation is just one use of sex able to be trumped by some other use ordered by God, Aquinas views procreation as a defining use of sex. I am arguing that Aquinas's exalting of the procreative purpose of sex stems from its contribution to the object of the divine creative will, namely, the order and perfection of the universe. As naturally procreative, sex makes this contribution by preserving the species. In other words, the ordering of sex to procreation is not a disposable ordering since the existence of multiple species is not a disposable element of a created order.

Milhaven might respond that the order and perfection of the universe about which I am speaking is a natural order and perfection. In that context my argument holds. But as I admitted in remarks on the Abraham and Isaac case, as far as the philosopher knows, the order and perfection of the universe may be wider than the natural. Hence, I pointed out that in the natural order the death of a child is a *quandoque* evil only permitted by the creator. But in the supernatural order the child's death might be a commanded evil for some good. Why cannot the same be said of sodomy? In the universe's natural order, sodomy flies in the face of the procreative nature of the sexual act and so strikes at the perfection and order of the universe. So does the killing of children. But God orders, or commands, the latter for some good, although supernatural, end, so why not possibly a divine command for sodomy?

Natural Corruptions 119

What breaks the analogy is that in the natural order God can take human life but never can order nonprocreative acts. For the natural good and perfection of the universe the existence of corruptibles is limited. What the Isaac case does is extend God's ability to take life to taking the life of a child. And the Isaac case does this by appealing to a wider order for the universe. But in the universe's natural order, as explained above, God never possesses the ability to command intrinsically nonprocreative acts. Since sex is of itself procreative, to command nonprocreative sex is to act against procreation as such. But that is to fly in the face of one of the necessary conditions for the universe of corruptible things, which in turn is necessary for a reflection of the divine. What a proponent of Milhaven's thesis would have to do is to show that just as God possesses an ability to take life that can be extended to those not yet mature, so too God possesses an ability to command nonprocreative acts that can be extended to sodomy. But it is metaphysically impossible that God command nonprocreative acts. So the analogy breaks down.

In sum, Milhaven's understanding of the twofold ordering to good skips something. His understanding skips the metaphysical ordering of things to God as God is reflected in the order and perfection of the universe. Milhaven has things ordered to the divine essence as such, while Aquinas has them ordered to the divine essence as reflected in the universe. Requirements related to this reflection veto many of Milhaven's suggested implications for a Thomistic sexual ethics. The crucial issue cannot be whether God has in some way extended to contemporary man his ability to order "any physical means to a good end." For Aquinas God never had that ability.

CONCLUSION

For the Thomist the meaning of death is opaque. It is opaque not because the Thomist has no idea as to death's meaning but because the Thomist has too many ideas. Death may be a natural defect willed by the creator for the good ordering of the universe. But then death may be a punishment for some primal human fault. If the Thomist is imaginative enough, both are discernable possibilities within a metaphysics of *esse*. Finally, there is a third philosophically discernable possibility, death is somehow meant to be a crucible to another and supernatural life. The disembodied soul has little or no natural means of operating. Yet, the philosopher could imagine the creator supernaturally bringing about operation in the disembodied soul. According to some Thomists, with whom I agree, this possible activity could extend all the way to the level of the beatific vision. Aquinas appeals to his metaphysics to establish the remote possibility of the beatific vision: "Since therefore a created intellect is naturally capable of apprehending the concreted form and the concreted being [*esse concretum*] in abstraction, by way of a certain resolution, it can by grace be raised up to know separate subsisting substance and separate subsisting being [*esse separatum subsistens*]."[62] The metaphysical formulation of *esse commune*, called here "*esse* in abstraction" shows some human ability to pierce the nature of *esse* and so some ability to receive it. All of these possibilities are irresolvable without an appeal to religious truth. In my opinion, the philosopher's epistemological situation here is analogous to what Aquinas describes as the philosopher's situation on knowing whether the world was created in time or from eternity. Both are possibilities for the creator; no philosophical arguments demonstrate one or the other to be the truth. One knows the first as true only because the creator has revealed that information to his believers.

In the light of so many possible explanations for the fact of evil, what should be the philosopher's final attitude? The answer is obvious. First, the philosopher should be humble and circumspect. Hence, the philosopher should not push the first scenario above too strongly as it includes the hard truth that this life may be the only

---

62. *ST* I, 12, 4, ad 3m; Pegis, *Basic Writings of Thomas Aquinas*, vol. I, 98.

one that we have to live. Second, in the wake of the realization that he lacks the definitive explanation for the existence of evil, the Thomist philosopher should be open to further information from religion. Beside the above possibilities, the philosopher should also be able to discern the possibility of religion. Characteristic of religion is the claim to have information from an absolute being about its designs for humans. The Thomist metaphysician's understanding of the deep structure of reality would certainly present this possibility. Reality does contain a creator who is personal and who possesses the power and knowledge to communicate in human history. Moreover, some religions, viz., those in the Judeo-Christian tradition, describe their God in terms strikingly similar to this philosophically knowable creator. Has the creator spoken to us in these religions? That is the question to which Aquinas's philosophy brings us. Though no religion can prove its truth as the philosopher can prove the truth of a creator, some religions can still offer the intellect powerful motives for credibility. These motives set the remote context for conversion. Hence, not as a philosopher but as a believer, the human will find the explanation of death.

5

Preliminaries to Aquinas and the Contemporary Discussion

I now wish to pivot to the massive contemporary literature on the evil problem. To keep my head above water, I want to grab a life preserver; second, I want to summarize Aquinas's position as I understand it from the investigations of the previous chapters.

C.G. III, 71: "IF EVIL EXISTS, GOD EXISTS"

Some have remarked that in the already centuries-old discussions of evil, the eighteenth-century British philosopher David Hume marks a turning point.[1] Before Hume, thinkers subsumed the problem of evil within a presupposed *religious* belief in God. Consequently, the problem took the guise of understanding *how* to reconcile God and evil. In short, the evil problem was the problem

---

1. Marilyn McCord Adams and Robert Merrihew Adams, eds., *The Problem of Evil* (Oxford: Oxford University Press, 1990), 2.

of formulating a theodicy. With Hume and continuing to the present, many philosophers exploit the atheistic implications of the evil problem. Hence, the evil problem becomes the formulation of a defense of theism.

Some truth exists in this observation. As my previous chapters make clear, Aquinas's concentration is upon the how question. Yet, as I will show, Aquinas's concentration upon evil as a how problem is not simply because of a presupposed religious belief in God. In three places, Aquinas raises the evil problem as a philosophical challenge to theism. The locations are: *De Ver.* X, 12, ad 10m of the second set; *C.G.* III, 71 *Per haec autem*; and *ST* I, 2, 3, ad 1m. The *Summa Theologiae* text occurs in the article on the famous five ways for demonstrating that God exists. I have already commented upon Aquinas's reply to the first objection. In sum, Aquinas answers that God permits evils to exist because God is so perfect that God can order the permitted evils to some good. Any permitted evil will be matched by a redeeming good. The permission talk indicates that the mentioned evils are what I called "*quandoque*" evils. Crucial to validating this defense of theism is whether the Thomistic category of *quandoque* evils can accommodate the horrendous evils detailed in contemporary discussion of the inductive atheological arguments from evil. I believe that ideas from my previous chapters can be marshaled to meet this demand. More on that issue in the next chapter. What interests me is the other two texts defending theism amidst evil. It will be my contention that in these texts Aquinas philosophically solves the theism problem of evil so decisively that the evil problem understandably becomes a theodicy problem for the remainder of the time. What is striking about these texts is Aquinas's claim that evil is never so great that all good is lost. In other words, if evil exists, God still exists. I begin with the *Contra Gentiles* passage.

In chapter 71 of the *Contra Gentiles*, Aquinas is intent upon arguing that divine providence is compatible with evil in things. At the close of the chapter, he says, "With these considerations we dispose of the error of those who because they noticed that evils occur in the world, said that there is no God. Thus, Boethius introduces a certain philosopher who asks: 'If God exists, whence comes evil?'"[2] Instead of using the stated ideas of chapter 71, Aquinas answers the question by taking a new tack: "But it could be argued to the contrary: 'If evil exists, God exists.' For, there would be no evil if the order of good were taken away, since its privation is evil. But this order would not exist if there were not God." "If evil exist, God exists" is quite a dramatic turning of the table on the atheistic use of the evil problem. It is worth the effort to see if Aquinas can make good on this claim. A brief commentary on Aquinas's argument follows.

First, in sum, Aquinas is saying that since evil is a privation in the order of good and since this order would not exist without God, then, if evil exists, God exists. Second, back in chapter 6, Aquinas provided an elucidation of the privation concept of evil:

> Now, evil is in a substance because something which it was originally to have, and which it ought to have, is lacking in it. Thus, if a man has no wings, that is not an evil for him, because he was not born to have them; even if a man does not have blond hair, that is not an evil, for though he may have such hair, it is not something that is necessarily due him. But it is an evil if he has no hands, for these he is born to, and should, have—if he is to be perfect. Yet this defect is not an evil for a bird. Every privation, if taken properly and strictly, is of that which one is born to have, and should have so, in this strict meaning of privation, there is always the rational character of evil.[3]

For Aquinas, evil is real. But the trick is to understand its manner of existing. Generally, evil is not real in itself but in something else; evil is real reductively. In that respect evil is like the accidents of a substance. For example, the accident of color is real but only as in and of something else, viz., a surface and ultimately a substance.

---

2. Thomas Aquinas, *Summa contra Gentiles*, vols. III–I, translated by Vernon J. Bourke (Notre Dame, Ind.: University of Notre Dame Press, 1975), 240–41.

3. Ibid., 44.

The experiential basis for this conception is twofold. The color cannot be found apart from the surface, but the surface can be found apart from the color. Evidently the color and the surface are two really different items. But in its real difference from the surface the color *qualifies* the surface. In the ontological scale of things, the color "bumps up" the surface. To do that qualifying, the really different item that is the color must be understood as existing in and of the surface. So an accident is something positive that makes an addition to the total situation in which it is derivatively present. Evil is derivatively real but not in that positive manner. Evil is not derivatively real in the positive manner of an accident. Rather, an evil is derivatively real as a type of absence or lack; it is the actual nonpresence of something positive. That absences or lacks are actual follows from the determinateness of things. For example, because I am pale complexioned, I am really neither tan nor ruddy. The pale complexion as something determinate actually excludes the others and grounds the reality of their absence. But evil is not a simple absence; evil is an absence of a certain kind. In the above text, Aquinas specifies evil to be an absence of something that should be there. Hence, the absence of sight in a rock is not an evil for the rock. But the absence of sight in a man is an evil. For example, the cataract in the eye is something determinate that excludes the due perfection of sight. This technical sense of real absence is called a privation and is distinguished from a mere negation of a perfection. So for Aquinas, evil is defined as the absence of a due perfection in a thing which because of its determinateness excludes that perfection.

This meaning of "privation" when used to speak of evil is a different sense of the word from when "privation" names one of the conditions of change. In his *De Principiis Naturae*, Aquinas speaks of three conditions for change: matter, form, and privation. Here privation expresses the exclusion of the form to be acquired insofar as matter is under another form: "for insofar as [matter] is under one form, it has a privation of another and conversely, just as in fire is the privation of air and in air is the privation of fire."[4] As is clear from the examples, privation here does not connote an imperfection in the thing subject to the privation; fire is not supposed to have the form of air and so as lacking that form fire is not suffering an evil. In that respect fire is not evil, it is something else. It is a principle of change. One would be wrong to conclude that since any changeable thing includes privation, then any changeable thing is evil.

Some object that Aquinas's notion of evil is insufficiently encompassing. One manner of objection I will present and respond to now; the second I will present and deal with later. Some say that though Aquinas's privation definition works for blindness and lameness as evils, it fails to fit the evils of pain and suffering. Pain and suffering seem to be more positive than any lack of a perfection could be, yet we do call them evil. In Aquinas's behalf one could note that both pain and suffering stand related to, but not within, the concept of evil as privation. To see this, consider their opposite, pleasure. Pleasure is the way sentient beings experience their well-ordered bodily functioning. As Aquinas says at *C.G.* III, 26, "Although pleasure is not the ultimate end, it is, of course, a concomitant of this end, since pleasure arises out of the attainment of the end."[5] The opposite should be true for pain. Pain and suffering should then be the ways that a sentient being experiences disorder in its physical organism. The disorder is the evil understood as a privation; the pain is how the disorder is experienced. So pain and suffering do not subvert Aquinas's definition of evil but are accommodated by it.

Back in chapter 71, Aquinas said that the order of good in which there is real privation would not exist without God. From my above remarks one knows that "the order of good" is the existing

---

4. "Inquantum enim est sub una forma, habet privationem alterius et e converse, sicut in igne est privatio aeris et in aere privatio ignis." Thomas Aquinas, *De Principiis Naturae*, vol. II, edited by John J. Pauson (Fribourg: Société Philosophique, 1950), 83.

5. Ibid., 109.

determinate substance that can lack what it ought to have and so be suffering evil. What, then, is the reduction from these substances to God? Help is provided by some passages in the earlier second book of the *Contra Gentiles*. At chapter 54, Aquinas remarks that for something to exist is for it to be a being (*ens*) but to be a being is for a thing to be composed with its *esse*: "the whole substance [of matter and form] itself, however, is that which is. And being itself (*ipsum esse*) is that by which the substance is called a being (*ens*)."[6] The reader will recognize Aquinas's metaphysics of the act of existing that I summarized in my chapter 2. The *Contra Gentiles* not only echoes that metaphysics of what it means to be a being, the *Contra Gentiles* also provides the causal reasoning that follows that metaphysical understanding. One argument for a cause of *esse* is found at C.G. I, 22:

> But whatever belongs to a thing and is yet not of its essence belongs to it through some cause; for if things that are not through themselves one are joined they must be joined through some cause. Being [*esse*], therefore, belongs to that quiddity through some cause. This is either through something that is part of the essence of that thing, or the essence itself, or through something else. If we adopt the first alternative, and it is a fact that the essence is through that being, it follows that something is the cause of its own being. This is impossible, because, in their notions, the existence of the cause is prior to that of the effect. If, then, something were its own cause of being, it would be understood to be before it had being—which is impossible.[7]

No act as an act, even the *sui generis* act that is *esse*, is found by itself. Rather, an act is found as in and of a subject. However, no chance exists to explain *esse* completely by the substance that is its subject. Substances that are complete explainers of an act are in some respect already in act. As a potency for its existential act,

---

6. Thomas Aquinas, *Summa contra Gentiles*, vol. II, translated by James F. Anderson (Notre Dame, Ind.: University of Notre Dame Press, 1975), 54, 157.

7. Thomas Aquinas, *Summa contra Gentiles*, vol. I, translated by Anton C. Pegis (Notre Dame, Ind.: University of Notre Dame Press, 1975), 22, 119–20.

substance cannot position itself to explain completely its *esse*. The need for complete explanation in the case of *esse* drives the mind to conclude a further being in which *esse* is not found as an act but as the very substance that is the further cause. Aquinas calls this further cause *esse subsistens* (subsistent existence), *esse tantum* (existence alone) and *esse purus* (pure existence). He also refers to it as *Deus* (God). Aquinas's stated reason at the end of chapter 22 is God's revelation to Moses in the Book of Exodus that God's name is *Ego sum qui sum*: I am who am.

A standard objection to this reasoning should be mentioned and addressed, one which Anthony Kenny raises in the course of his discussion of the *prima via* of Aquinas's *ST* I, 2, 3.[8] According to Kenny we can never be sure of the identity of the cause. Hence, claims that the cause actually contains what is seen in its effect are suspect. The basis for skepticism is the often observed disjunction between the nature of the effect and the nature of the cause. For example, though sometimes what is in the effect corresponds to what is in the cause (heat in the water, heat in the fire), that is not always the case (heat is the effect, rubbing hands is the cause). So, it could be asked how we can be sure that *esse* is caused by subsistent *esse*.

But Kenny's observation leads to problems only where something can be the incidental effect of a proper line of causality. So, in the proper line of causality, the effect is the hands moving to a place, and the cause is the stationary shoulders. What is in a place is causing motion toward a place. The heat is thrown off as an incidental effect of this line of causality. Properly understood, the claim of a likeness between effect and cause is true. The claim is not about any effect but about effects in a *per se* causal line. If the effect might be one incidental to this line, then all bets of a likeness between it and the cause are off.

---

8. Anthony Kenny, *The Five Ways: St. Thomas Aquinas' Proofs of God's Existence* (New York: Schocken Books, 1969), 21–22.

But can Aquinas be sure that the *esse* of a thing is not an incidental effect? I believe that Aquinas can be certain. What provides confidence is the grasp of *esse* as the act of what is of itself existence neutral, or nothing. In other words, *esse* is absolutely basic and fundamental. It cannot presuppose something else and so cannot be construed as the incidental effect of a more basic line of causality.

This metaphysical thinking from a proper, or nonincidental, effect is the basis for Aquinas's claims that we cannot know that a cause exists without knowing at least confusedly and imperfectly what the cause is.[9] Hence, as he also remarks, in thinking about the cause we can substitute in our minds the nature or quiddity of the effect.[10] In Aquinas's metaphysics, this should mean that the nature of *esse* in things will give us some knowledge of *esse* in God, the first cause. Some of this knowledge I will mention shortly.

Reaching a first cause of *esse* in which *esse* is not an act of the substance but the substance itself, viz., *esse subsistens*, Aquinas can argue further that the first cause of *esse* is all good in the moral

    9. "Similarly, therefore, we cannot know that God and other immaterial substances exist unless we know somehow, in some confused way, what they are." Thomas Aquinas, *In de Trin.* VI, 3c; Thomas Aquinas, *On the Division and Methods of the Sciences*, translated by Armand Maurer, (Toronto: Pontifical Institute of Mediaeval Studies, 1963), 77.
    10. "When something is not known through its form but through its effect, the form of the effect takes the place of the form of the thing itself, for from the effect itself it is known that the cause exists." Aquinas, *In de Trin.* I, 2, ad 5m; Thomas Aquinas, *Faith, Reason and Theology*, translated by Armand Maurer (Toronto: Pontifical Institute of Mediaeval Studies, 1987), 24. Also, "When causes are known through their effects knowledge of the effect takes the place of the knowledge of the essence of the cause." Ibid., II, 2, ad 2m; Aquinas, *Faith, Reason and Theology*, 43. Finally, "If the effect is proportionate to its cause, we take the quiddity itself of the effect as our starting point to prove that the cause exists and to investigate its quiddity, from which in turn its properties are demonstrated. But if the effect is not proportionate to its cause, we take the effect as the starting point to prove only the existence of the cause and some of its properties, while the quiddity of the cause remains unknown. This is what happens in the case of the separate substances." *In de Trin.* 6, 4, ad 2m; Aquinas, *Division and Methods*, 84. I take it that demonstrating "some of its properties" means that there is some quidditative knowledge of separate substance. For a more strict ignorance of immaterial quiddity and a more loose interpretation of like follows like, see Brian Davies, *The Reality of God and the Problem of Evil* (London: Continuum, 2006), 64–65, 206–7. For a discussion of Davies, see my chapter 8.

sense and all powerful. Aquinas's understanding of God's morality is approachable from what we know of morality in ourselves, as some philosophers have insisted.[11] From my previous discussion of Aquinas's natural law ethics in chapter 2, one can say that morality consists in a respect and solicitude for epiphanies of being, for those analogates that present the analogon of being in a heightened way. Turning to the metaphysically reached creator, one can say further that the creator is necessarily moral in all of its free acts because the creator acts in light of itself who is, as subsistent esse, an epiphany of being *par excellence*. As subsistent *esse*, the creator is an analogate of *esse* that is the analgon of *esse*.[12] The creator is the intelligible heart of the *ratio entis*. By conforming its free actions to itself, the creator fulfills the moral norm of a respect and solicitude for an epiphany of being.[13]

Bruce Reichenbach objects to the attribution of moral goodness to God. A person who does good without the possibility of doing evil is neither morally good nor praiseworthy.[14] Reichenbach concludes that this is God's nature as conceived of by Aquinas. But I think that Reichenbach misses the point. Aquinas can say that God is praiseworthy not because God does not do evil but just because God does not have to act, that is, create anything. Is not the gratuity of God's necessarily good act a basis for praise? Even among us gratuitous acts of kindness are praiseworthy.

11. "I wish to conclude from this set of theses that in calling God good a theist is committed to saying that God's reasons for permitting evils must be reasons that are acceptable according to the believer's own set of moral standards." Terence Penelhum, "Divine Goodness and the Problem of Evil," in *The Problem of Evil*, edited by Marilyn McCord Adams and Robert Merrihew Adams (Oxford: Oxford University Press, 1990), 76.

12. For texts and explanation, see "Thomistic 'Natural Desires' and the Human Person," in chapter 6.

13. Bruce Reichenbach, *Evil and a Good God* (New York: Fordham University Press, 1982), 138, misses this approach to God's moral goodness from the metaphysical basis of Aquinas's natural law ethics. But Reichenbach correctly notes that many texts of Aquinas speak not of God's moral goodness but his ontological goodness. Likewise, Davies, *Reality of God*, 202-8. For Davies, God cannot be morally good because that would place God under a norm, 203–4, and would imply that God acts for a reason which requires a need, 216.

14. Reichenbach, *Evil and a Good God*, 133–35.

Second, Aquinas argues that God can do all things except contradictions. Contradictions are precisely the denial of the thing required by *esse* other than the one and only subsistent *esse*. First, subsistent *esse* is infinite and unique. As realizing the intelligible heart of the *ratio entis*, *esse* in a subsistent configuration has the infinite perfection of the *ratio entis*.[15] That infinity is a basis for knowing its unicity. Two all-perfect beings would require for their distinction that one have something the other lacks.[16] From these two conclusions follows a third. If *esse* is to be anywhere else, *esse* must be in a nonsubsistent configuration and so with something. But a contradiction is precisely the denial of a thing. For example, a square circle means either square plus nonsquare or circle plus noncircle. In both cases, one sees that square circle involves the denial of a thing that can have *esse*. Precisely because a contradiction is a denial of a thing, Aquinas insists that the more proper way to speak is to say that contradictions cannot be made rather than to say that God cannot make contradictions.[17]

In sum, if evil exists, God exists. Since evil exists only because of existing substances and substances exist only because of subsisting *esse* which is identifiable with the God of Exodus as well as the all-good and omnipotent God of Christianity, then evil proves God. This earlier reasoning explains how Aquinas can say at *C.G.* III, 71 that God is compatible with evil. If a problem of evil remains, it is a how problem, viz., how are God and evil compatible. Whether Aquinas succeeds in answering this how question, we can be assured that God and evil are compatible. F. C. Copleston reiterates my point:

15. "But for a thing that is its own being [*esse*] it is proper to be according to the whole power of being [*potestatem essendi*]." *C.G.* I, 28; Aquinas, *Summa contra Gentiles*, vol. I, 135.
16. "For, if none of these perfect beings lacks some perfection, and does not have any admixture of imperfection, which is demanded for an absolutely perfect being, nothing will be given in which to distinguish the perfect beings from one another. It is impossible, therefore, that there be many gods." *C.G.* I, 42; Aquinas, *Summa contra Gentiles*, vol. I, 158. Also, *ST* I, 11, 3c
17. *ST* I, 25, 3c.

[Aquinas] was convinced that the metaphysician can prove the existence of God independently of the problem of evil, and that we therefore know that there is a solution to the problem even though we cannot provide it. And this, of course, is one of the ways in which he differs from the modern agnostic who is inclined to start with the problem in mind rather than to regard evil as something which has to be reconciled, so far as this is possible, with an already established truth.[18]

As a concluding comment, I wish to address a second objection to Aquinas's privation understanding of evil. In an incisive observation, John Crosby claims that in a further way Aquinas's definition of evil is not sufficiently encompassing.[19] For example, the definition makes sense for evils like blindness or lameness. But how does it apply to the evil of corruption, an evil that involves the complete destruction of a being? As noted, Aquinas does use the term "evil" of corruptions. For instance, there is the evil of natural corruption that God wills insofar as God wills the perfection of the universe. In this case of corruption, where is the subject that is required by the privation that is evil?

In reply, let me begin by saying that as obvious as Crosby's remark is, Aquinas does not seem to be bothered by it. In the very text of the *Contra Gentiles* that describes evil as a privation, Aquinas has no problem describing the privation of a substance's substantial form as an evil for the substance. Now this privation is obviously more radical than the privation of hands from the man. Without his form, the man does not exist. So Aquinas acknowledges Crosby's case of evil that is the complete destruction of a being, yet Aquinas feels no incompatibility of this case with his textually very proximate definition of evil as a privation. It is no use to say that the presumed subject for the privation is matter, because Aquinas points out "the privation of such forms [of water or of fire] in relation to matter is not an evil for the matter, but in relation to

---

18. F. C. Copleston, *Aquinas* (Baltimore: Penguin Books, 1961), 149.
19. John Crosby, "Is All Evil Really Only Privation?" *Proceedings of the American Catholic Philosophical Association*, 75 (2001), 197–210. For more on Crosby, see chapter 7, n. 61.

the thing whose form it is."[20] Aquinas may have made the slip to which Crosby is drawing attention, but I do not think it is likely for such a profound thinker as Aquinas. So what can Aquinas be thinking? My suggested answer is this. When Aquinas says that evil is a privation in a being, he does not necessarily mean a presently existing being. If the privation is a profound one, like the privation of form or of *esse*, then the privation is called evil in respect to a past existent. So evil is a privation in a being past or present. I am confident about this interpretation because the interpretation would still enable Aquinas to say that if evil exists, God exists. The argument for the present existence of God would begin from the recalled past existence of the order of the good that suffered the privation.

WILLIAM ROWE ON COSMOLOGICAL REASONING

Before going on to *De Ver.* X, 12, ad 10m, it would be helpful to comment on William Rowe's critique of cosmological reasoning. Does it have an impact on Aquinas's reasoning from the *esse* of things? Of course, at this time any critique of cosmological reasoning could be offered. Yet Rowe's opinion deserves attention because it appears in his atheistic argument from evil which I will look at in my next chapter. Briefly, Rowe claims that the existence of pointless evils, viz., those whose goods could have been attained without the evils, disproves God because a moral being, which God is assumed to be, would never permit such evils. Rowe admits that one way to defeat his argument is in and through an independent argument for God. That argument cancels Rowe's argument because knowledge of God's existence assures us that what looks like a pointless evil in fact is not so.[21]

Rowe regards Samuel Clarke's contingency argument as the

---

20. C.G. III, 6; Auinas, *Summa contra Gentiles*, vol. III–I, 45.
21. William Rowe, "Evil and Theodicy," in *William L. Rowe on Philosophy of Religion: Selected Writings*, edited by Nick Trakakis (Burlington, Vt.: Ashgate Publishing Company, 2007), 121.

version of the cosmological argument most useful for philosophical discussion. In Clarke's argument Rowe isolates what he calls the strong form of the principle of sufficient reason (PSR). The strong form has both an existential and an essential variant. The existential variant claims: whatever exists has either in itself or in something else a reason for its existence. The essential variant claims: every actual state of affairs has a reason either within itself or in some other state of affairs.[22] Of these two variants Rowe considers the existential form as central for the cosmological argument.[23] Rowe makes a good case that neither by intuition nor by demonstration do we know the PSR is true. Rowe's conclusion is that the strong existential form of PSR may be true, but we just do not know. Hence, the cosmological argumentation may be true, but we do not know. The following is a summary of Rowe's critique of our knowledge of the existential PSR.

First, the PSR is not demonstrated *a priori*. *A priori* demonstration takes two forms. Both forms are *reductio ad absurdum*. In the first form, denial of the principle leads to a denial of the principle of noncontradiction.[24] If something exists without a sufficient reason, then it has no sufficient reason and so should both exist and not exist at the same time. Rowe counters that this reasoning seems to assume PSR while trying to prove it. For without the PSR, that something exists without a sufficient reason does not entail that this something does not exist. It only entails that the thing is a brute fact. Neither is the PSR demonstrated *a priori* by showing that the denial is self-contradictory. That we cannot deny the principle without affirming it may only be bringing out how we have to think and not how reality is itself.[25]

Second, neither is PSR demonstrated *a posteriori*, or from experience. As Rowe points out, at best experience would lead us to

22. William L. Rowe, *The Cosmological Argument* (Princeton: Princeton University Press, 1975), 37 and 98.
23. Ibid, 112–13.
24. Ibid., 75–76.
25. Ibid., 91.

formulate only the weak sense of PSR, viz., whatever comes into existence must have a reason for its existence.[26] And perhaps this is even saying too much. Hume's critique of causality must be faced. Hume strongly argued that in our experience of the happening of things, we neither perceive causality nor anything that would allow causality to be demonstrated.

Finally, third, the PSR does not seem to be intuitively true. Intuition fails to perceive either an analytic or a synthetic link between an existent and an explanation.[27] An analytic link is found when the meaning of the predicate is contained in the subject. A synthetic link is found when subject and predicate are necessarily connected, though not on the basis of containment nor experience. Now there is no analytic link because there is no containment of the notion of explanation in the notion of being. "A being is something to be explained" is not analytically true.[28] There is no synthetic link because we can think a being without thinking of explanation.

My opinion is that Rowe's critique is correct at least with respect to Leibniz and Clarke. Does Rowe's critique of Leibniz apply to Aquinas's metaphysical reasoning for God? In other words, does Aquinas use the existential PSR? *Prima facie*, I do not think that Aquinas employs the principle. The only text that comes close is one similar to the weak existential form of sufficient reason. At *C.G.* I, 13, Aquinas

26. Ibid., 89.   27. Ibid., 83.
28. Likewise Aquinas, "But, since to be caused does not enter into the nature of being taken absolutely [*de ratione entis simpliciter*], that is why there exists a being that is uncaused." *ST* I, 44, 1, ad 1m; Anton C. Pegis, ed., *The Basic Writings of St. Thomas Aquinas*, vol. I (New York: Random House, 1945), 427. Interestingly, at 44, 2, Aquinas presents a three-stage history of philosophy in which progressively deeper understandings of being, *ens*, lead to more universal causes. But the knowledge of causes from *ens* is tied to discoveries of deeper compositions of subject and attribute within *ens*. At stage one we have the substance and accident composition; at stage two the matter and form composition; at stage three the matter, form, and *esse* composition. This description indicates the centrality of the subject and attribute model of thinking and its causal implications. In other words, only when the philosopher discovers a subject and attribute composition within *ens* does the search for an explanation begin. By itself the *ratio entis* does not imply the need for a cause.

speaks about the obviousness of a cause for what begins to be. This idea is similar to the idea of causality critiqued by Hume, viz., that what happens has a cause. Yet, as I will note, in Aquinas the idea of causality for happenings is rooted in thinking not suspected by Hume and not obvious in defenses of the PSR. Yet famous Thomists have maintained the PSR. In fact Pope Pius XII in paragraphs 48–49 of the encyclical *Humani generis* (1950) named PSR along with the principles of noncontradiction and finality as "unshakable" and "self-evident" metaphysical principles that every Catholic philosopher should affirm, though the Pope acknowledged that Catholic philosophers could disagree on how to do this. I will consider a famous Thomist's treatment of the PSR. I believe that his interpretation of the principle can be defended but that his own defense falls victim to Rowe's remarks.

In his *God: His Existence and His Nature*, Réginald Garrigou-Lagrange expresses the PSR in a way in which it can be taken both existentially and essentially: "Every being has a sufficient reason for being what it is, either in itself or in something else."[29] If being a being is included in a being's being what it is, then this expression of the PSR includes Rowe's existential variant. Interestingly, Garrigou-Lagrange interprets each alternative of the PSR, viz., "in itself" or "in something else," as expressing a form of the principle. The first alternative expresses the "intrinsic" form of the principle. Garrigou-Lagrange regards it as a "determination" of the principle of identity, which in turn is the positive form of the noncontradiction principle.[30] Accordingly, the defense of the first half of the PSR boils down to a defense of the principle of noncontradiction. Here Garrigou-Lagrange uses the method of retorsion: because I cannot deny the principle of noncontraction without affirming it in my denial, I cannot deny the principle. Despite being an aposteriorist in epistemology, in a moment of rationalism Garrigou-Lagrange claims

---

29. Reginald Garrigou-Lagrange, *God: His Existence and His Nature*, vol. I, translated by Dom Bede Rose (St. Louis: B. Herder Book Co., 1939), 183.
30. Ibid., 184.

elsewhere that this defense is so autonomous that the abstractive origin of our concepts can be set aside.[31] Here I agree with Rowe's above observation that this procedure may only be bringing out how we have to think and not how reality is.

Garrigou-Lagrange calls the second alternative in the PSR the "extrinsic" form of the principle: a thing without a sufficient reason in itself has its reason in another. Garrigou-Lagrange's defense is a *reductio* to the principle of noncontradiction. If something exists without a sufficient reason, it has no sufficient reason and so should both exist and not exist at the same time.[32] As Rowe has noted, the problem is that the reasoning seems to assume the PSR while trying to prove it. For without the PSR, that something exists without a sufficient reason does not entail that this something does not exist. It only entails that the thing is a brute fact. Garrigou-Lagrange is aware of this criticism and tries to respond, although no reply convinces me.[33]

In sum, Rowe's critique of the *a priori* demonstrations of the PSR are applicable to Garrigou-Lagrange's defenses of the PSR. A minor difference is that Garrigou-Lagrange uses retorsion to defend the noncontradiction principle while Rowe mentions retorsion to defend the PSR. Yet Rowe's critique of retorsion extends to Garrigou-Lagrange's use of it for knowing the noncontradiction principle. Unlike Garrigou-Lagrange, I would not employ *a priori* means to defend what he calls the intrinsic and extrinsic forms of the PSR.

---

31. "We see at once that it is not only inconceivable, but *really impossible*, for a thing at once to be and not be. And we thus affirm already the objective and ontological value of the principle of contradiction *before any judgment of existence*, before reflecting that this primary affirmation presupposes ideas, and before *verifying* the fact that these ideas come to us, by abstraction, from sensible things grasped by our senses." Reginald Garrigou-Lagragne, "Le réalisme thomiste et le mystère de la connaissance," *Revue de Philosophie* 38 (1931). Cited by Jacques Maritain, *The Degrees of Knowledge*, translated by Gerald B. Phelan (New York: Charles Scribner's Sons, 1959), 134, n. 2.

32. Garrigou-Lagrange, *God: His Existence and His Nature*, 185. See also Jacques Maritain, *A Preface to Metaphysics: Seven Lectures on Being* (New York: Mentor Omega Book, 1962), 99.

33. Garrigou-Lagrange, *God: His Existence and His Nature*, 186–89.

First, when Aquinas follows Aristotle's defense of the noncontradiction principle at *Meta.* IV, 4, I do not believe that Aquinas is transiting from thought to reality via retorsion. Aristotle, Aquinas, and their opponents (Heraclitus, Protagoras, Empedocles, Democritus, and Anaxagoras) are all realists. Everyone thinks that they know reality. Aristotle and Aquinas think that reality is consistent, while their opponents think that reality is contradictory. The defense of Aristotle and Aquinas is to observe that the realism of their opponents should render their thinking contradictory and so reduces them to the level of plants. On the other hand, if the opponents want to keep their thinking consistent, then in the light of their realism they should acknowledge that reality is consistent. No party begins by claiming that the noncontradiction principle could be a law merely of the mind. Again, everyone is already a realist. A better interpretation of the noncontradiction defense roots the defense, *pace* claims against immediate realism, in an intellectual perception into sensible things.[34]

Second, the Thomistic texts of the extrinsic form of the PSR cited by Garrigou-Lagrange provide a better defense than his own defense of the extrinsic form. Garrigou-Lagrange cites *C.G.* II, 15: "For everything that belongs to another but not insofar as what itself is, belongs to it through some cause, just as white to man: omne enim quod alicui convenit non secundum quod ipsum est, per aliquam causam convenit ei, sicut album homini."[35] This proposition is not self-evident from Garrigou-Lagrange's above-mentioned reduction. The proposition is self-evident in and through its subject. What belongs (*convenit*) to a thing is an Aristotelian accident. The example of white also indicates this. As experience shows, an acci-

---

34. For the intellectual insight approach see Joseph Owens, *An Elementary Christian Metaphysics* (Houston: Center for Thomistic Studies, 1985), 269–70, and Robert J. Henle, *Method in Metaphysics* (Milwaukee: Marquette University Press, 1980), 56. For a critical discussion of immediate realism and what it can underwrite, see John F. X. Knasas, *Being and Some Twentieth-Century Thomists* (New York: Fordham University Press, 2003), 4–17, ch. 3, and 289–92.

35. Garrigou-Lagrange, *God: His Existence and His Nature*, 185.

dent is not so distinct from its subject that it fails to modify it. But to modify the subject, the accident must exist in and of the subject. Accordingly, as a modifier an accident is an *ipso facto* dependent item. The recognition of the accidental gets the idea of explanation going. The explanation continues by noting that as potential to the accident, no subject *qua* subject can completely explain the accident. So the extrinsic form of the principle of sufficient reason is *per se notum* through the idea of the accidental.[36]

As should be obvious from my summary of Aquinas's metaphysical reasoning, Aquinas uses this thinking about accidents to reach a subsistent instance of *esse*. Not only in the very *Contra Gentiles* text cited by Garrigou-Lagrange but also in Aquinas's *De Ente et Essentia*, we find Aquinas applying the same thinking about a cause to what belongs to a thing.[37] Also, it is this same thinking that lies behind Aquinas asserting that what happens has a cause, for a happening is analyzable into a subject and attribute situation. Once one has discerned an attribute, one is offered a dependency for which one can seek the full explanation. Hume's

---

36. If we understand "state" as an accident, Davies, *The Reality of God*, 39, may be saying the same thing in the following: "Or we can say that something which undergoes change cannot itself totally account for the state in which it comes to be, since that state is a way of being which is not present in the thing before the change it undergoes, and since something cannot give itself what it does not have to start with (surely another reasonable assumption?)." In any case, Davies says the argument only provides a "reasonable ground" for knowledge of causality. On 36–37, Davies rests his case against Hume on three observations. Hume's denial of a cause for what happens rests upon imagination which is not necessarily indicative of reality. Second, knowing that something has genuinely begun rather than simply relocated presumes a knowledge that the thing was caused. Third, "could" in "Could x come about?" "normally means 'is able to come about given the existence of what is able to bring about certain effects.'"

37. "Whatever belongs to a thing [*convenit alicui*] is either caused by the principles of its nature (as the capacity for laughter in man) or comes to it from an extrinsic principle (as light in the air from the influence of the sun). Now being itself [*ipsum esse*] cannot be caused by the form or quiddity of a thing." Thomas Aquinas, *On Being and Essence*, translated by Armand A. Maurer (Toronto: Pontifical Institute of Mediaeval Studies, 1968), 56. Again, the examples of risibility and illumination indicate that what belongs to a thing is an accident. For the Thomist discussion of whether this *De Ente* text is a proof for God, see Knasas, *Being and Some Twentieth-Century Thomists*, 224–36.

enumeration of the possible bases for knowing the causal proposition omits the Aristotelian idea of the accidental.[38] In sum, for Aquinas the need for explanation is not original. It is derived from, or follows in the wake of, a recognition of the need of a cause. For proponents of the PSR, causality is one of the things we come to know in the wake of an original need for explanation.

A subsequent issue that Rowe might raise is whether Aquinas is correct to regard the thing's existence as *esse*, that is, as a *sui generis* accident or act.[39] Aquinas's view clashes with Kant's claim that existence cannot be a predicate because existence cannot add something determinate to the thought of the subject. Existence cannot add something determinate because "[the thing as thought] would not be exactly the same thing that exists, but something more than we had thought in the concept."[40] Hence, "the real contains no more than the merely possible." Aquinas could sidestep this critique. *Esse* is a *sui generis* attribute not simply because of its priority to its subject. As the act of all form, both substantial and accidental, *esse* is a nonformal act.[41] It is the act of all deter-

---

38. For a discussion of Hume's objections to knowing causality, see Knasas, *Being and Some Twentieth-Century Thomists*, 216–21. Like Hume, Rowe, *The Cosmological Argument*, 45, holds that something happening could be just a brute fact. Hence, Rowe thinks that when Aquinas holds in the *Tertia Via* that happenings require explanation, Aquinas can have only one possible reason for the requirement, viz., the principle of sufficient reason: no thing can exist and no fact can obtain without there being an explanation for that thing's existence or for that fact's obtaining. Rowe is missing the context of the accidental or attributive to deal with a change. Explanation is initiated precisely insofar as a change involves the acquiring of an accident or an attribute. Furthermore, because the subject of the attribute precisely as subject is a potency for the attribute, then a full explanation of the attribute shifts to something else, viz., the subject in some other respect or some other subject. The demonstrative need for something else is what is behind Aquinas's claim that in a regress of causes if the first is removed then the others are removed. Hence, when Aquinas uses this claim to refute an infinite regress, Aquinas is not begging the question as claimed by Rowe, *The Cosmological Argument*, 18–19.

39. Rowe, ibid., 215, admits hesitancy about the following critique.

40. Immanuel Kant, *Critique of Pure Reason*, A 600/B 628; translated by Norman Kemp Smith (New York: St. Martin's Press, 1965), 505

41. "[T]he actuality [*actualitas*] which the verb 'is' principally signifies is the actuality of every form commonly, whether substantial or accidental." *In I Peri.*, lect. 5, n. 22; Thomas

mination without being a determination. Hence, a Thomist can do justice to the surprised reaction most have to Kant's claims that the actual contains no more than the possible, and yet the something more does not render thought of the possible different from the actual. Among current analytic Thomists a tendency exists to understand Aquinas's *esse* talk as second order talk for something else, for example, form. The reader is directed elsewhere for a presentation of this view and a discussion of it.[42]

In conclusion, if one form of the PSR is Aquinas's claim that what belongs to a thing belongs to it through some cause, then Aquinas's metaphysical proof for God uses the PSR. But as asserted by Aquinas, the proposition is not true by reducing its opposite to a question begging self-contradiction. It is true self-evidently in and through the meaning of its subject—what belongs to a thing, a point missed by opponents as well as proponents of the PSR.

DE VER. X, 12, AD 10M: "IF NOT GOD FROM JUSTICE, THEN GOD FROM SOME OTHER EFFECT"

Just earlier in his *De Veritate* at question X, article 12, Aquinas discusses whether "God exists" is self-evident or *per se notum*. His conclusion is that "God exists" is not self-evident to us, yet the proposition is known by demonstrations taken from God's effects (*ex effectibus*). In his reply to the tenth objection of the second set, Aquinas specifies what he understands by effects. He says: "God is known not only in the effect of justice, but also in his other effects: whence given that God is not known by someone as just, it does not follow that he is not known in any way. It is impossible

---

Aquinas, *On Interpretation*, translated by Jean T. Oesterle (Milwaukee: Marquette University Press, 1962), 53.

42. John F. X. Knasas, "Haldane's Analytic Thomism and Aquinas's *Actus Essendi*," in *Analytical Thomism: Traditions in Dialogue*, edited by Craig Paterson and Matthew S. Pugh (Burlington, Vt.: Ashgate Publishing Company, 2006), 233–52. For an attempt to compare the contemporary discussions of necessity in cosmological reasoning with Aquinas's *Tertia Via* from the possible and the necessary, see my " 'Necessity' in the *Tertia Via*," *The New Scholasticism* 52 (1978), 373–94.

that none of his effects are known, since his effect is common being [*ens commune*], which is not able to be unknown."⁴³

The objection itself denies divine justice because evils are pleasing to God (*Deo placere mala*). The objection does not elaborate but it seems clear that what is meant is the observation that the wicked prosper. Aquinas's reply concedes this observation and so indicates Aquinas's realization of the weight of this observation. The strategy of the reply is to remind the reader that God is already known through his other effects, for God's effect of common being cannot be unknown. What is *ens commune*, this effect that provides an unmistakable starting point for demonstrating God?

A reader of the *De Veritate* would discover that in its first article, Aquinas takes great pains to spell out his understanding of *ens*. Our intellect conceives *ens* as most known (*notissimum*) and as that into which it resolves all of its concepts. For every nature is essentially a being. Aquinas further concludes that other concepts add to being, not by bringing in something extrinsic, but by expressing something already implicitly contained within the meaning of *ens*.

This expression takes two general forms. First, certain special modes of *ens* can be what are expressed. Examples are the diverse genera of things (*diversa rerum genera*), namely substance and the various kinds of accidents, such as quantity, quality, relation, action, and so forth. Both substance and accidents express special regions within the larger notion of *ens*.

Second, some of our concepts can express different meanings true of every being. These are general modes of being. These general modes are of two kinds: those true of every being of itself and those true of every being in its relation to another. As regards meanings true of every being in itself, Aquinas says that we can speak affirmatively or negatively. Affirmatively speaking, essence is found in every being. At this point Aquinas makes some remarks

---

43. Thomas Aquinas, *Disputed Questions on Truth*, vol. II, translated by James V. McGlynn (Chicago: Regnery, 1953), 71.

about *ens* that draw upon his metaphysics. Aquinas distinguishes the meanings of the terms *ens* and *res* in the following manner: "Being [*ens*] is taken from the act of being [*actus essendi*] but the name of thing [*res*] expresses the quiddity or essence of the being." What is meant by *actus essendi* here? Aquinas's reply to the third objection of the second set is relevant. There Aquinas says: "In the statement, 'To be [*esse*] is other than that which is [*quod est*],' the act of being [*actus essendi*] is distinguished from that to which that act belongs. But the name of being [*ens*] is taken from the act of existence [*actus essendi*], not from that whose act it is."[44]

By *actus essendi* Aquinas means *esse*. *Esse* is the act of the *quod est* to which *esse* belongs. The *quod est* is what he called quiddity or essence and with which he identified thing (*res*). This leads to an important conclusion. The term *ens* is given to the various genera of things (*diversa rerum genera*), for example, substance and accident, on the basis of the *esse* that belongs to them. In other words, by *ens* Aquinas is referring to a composition of *essentia* and *esse* that can be specialized into compositions of substance and *esse* or the various accidents and their *esse*.[45]

A reader's look at *De Ver.* I, 1c, indicates that by *ens commune* Aquinas is referring to a composite intelligibility drawn from, "*resolvit*," a field that includes as its members various substances and accidents actuated by their existences. *De Ver.* I, 1c, also makes plain that when Aquinas spoke of God's effects of justice and of *ens commune*, he was not considering two different but equal effects. Rather, the effect of justice appears to be englobed within *ens commune* as an instance of it. If the instance of justice goes unnoticed, some other instance of *ens commune* will be apprehended, for everything is a mode of *ens*. From that instance God

---

44. Thomas Aquinas, *Disputed Questions on Truth*, vol. I, translated by Robert W. Mulligan (Chicago: Regnery, 1952), 8.

45. This division of *esse* is also acknowledged in the *Contra Gentiles* I, 26: "This being [*esse formale*] is divided into the being [*esse*] of substance and the being [*esse*] of accident. On the Thomistic debate about whether accidents like substance have their own *actus essendi*, see Owens, *An Elementary Christian Metaphysics*, 160, n. 5.

can be known by Aquinas's causal reasoning summarized above in chapter 2. Finally, as just detailed in the last section of the present chapter, as subsistent *esse*, God is morally good and all-powerful.

The thinking of the twelfth reply illustrates how minimal is Aquinas's approach to God. The approach does not presume things that are just but simply things that exist; and the things, *rei*, do not even have to be substances, but they can be their accidents. In these cases Aquinas does not get to a good God from a good or from an ordered world. To insist that Aquinas's God proof requires more than existence is to create a red herring. Injustice can even be overwhelming, but as long as something exists, God exists. As Maritain remarked, "Let us but grant to a bit of moss or the smallest ant its due nature as an ontological reality, and we can no longer escape the terrifying hand that made us."[46]

46. Maritain, *The Degrees of Knowledge*, 110. In his *The Reality of God and the Problem of Evil*, Brian Davies takes an approach to God and evil similar to the one described in this section. He calls the approach the "I know God exists approach," (17). Yet Davies (65–67) reinterprets the essence and *esse* distinction. It becomes the individual and nature distinction mentioned by Aquinas at *ST* I, 3, 3. Davies then argues that the nature of no individual explains that individual because no nature includes the designated matter (this flesh and these bones) that are in the individual (Step four, 41). If all individuals in the universe include this distinction, then the universe is caused by a creator. Yet I wonder if the conclusion of a creator follows. If the cause accounts for the nature being in this designated matter, is not the cause a mover, or generator? Moreover, is the cause even necessarily immaterial? As I noted John Quinn to say (supra ch. 3, n. 10), matter and form reasoning reaches a first physical cause that in comparison to terrestrial bodies is equivocally a body. This is the conclusion that Aristotle and Aquinas *de facto* identified with the heavens of the astronomy of the time. It is also worth noting that Aquinas denies the individual and nature distinction in these heavenly bodies. Aquinas uses the denial to argue for the lack of this distinction in truly immaterial substances: "But in heavenly bodies, on account of their very perfection, we find that one species contains only one individual; both because each of them exhausts the entire matter pertaining to its species, and because each heavenly body possesses perfectly the power of its species to fulfill in the universe that to which the species is ordered, as the sun and the moon exemplify conspicuously. For all the more reason, then should we find in separate substances but one individual of the one species." *C.G.* II, 93; Thomas Aquinas, *Summa contra Gentiles*, vol. II, translated with introduction and notes by James Anderson (Notre Dame, Ind.: University of Notre Dame Press, 1975) 321–22. In my approach, since *esse* is most prior and deeply set in the existent, then in causing *esse*, subsistent existence causes the thing without presupposing anything else. In other words, subsistent existence is a creator. Accordingly at *ST* I, 44, 2c, a cause of *esse* is a creator of matter. For

SUMMARY OF AQUINAS ON THE EXISTENCE OF EVIL

Another useful preliminary before engaging the contemporary debate is to summarize my findings on Aquinas and the problem of evil.

First, Aquinas does acknowledge the problem as a theistic challenge. But because of his metaphysics of *esse*, Aquinas quickly neutralizes the challenge even so far as to argue that if evil exists, then God exists.

Hence, second, the persistent problem of evil is a how question. Given that evil exists as a fact of experience and that God exists as a conclusion to metaphysical reasoning, how are these two givens related, how are they compatible?

Third, to answer this how question a distinction among evils is important. On the one hand are "natural corruptions"; on the other are *"quandoque* evils." At *ST* I, 19, 9c, Aquinas explains the former as willed by God insofar as God wills the natural perfection of the universe. Elsewhere in the *C.G.* III, 6, Aquinas describes this psychology of willing as intending evil *per accidens*. The general psychology appears to be one of means to ends. As regards the evil of natural corruption, Aquinas's thinking seems to be that if some class of generable and corruptible substances is privileged with incorruptibility, then matter would be taken up into that class to the detriment of other classes. Hence, the universe's perfection which consists in reflecting God's simple perfection in a multiplicity of different substances is destroyed. Of course in the eyes of the Thomistic metaphysician, a supernatural override of this situation is a possibility. The creator could constantly provide new matter to replace the matter taken up into the higher species. But as supernatural this override is not something that the creator is required to provide, nor is the override something that the metaphysician is in a position to know.

---
the same reasoning, one understands that subsistent existence's causing of the *esse* of the substance must be continuous.

The human person is not an exception here. Death is not an "utter anomaly" for the human as Maritain claimed. As Aquinas notes in *C.G.* III, 112, the dignity of the human derives from the intellection of being. But the intellection of being is analogical. Hence, being does not so perfectly seat itself in the human intellect that the human becomes a whole or a universe unto itself, as Maritain said at one point. Rather, Aquinas goes on to describe the human as: "more like a whole than a part," a "principle part," and the most perfect "in all of nature." In short, the dignity natural to a human never catapults the human outside the whole of nature. Consequently the human naturally suffers the corruption that God wills any part of nature for the perfection of the whole. In this context, to protest one's eventual demise is to ignore one's natural status as a part of the cosmic whole, albeit a principle part.

Fourth, the evils about which Aquinas becomes exercised are *quandoque* evils. As the attack of the lower on the higher, these evils wreck the perfection of the whole so that they constitute a challenge to God's existence and to his providence. How are they compatible with God? Aquinas insists that they are not willed even indirectly by God. Their relation to God's will is simply one of permission. They are not willed either *per se* or *per accidens*. At *ST* I, 48. 2, ad 3m, for example, Aquinas presents a twofold reason for their divine permission. The first reason is the antecedent good which consists in the natural functioning of things. The thinking seems to be that creatures act as movers and movers presuppose a material upon which to act. But there is no natural guarantee that the material does not contain radicals that can interfere with the causality of the mover. Hence, natural things attain their ends "for the most part" and fail to do this "in a few cases." In other words, contingency is part of the warp and woof of the natural order, and not all contingent events are good, as finding a treasure is good. When fallible and limited human intelligence is added to this mix, the *quandoque* evils increase exponentially. For example, a tribe believes that it makes good sense to leave the pestilence of the jungle for the health of the coast only to find that they are now victims of tidal waves. They then move to the mountains only to be ambushed by earthquakes. These ideas entail that the realization of the good of which we are naturally capable, viz., a metaphysics of the intellection of being and an ethics based upon the human as an intellector of being,[47] will be by its nature agonizingly slow, never fully realized, and realized if at all only after many failures. Even though there is a good that we can naturally attain, it is a good that is difficult to realize. And difficult things are accomplished rarely. For example, if we have two hands and ten fingers, we are naturally capable of playing Rachmaninoff. But how many of us can play Rachmaninoff well? It is the same for metaphysics and ethics. As I explained in chapter 2, even though the principles of metaphysics and ethics are self-evident to all, the explicit and formal development of these principles is fraught with pitfalls. The human condition is naturally a messy and laborious affair, and to believe that the slings and arrows of fortune should be less is the height of naivety. The hope of the pure philosopher is that someone, somewhere, at some time will get through and realize human potentiality. This hope consoles him even in personal adversity. Because the basic object of his love is being which is found in other intellectors, his life was never just about himself but about the proliferation of the knowledge and choosing of being. There is no jealousy here. The philosopher takes his pleasure in knowing that where one fails or falls short, others will succeed. Just as a good team member is happy about a teammate getting the hit or making the basket that one missed, so too a human should rejoice that others realize the life of the intellector of being.

Finally, neither does this sober understanding of the history of the natural order disqualify it as an object of the creator's will. Even such a history will provide some reflection of the intelligence of the creator. Both a flickering candle and a steady flame illumi-

---

47. For the texts, see my chapter 6 at nn. 66 and 67.

nate. Insofar as the corruptible order, through humans, achieves some reflection of the intelligence and love of the creator, that order is a legitimate object of the creative will. This is to reiterate the first reason for the divine permission of *quandoque* evils.

The second reason for the divine permission of *quandoque* evils is the divine perfection. Aquinas employs this idea to claim that insofar as *quandoque* evils attack the order that God wills, then God has the motivation and the resources to order these evils for some good. *Quandoque* evils will not be the last word; they will not stand unresolved into good. In a contemporary idiom, pointless evils will not exist. Even though Aquinas is metaphysically sure of this second reason, he is admittedly metaphysically ignorant about the identity of the consequent good to which God orders the permitted *quandoque* evil. But Aquinas is ignorant not because he has no idea about its identity but because he has too many ideas. Aquinas's stock example is the suffering of the martyrs giving way to the good of their exemplary patience. But the consequent good does not have to accrue to the sufferer. The examples of the killing of the stag rebounding to the good of the lion and God commanding the slaying of Isaac to manifest Abraham's faith in God show that permutation. Nor does the consequent good have to be a new good as was the case with the patience of the martyrs. The consequent good can be a previously mentioned antecedent good. Aquinas notes that by feeding the lion the killing of the stag keeps the species in existence. Finally, if the consequent good is a new good, it does not have to be a natural good like the continuance of the feline species. The possibility exists that the consequent good intended by the creator is a supernatural good, for example, the consequent good could be what Christian theologians call the beatific vision. Such a good is not totally unknown to the metaphysician. If the Thomistic philosopher is imaginative enough, the Thomistic philosopher just as a philosopher would know that the human's intellection of being establishes the remote condition for the human to cognitively receive the creator who as *esse subsistens* realizes the intelligible heart of the *ratio entis*.[48] The human intellect is to the creator not like the eye is to sound. The eye has no capacity, remote or proximate, to receive sound. Unfortunately, even at the peak of the philosopher's abilities, the philosopher has no way of demonstrating that the creator does in fact intend to order all to this supernatural consequent good. As supernatural it is not a known fact but a known possibility. Naturally speaking, the human intellect is geared to know being only through its analogates. That is why natural happiness is imperfect. True, after the philosopher knows the existence of the creator, Aquinas says that there arises a natural desire to know the essence of the creator. But this desire causes no exigency for the beatific vision. Without the vision the human situation is not one of total frustration. The human has the natural happiness of the analogical knowledge of being and of its creative source. Just as a parent need not completely satisfy a child's desire to eat in order to satisfy nutritional requirements, so too the creator, without dereliction, need not complete the human's desire for vision of the creator's essence. As is his prerogative as a Christian theologian, Aquinas appealed to the datum of heavenly reward when he spoke of the patience or virtue of the martyrs.[49] But the practitioner of a pure Thomistic metaphysics would have to be more circumspect. On the basis of the data available to the philosopher, the philosopher would not know exactly what is going on.

There are still other unresolved possibilities for the consequent good. A further possibility is a life after death less than the beatific vision. Even though the metaphysician knows that intellectual soul is incorruptible, the metaphysician does not know if it is im-

---

48. See *ST* I, 12, 4, ad 3m in which the intellect's ability to know the concreted being (*esse concretum*) in abstraction establishes the remote possibility for reception of the divine essence.

49. "But the death of a man killed by a lion is directed not merely to the good of the lion, but principally to the man's punishment or to the increase of his merit; for his merit can grow if he accepts his suffering." *De Ver.* 5, 6c; Aquinas, *Disputed Questions on Truth*, vol. I, 226.

mortal. By "immortal" is meant operating in separation from the body. In Aquinas's philosophical psychology volition is naturally dependent upon intellection and intellection as abstractive is dependent upon sensation. Hence, a human soul bereft of the body seems to be naturally inert. Nevertheless, the metaphysician can know that what nature fails to supply to the separated soul, the creator can supply and so activity in the separated soul is a possibility. But as over and above the nature of the soul, this divine aid is supernatural and so gratuitous.⁵⁰ Hence, perhaps God is ordering evils suffered now for an afterlife that is less than the beatific vision. Obviously, this possibility admits the alternative possibility that the creator has established us simply in the natural state in which we have just one life to live in which evils would be ordered to natural knowledge and virtue.

Finally, the philosophically discernable category of the supernatural also neutralizes any antecedent good as a definitive explanation for natural corruptions and *quandoque* evils. If the philosopher is familiar with the narrative of Christianity, the philosopher would become acquainted with the episode of original sin. Using metaphysics, the philosopher should see no inherent impossibility in that episode. That humans were created in an initial state of supernatural benefaction which they lost through some fault is not like a square circle. The creator has the power to create such a state and human nature presents no inherent obstacle to be raised to this state. That realization by the metaphysician means that the evils of the present time are possibly punishments just as Christianity claims. As noted in the discussion of the Abraham and Isaac incident and in the discussion of original sin, Aquinas treats evils

---

50. See *ST* I, 12, 5, for what I take to be a philosophical argument for grace as necessary for the beatific vision. The major premise of the *responsio* of article five is: "Everything which is raised up to what exceeds its nature must be prepared by some disposition above its nature; as, for example, if air is to receive the form of fire, it must be prepared by some disposition for such a form." The example shows that the major premise is derived from ordinary experience available to the philosopher. The prerequisite grace Aquinas calls the light of glory.

as punishments. Moreover, the possibilities become more dizzying to contemplate. After mentioning the punishment character of present evils, Aquinas himself says that for the baptized these evils are something else; they are ways for the Christian to participate in the redeeming action of Christ.[51] To which again a metaphysician would have to say, "Yes, it is possible."

What these reflections amount to is the realization that in respect to evil the Thomistic philosopher is in a state of ignorance similar to the ignorance regarding the creation of the world in time or from eternity. Contrary to the followers of Bonaventure who claimed that human reason could demonstrate a first moment of the world's existence and contrary to the followers of Aristotle who claimed that human reason could demonstrate that no such moment existed, Aquinas claimed that both positions were creative options for God and that we only know the truth of the first because God has told us what God did. In other words, working with the data available to natural reason, the philosopher can demonstrate that at any moment *esse* is dependent upon *esse subsistens*. What the philosopher is unable to do is show that past moments include a first moment. The data indicate` that God could have given *esse* to a first moment for the world or given *esse* without such. The philosopher cannot answer the question of whether the world was created in time or from eternity, not because there is no idea of an answer but because there are too many ideas. The situation is the same for the philosopher and the question of why does evil exist. No natural explanation, like the antecedent good explanation for natural corruptions and *quandoque* evils is final and definitive because they fail to eliminate a possible supernatural explanation, for example, punishment for original sin or some kind of prepara-

---

51. "For it is right that we should first of all be conformed to Christ's sufferings before attaining to the immortality and impassibility of glory, which was begun in Him, and by Him acquired for us. Hence it is necessary that our bodies should remain, for a time, subject to suffering, in order that we may merit the impassibility of glory, in conformity with Christ." *ST* I-II, 85, 5, ad 3m; Pegis, *Basic Writings of Thomas Aquinas*, vol. II, 702.

tion for an afterlife. Likewise no supernatural explanation is philosophically definitive because by definition the supernatural, as a fact, is beyond the ability of natural reason to determine. This situation is not the same as that in which many contemporary theodicies find themselves. In the contemporary discussion we find many theodicies because no one theodicy is comprehensive. So a solution for one kind of evil fails to explain another. For instance, Hick's soul-making theodicy fails to explain why animals suffer. Or the best possible world may explain why animals suffer but seems inappropriate for human dignity. In Aquinas's thinking one can find ideas to address these gaps, but the result is still no one true theodicy. Each will be comprehensive but not definitive.

A STRATEGY

This result of my study of Aquinas on evil creates the strategy to follow in canvassing the contemporary discussion. Theistic explanations will be neutralized while at the same time their possibility will be defended. For example, the perfection of the universe solution will not be definitive because there exists the possibility that cannot be eliminated that the human has been supernaturally raised to a divine life that makes the human more than a principle part of the whole. In sum, the possibility here is the one described by Maritain in his Marquette Aquinas lecture. On the other hand, since the human's status as a whole is a supernatural realization, there is the possibility that the human is in fact still a principle part of the created whole and so suffers evil as a result of that status. The Thomistic philosopher will defend one against the other and will defend both against atheists. Just as Aquinas's discussion of the world's temporal inception or creation from eternity is complicated, so too will be my discussion of the contemporary literature on evil. But given the massiveness of that literature, this strategy has the advantage of providing the philosopher with some orientation of his mental energies.

6

The Thomist and the Contemporary Discussion

PERSONALIST THEODICIES

The present chapter develops the strategy mentioned at the end of chapter 5. In the current debate, theists as well as anti-theists argue in either of two ways, for which Maritain's Marquette Aquinas lecture provided the categories. One theistic group explains evil in the light of the perfection of the whole created cosmos. In other words, it is not irrational to explain the evils that one human being suffers by the good brought about elsewhere. Another group explains evil by the perfection of the individual human being. In other words, the dignity of the human being requires that the evils suffered rebound at least to the good of that human sufferer. In sum, the theistic explanations are either cosmological or personalist.[1] If I am

---

1. I am indebted to Paul St. Amour, "The Scale-Wielding God and the Limits of Philosophical Theodicy," *Proceedings of the American Catholic Philosophical Association* 74

correct about Aquinas, the Thomist must oppose both theodicies as *the* explanation of evil. In other words, neither the cosmological nor personalist explanation can validate the claimed definitiveness of their explanations. The reason for the lack of definitiveness is that the philosopher fails to determine if the creator has brought humans into existence with a natural end or with a supernatural end, respectively. Both theists will be making philosophical arguments not for truths but only for possibilities. A Thomist is bound to displease fellow theists somewhat as Aquinas was bound to displease Bonaventurians and Aristotelians about the failure of demonstrations for the world's temporal inception and for the world's existence from eternity.

How will I develop the strategy? Since my monograph began with Rachel, I want to begin with the personalists. My critique of the personalists will focus on their understanding of the human person. From a strictly philosophical viewpoint, the understanding may be too exalted. Hence, a cosmological explanation of evil will always be possible. Personalists should realize that their assumed exalted view of the human person is a truth of religious revelation and they should not inappropriately inject it into a philosophical discussion. Somewhat similarly Aquinas did not inject the Biblical revelation of a temporal cosmic inception into philosophical debates about the same.

(2000), 259–71, for the last label. He critiques many contemporary theodicies (Plantinga, Hick, Swinburne) on the basis of the "personalist intuition"—namely, when the parts in question are persons, evil done to these parts cannot (morally) be justified by reference to the harmony of the whole," 266. In his behalf, St. Amour cites both Maritain's *The Person and the Common Good*, 266, and Aquinas's natural desire in rational creatures for the fullness of being, 264. I have already discussed Maritain. For my treatment of Thomistic natural desires, see this chapter's last section. As mentioned in chapter 1, it is unclear that Maritain is a philosophical personalist in St. Amour's sense. It is the thesis of this book that Aquinas is not. Yet I would be hesitant to deny that both thinkers are personalists. The philosophical case for human dignity need not be made on the basis of knowing that the person is a whole, or universe, unto itself. A more modest basis is that the human is the "principal part" in the cosmos. Aquinas argued from that basis for the conclusion that the human as rational is divinely governed for its own sake. Maritain was aware of this text. Nevertheless, my discussion will proceed by employing St. Amour's definition of "personalist."

MARILYN MCCORD ADAMS AND "HORRENDOUS EVILS"

In the concluding article of her anthology, *The Problem of Evil*, Marilyn McCord Adams makes an impassioned argument for the following claim: "In the spirit of Ivan Karamazov, I am convinced that the depth of horrific evil cannot be accurately estimated without recognizing it to be incommensurate with any package of merely non-transcendent goods and so unable to be balanced off, much less defeated, thereby."[2] By horrific evils she means "evils the participation in (the doing or suffering of) which gives one reason prima facie to doubt whether one's life could (given their inclusion in it) be a great good to one on the whole."[3] Consequently, she has in mind not only sufferers of these evils but perpetrators as well. Examples of the latter include cannibalizing one's own offspring, child abuse as described by Karamazov, participation in the Nazi death camps, unwittingly causing the disfigurement or death of loved ones. With these instances in mind, Adams illustrates the inadequacy of generic and global theodicies in which some general reason and some feature of the world as a whole, for example, the best possible, is called upon to do the explaining. The problem is that the theodicy explains evil to the world but not to the individual. Here are two cases by which she makes her point:

> Suppose for the sake of argument that horrendous evil could be included in maximally perfect world orders; its being partially constitutive of such an order would assign it that generic and global positive meaning. But would knowledge of such a fact defeat for a mother the prima-facie reason provided by her cannibalism of her own infant to wish that she had never been born? ... Could the truck-driver who accidently runs over his beloved child find consolation in the idea that this middle-known but unintended side-effect was part of the price God accepted for a world with the best balance of moral good over moral evil he could get?[4]

---

2. Marilyn McCord Adams, "Horrendous Evils and the Goodness of God," in *The Problem of Evil*, edited by Marilyn McCord Adams and Robert Merrihew Adams (Oxford: Oxford University Press, 1990), 217.

3. Ibid., 211.   4. Ibid., 214.

She even suggests that such explanations would make horrific evils more horrific because they would "draw a picture of divine indifference or even hostility to the human plight."[5] Adams's solution is to insist that challenges to the consistency of Christianity should bear in mind the totality of Christianity. In that respect, she enlists the doctrine of the beatific vision as the only good capable of defeating evils in individual lives.[6] Moreover, her use of this Christian point is not so much to provide a *why* to evil but a *how*. She illustrates the latter by the way "the two-year-old heart patient is convinced of its mother's love, not by her cognitively inaccessible reasons, but by her intimate care and presence through its painful experience."[7]

My contention is that Adams's category of horrendous evils makes the same personalist assumption that was noted in Maritain, Camus, and Flew. That is why for her no nontranscendent good can defeat horrendous evils. Likewise Maritain's Rachel and Camus's Rioux regard the child as a whole onto itself and so these authors render blasphemous any explanation of the child's suffering by a good brought to be somewhere else. Also, Flew assumes that if the creator loves us, the creator must love us as a father. From the perspective of Aquinas's philosophy these assumptions are possibilities but not truths that the philosopher can establish. For example, Christian belief holds that by grace we have been made children of God and so God is our father. Hence, Flew's complaint should be taken up within that perspective and not restricted to the perspective of philosophy. In the wider Christian perspective Flew will find other points that address his complaint, such as those mentioned in Maritain's Aquinas lecture.

One can see the play of this personalist assumption in the examples of horrendous evils. Why can the mother who cannibalizes her child only wish that she had never been born? Even if she is made a pariah because her action is known, why does she not re-

5. Ibid., 214.
6. Ibid., 219–20.
7. Ibid., 217.

spond with profound regret and with resolve to live for the good of her fellows? Why does she regard her life as finished? I believe that her thinking goes like this. The child that she killed was unspeakably precious, a good unto itself. Hence, the mother cannot make up for her assault by bringing about a good elsewhere. But since the child is dead, the mother cannot address her wrong to the child by returning a good to the baby. Such is the checkmate situation of the murderer. Once the murder is done, it appears to be humanly irremovable. For the mother the only solution is to wish that she had never been born and so the act never committed. The same dynamic can be used to deal with the prison guard and the truck driver. If the victims are accorded an unspeakable preciousness, then no nontranscendent good will defeat the suffering of the victims. And so no generic and global theodicy will satisfy.

But do we know that this unspeakable preciousness is true? Not philosophically. As a result of his philosophical psychology, Aquinas establishes human dignity on the basis of the intellection of being. Such an understanding is enough to ground primary and secondary precepts of natural law that are invariable both in rectitude and in knowledge. But since that intellection of being is analogical, viz., the grasping of sameness in difference, the *ratio entis* never perfectly seats itself in the human intellect. By its nature, then, the human is only "closer to a whole" and only "the principle part" of the created whole. By its nature the human is precious but not unspeakably so. In this perspective murder is not a checkmate situation. There exists the possibility that the evil done be made right by a good brought about elsewhere. In Christianity where, by supernatural means, the human is unspeakably precious, other factors endemic to the religion exist to deal with the remorseful killer. A checkmate situation arises only when one conflates religion and philosophy. In sum, evils are "horrendous" only up and against a certain exaggerated view of the human.

But such a conflation is understandable. All of us, Christian or not, have experienced the unspeakable pains of loss and of guilt. If what Aquinas says is true, why should this happen? Are not these unspeakable experiences reactions to unspeakable evils? Not necessarily. As I tried to explain at the end of chapter 2, the notion of being can produce faux epiphanies of itself. The contemplation of the great and of the small can so aggrandize the use of the notion of being that the great or the small can take on all the preciousness of being itself. And it is interesting to note that like the cases of Maritain, Camus, and Flew, so many of Adams's examples all involve something small, viz., children. My contention is that the personalist enters the discussion about evil with a presupposition about the status of the human. That presupposition is philosophically unvalidated and in truth is an appearance created by an unwitting association of being, the good, with either the great or the small.

WILLIAM HASKER: PERSONAL SATISFACTION AND WORLD APPROVAL

In my opinion, another strong personalist is William Hasker. Hasker ventures a novel argument against the atheologian in his "On Regretting the Evils of This World."[8] As I will explain, Hasker's argument is not without a cost to the theist.

Hasker's argument begins with a very personal and admittedly "existential" question. "Am I glad that I exist or do I wish that I had never been born?" After asking us to consider the question very carefully, he affirms an embodied view of personal identity.[9] This embodied view roots me in the "major or significant events in the world's past history."[10] Hasker argues for a principle that governs the logical relation between certain attitudes: (E) "If I am glad on the whole that P, and I know that P entails Q, than (sic) I rationally must be glad on the whole that Q." With these previous thoughts

8. William Hasker, "On Regretting the Evils of This World," in *The Problem of Evil: Selected Readings*, edited by Michael L. Peterson (Notre Dame, Ind.: University of Notre Dame Press, 1992), 153–68.
9. Ibid., 156.
10. Ibid.

set forth, Hasker draws them together in a surprising conclusion: (G) "If I am glad on the whole about my own existence and that of those whom I love, then I must be glad that the history of the world, in its major aspects, has been as it has."[11]

Turning to the problem of evil, Hasker thinks that now he has the atheologian caught in a dilemma.[12] On the one hand, the atheologian's complaints about the world ramify to complaints about himself and those he loves. On the other hand, gladness about his own existence and of those he loves ramify to gladness about the way the world is and has been and so contradict his complaints about the way the world is. The atheologian is either a cad or toothless.

The argument is clever but, as I noted, it carries a cost that some theists may not want to bear. This cost also evinces the personalism that I claimed was implicit in Hasker's position. To make the cost obvious, let us suppose an illegitimate child, namely, someone born through fornication. If the child makes a moral complaint to or, in other words, disapproves of his fornicating parents, the child invites his parents to reply that if they did not fornicate, the child would not exist. So the child should stop disapproving. Who would be so bold to say that for immorality not to exist, it is better that they would never have been born? That is Hasker's appeal to personalism. But the cost here is that human existence would seem to justify everything, hence anything, even immorality. Some theists would not want to say that.[13]

So what is to be done? As it looks to me, Hasker's argument amounts to saying that if I approve my existence, then I have to approve what got me here, even immorality. But it also seems to make sense to say that if I value myself, then I disapprove of the immorality that got me here. There seems to be some ambiguity

11. Ibid., 159.
12. Ibid., 162–63.
13. On the problem of a denial of genuine evil, see the discussion of John Hick, below at "David Ray Griffin and the Denial of Genuine Evils."

that cries out for clarification. Hasker's argument appears to have a point but not the very one that he wants. To get to the bottom of the puzzle, I think that it is worth remembering how Aquinas said that *quandoque* evils are related to consequent goods.[14] They were causes but accidental material causes. This characterization is important because it allows for a dissimilarity to exist between effect and cause. As Aquinas said, the effects of an accidental cause are infinite. In other words, the effects need not be of one nature because they correspond to the nature of the cause. At *ST* I, 19, 9, ad 1m, Aquinas also mentioned the example of the patience of the martyrs being outside of the intention of the persecutors. Also, to return to the fornicating parents, they, *precisely as fornicators*, will or intend only the sexual pleasure and so in that respect are only accidental causes of the child.

So, insofar as an accidental cause is a cause, then it should be acknowledged. That is the point Hasker's argument makes. But insofar as an accidental cause can be of a different nature than its effect, then it need not receive the same approval as the effect receives. In other words the child can approve its own existence but not approve the existence of the fornication. And so when the parents tell the child to stop disapproving because the child would not exist if they did not fornicate, the parents are claiming for themselves as fornicators too much causality. They are claiming that they are *per se* causes instead of accidental ones. Hasker's discussion of my rootedness as an embodied person in the major or significant events in the world's past history does not include this distinction between accidental and essential causes. Accordingly, he too quickly concludes to (G) and so does not trap the atheological in the above dilemma.

Finally, Aquinas's thinking on the dissimilarity between accidental causes and their effects is also important for understanding the lines from the Roman liturgy of the Easter vigil that Hasker

---

14. See "Bracketing *Quandoque* Evils between Goods" in chapter 3.

quotes:[15] "O truly necessary sin of Adam, that is wiped out by death of Christ. O happy fault, that was worthy to have such and so great a redeemer." A Thomist would understand the necessity of the sin as the necessity of an accidental cause. As such the Thomist would never extend to the sin the approval that he takes in the redemption. A happy fault is still a fault. The adjective does not remove the noun.

JOHN HICK: CREATION AS A GYMNASIUM FOR THE DEVELOPMENT OF OUR VIRTUES

I am categorizing John Hick as a personalist because he begins from the Christian idea that we are the apple of God's eye and are destined for eternal life.[16] God is our father, not simply our creator. Unlike Maritain, however, Hick attempts to deal with evil without an appeal to the traditional account of the temptation and the fall. In that account the initial humans were tempted by a fallen angel, Satan. Having sinned, humans lost the supernatural gifts enjoyed in the garden and as punishment returned to the state of nature. The natural state is inherently messy. As Aquinas mentioned, hu-

---

15. Hasker, "On Regretting the Evils," 161.

16. In fact for Hick, since the idea of eternal damnation is bogus, all humans will be saved. Since that is hardly achieved in this life, Hick ventures an afterlife of continued soul-making. Hick mentions two reasons for jettisoning the traditional notion of hell: "The sufferings of the damned in hell, since they are interminable, can never lead to any constructive end beyond themselves and are thus the very type of ultimately wasted and pointless anguish.... Further, the notion of hell is no less fatal to theodicy if, instead of stressing the sufferings of the damned, we stress the fact that they are unendingly in sin. For this is presumably an even greater evil—a greater frustration of the divine purpose,—than their misery. Thus in a universe that permanently contained sin, good and evil would be co-ordinates, and God's creation would be perpetually shadowed and spoiled by evil; and this would be incompatible either with God's sovereignty or with His perfect goodness." John Hick, *Evil and the God of Love* (New York: Harper & Row, 1978), rev. ed., 341–42. Aquinas sees it differently. Hell is not unmitigated evil. It contains the good of punishment brought about by a just God. "For example when a man sins, God orders the sin to the sinner's good, so that after his fall, upon rising again, he may be a more humble person; or it is ordered at least to a good which is brought about in him by divine justice when he is punished for his sins." *De Ver.* V, 5c; Thomas Aquinas, *The Disputed Questions on Truth*, vol. I, translated by Robert W. Mulligan (Chicago: Regnery, 1952), 223.

man nature absolutely considered suffices to see that material and spiritual defects might well be natural defects and not penalties, and so the doctrine of original sin is not demonstrated from our present condition. Hence, to suffer a return to the natural state is more like a punishment. In other words, a Christian theologian like Aquinas is a personalist but also has as part of his theology the doctrine of the fall. But for Hick, the personalism remains, yet the fall is reinterpreted.

Hick's problem with the traditional account is the plausibility of Satan. Hick describes the sin of Satan in this oxymoronic way: "the incomprehensible rebellion of finitely perfect beings who were enjoying the full happiness of God's presence."[17] Consequently, Hick offers his own understanding of the fall. God spiritualized man as the product of a long evolutionary process. Hence, man came to exist as essentially free and self-directing in a world that hid God. This locus made it "virtually inevitable" that man would center his life upon himself. God lifts man from such a condition of "fallenness."[18]

In a context of answering Hume's four objections to theism from evil, Hick says that God uses evils in this world to develop the moral virtue aimed at eternal life.[19] That evils play this role is illus-

---

17. Hick, *Evil and the God of Love*, 249–50. On angelic sin for Aquinas, see chapter 7, n. 60. Hick seems to be considering the prelapsarian state as the beatific vision with its characteristic of impeccability. For Aquinas on impeccability in the beatific vision, see chapter 7 at n. 56.

18. Hick, *Evil and the God of Love*, 322–23, especially "Man can be truly for God only if he is morally independent of Him, and he can be thus independent only by being first *against* Him!" Ibid., 287. It is worth mentioning Christopher Dawson here. From the standpoint of anthropology Dawson locates the "religious impulse" as the motor for human culture. Even the most primitive cultures were religious. They were not self-centered. They experienced nature as divine and organized their societies around nature's rhythms. See Christopher Dawson, *Progress and Religion: An Historical Inquiry* (Washington, D.C.: The Catholic University of America Press, 2001), ch. 5. In the light of Dawson's anthropological reflections, Hick's description of our initial state as implicitly the state of modern science in which things receive spatiotemporal explanations (Hick, *Evil and the God of Love*, 284) appears anachronistic. Strangely, Eleonore Stump, "The Problem of Evil," *Faith and Philosophy* 2 (1985): 417, describes Hick's theodicy as "an evolution from good to better."

19. "If, then, God's aim in making the world is 'the bringing of many sons to glory,'

trated by various counter-factual hypotheses. The first envisages a world without any evil. Money would miraculously appear in the vaults of robbed banks, murders would not exist because bullets would melt in the air, injury from falling debris would disappear because gravity would be partially suspended, and so forth. Such a world would suspend moral qualities whose list includes: self-sacrifice, care for others, devotion to the public good, courage, perseverance, skill, and honesty. Extreme and crushing evils are handled in the same counter-factual way. In a world that is to be the scene of compassionate love and self-giving for others, suffering must fall upon mankind in the present haphazard and unequal way. For instance, if suffering were in proportion to virtue or the lack thereof, we would not seek to ameliorate suffering for fear of interfering with someone's soul-making. Also, if virtue were always rewarded, we would do the virtuous act for the reward rather than for its rectitude. Hick concludes, "Once again, then, we are confronted by the integral character of the existing order of things such that bane and blessing are intimately bound together within it, and such that not even an unfettered imagination can see how to remove the possibility of the one without at the same time forfeiting the possibility of the other."[20]

In the end Hick admits that when he turns his eyes to the actual world, soul-unmaking seems as true as soul-making. Both regular and excessive evils might be employed in soul-making but in far too many cases that occurrence is hidden from our eyes.[21] Hick ventures another life in virtue of which the soul-making would continue or get back on track.[22]

---

that aim will naturally determine the kind of world that He has created." Ibid., 256. On the value judgment, "not capable of demonstrative proof," in Hick's conception of God's aim, see ibid., 255–56. For Hume's objections see my chapter 7.

20. Ibid., 181.

21. "And yet, so far as we can see, the soul-making process does in fact fail in our world at least as often as it succeeds." Ibid., 336.

22. "Belief in an afterlife is no less crucial for theodicy." Ibid., 338. On the continued soul-making in the afterlife, see ibid., 345–49.

How does Hick's treatment of evil compare to Aquinas's? As a theologian Aquinas, like Hick, is a thinker who rests his thinking upon his religious beliefs. So for both, humans have a divinely intended eternal end and so both are personalists; evils are meant to rebound to one's good, not simply to a good brought about elsewhere. But Hick is trying to do a personalist theology without the traditional account of original sin. This omission creates intractable problems of which two are the following.

First, without the traditional account's reduction to the natural state, Hick cannot distinguish types of evils. In the natural order, according to Aquinas, there exist both natural corruptions and *quandoque* evils. Aquinas's second kind of evil seems to be what is on Hick's mind. For Aquinas *quandoque* evils follow the workings of natural things. As a realm of movers, the natural order is not so perfectly arranged that "free radicals" are absent. Their impact upon things can bring about the full panoply of *quandoque* evils that afflict humans. Also when humans are introduced to this state, the possibilities for tragedy increase. By its nature human intelligence proceeds from potency to act and so along the path of its development many opportunities for misfortune exist. So, *quandoque* evils are the incidental effects of a generable and corruptible order that God wills because its level of being contributes to the universe's reflection of God's goodness. As incidental effects, *quandoque* evils are properly speaking "permitted" by God. Their wreckage is then ordered by God to some good.

But without the traditional account of original sin, Hick does not have the natural order to fall back upon. In other words, unlike Aquinas, Hick cannot appeal to an antecedent good to explain evil. In Thomistic terms, the entire basis of Hick's theodicy is consequent goods.[23] Again, in Aquinas the evils humans suffer are substantially accounted for by the antecedent goods to which

---

23. "That is to say, instead of looking to the past for its clue to the mystery of evil, [theodicy] looks to the future, and indeed to that ultimate future to which only faith can look." Ibid., 261.

they are joined as incidental effects. For Hick the future has to do all the explanatory work. As Aquinas admitted, in that direction things are dark. Hence, it is not a surprise that Hick's account has difficulty dealing with animal suffering and with a standoff on the soul-making role claimed for evil in this life.[24]

Second, Hick's silence about a natural state with *quandoque* evils that are only divinely permitted and ordered creates the impression that evils are "willed" by God, not "ordered" by God as in Aquinas, as a means to the end of human virtue. Hick does remark, "For if our general conception of God's purpose is correct the world is not intended to be a paradise."[25] This remark seems to imply that the world is intended insofar as it is not a paradise. Likewise, "In this faith the prophets saw both personal and national tragedy as God's austere but gracious disciplining of His people."[26] Later, again speaking of the prophets, Hick speaks of evil as an instrument: "The prominence of the monotheistic instrumental view of evil at several points in the Old Testament is due to the fact that the faith of the prophets reached beyond our human scene, and looked upward to God."[27] Since instrumental causes are means to

---

24. For a listing of Hick's difficulties with animal suffering, see David Ray Griffin, *God, Power, and Evil: A Process Theodicy* (Philadelphia: The Westminster Press, 1976), 190–92.

25. Hick, *Evil and the God of Love*, 258.

26. Ibid., 243. Despite her noted difference from Hick, Stump remarks, "Furthermore, God as parent has a right to, and a responsibility for, painful correction of his creatures." "The Problem of Evil," 413. Like Hick, Stump insists upon a larger Christian context to deal with the evil problem. The larger Christian context includes ideas of Adam's fall, the subsequent entrance of natural evil, and an afterlife of heaven or hell. It also includes the Christian belief in the dignity of each human being such that the suffering of one human should be justified by some good accruing to that person. Ibid., 411. Hence, in my opinion, we are not dealing with a philosophical account. See my chapter 8 for more on Stump. In "The Problem of Evil," Stump's theodicy consists in God using both natural and moral evils to discipline us to humbly petition God to reorder our wills so that they are not disposed to will evil. In a nod to a lack of universalism in her theodicy, Stump recognizes the difficulty in making this claim about the suffering of children and of infants. Ibid., 411. Stump claims that any resemblance of her theodicy to Hick's theodicy is only "superficial." Ibid., 416. Hick's virtues are not strictly necessary in heaven and could be brought about simply through the challenge of writing a doctoral dissertation, for example.

27. Ibid., 358–59.

an end, then they are willed. Hence, Hick seems to have God willing evils.[28] This impression invites the comment, "I'll take a pass on my moral development, if my moral development means the death of my child." We have seen that in Aquinas's metaphysics there is the logical space for God's willing evil as a means to some good. For example, that space is involved in Aquinas's explanation of the Abraham and Isaac incident. Though God cannot order Abraham to sexually abuse Isaac for some end, even a supernatural one, God, as already a willer of death for the natural perfection of the universe, can order the execution of an immature and unbaptized human being for some supernatural end, in this case a manifestation of Abraham's faith in God and in God's promises for Abraham's descendents. Could, then, God be commanding the hurricanes, earthquakes, pestilences, and famines to some end just as God commanded Abraham to sacrifice Isaac? Yes, it is possible according to Aquinas's thinking but not probable. As noted, God's first intention is to preserve the nature that God has created. And so unless we are divinely informed to the contrary, we should regard all of these evils as *quandoque* evils, namely evils that God does not will but permits in willing a generable and corruptible order that, though it can sometimes fail, still evinces the perfection of the creator. Fr. Paneloux's explanation to Rioux too quickly assumed the contrary.

But the second problem with Hick's theodicy is not simply that the exceptional morphs into the ordinary. The problem is that

28. For more on Hick's apparent view that God in some sense wills evils, see my next section on Hick and Griffin. But what I am saying now is that like Aquinas's objector at *ST* I, 19, 9, 1 obj., Hick seems to think that it is good that evil be done and that this fact is what God wills. Also, a reader might recall that at *De Ver.* V, 5, ad 6m, Aquinas compares *quandoque* evils to tools (*instrumenta*) about which a noncarpenter would not know the use. Hence, is not Aquinas like Hick regarding evils as God's instruments? But Aquinas's analogy is self-admittedly inexact. The sixth reply's mention that God "directs" (*ordinat*) these evils returns the reader to *De Ver.* V, 4c, in which an evil of generation such as a monster, in other words a *quandoque* evil, is "directed" (*ordinatur*) and their occurrence falls not under God's providence of approval but under his providence of permission. So even though Aquinas calls evils "instruments" or "tools," Aquinas does not mean that evils are intended by God.

without a natural order there seems to be no brake on what God can will for soul-making. As noted in discussing Milhaven's interpretation of the Abraham and Isaac case, without a metaphysics of the world's perfection and of what that consists, Milhaven ventured to suggest that God can will all manners of sexual aberration if it is for some good, just as God commanded the sacrifice of Isaac for some good. Such is the prerogative of perfection. But by understanding the ordering of sex to the good of the species which in turn contributes to a reflection of the divine perfection in the world, Aquinas would regard God commanding essentially nonprocreative sex as like a general telling his soldiers to commit treason. In other words, if "bane and blessing are intimately bound together," then for God to will the human virtues mentioned previously is also for God to will the circumstances that realize these virtues. But what are the limits on the bane? How far can it go? Hick leaves this loose end. He does say, "In His original decision to create He was accordingly not responsible *under* any moral law or *to* any existing person."[29] And so the impression remains that some virtues are just not worth the willing of the evil that makes them possible.

DAVID RAY GRIFFIN AND THE DENIAL OF GENUINE EVILS

A third problem for Hick is raised by David Ray Griffin in his *God, Power, and Evil: A Process Theodicy*. It is an interesting problem. Even though I would concur with Griffin's critique, Griffin claims that this problem infects all traditional theodicies involving an omnipotent deity. In other words, it applies to both personalist and cosmological theodicies. Since I am arguing that both are possible but not philosophically definitive, then I cannot concede Griffin's critique of Hick without damaging my own position. Also, Griffin poses the same problem for Aquinas, and so I will have to respond. In sum, the current discussion of Hick presents the op-

---

29. Hick, *Evil and the God of Love*, 290.

portunity to discuss something of much wider implication. I would like to take advantage of that opportunity.

What is Griffin's problem with Hick's theodicy? It is closely related to my second criticism above. Griffin astutely observes that Hick's theodicy ends up denying genuine evil. By "a genuine evil" Griffin means "anything, all things considered, without which the universe would have been better."[30] Elsewhere, in terms similar to Rowe's pointless evils, Griffin says that a genuine evil is an evil "thought not to have been logically necessary for some compensating good."[31] He then initially describes the problem:

> But the key question in regard to the logical statement of the problem of evil is whether the theologian, regardless of how he defines evil, believes there is any genuine evil in the universe. For example, if the theologian says that evil is a privation of being, and believes that some instances of such a privation have occurred, the key question is whether he thinks that the universe would have been better off in the long run if these instances had not occurred. If he does not think so, then he has denied that there is any genuine evil, and the problem of evil does not exist for him. But if he does think there is genuine evil in this sense, then the issue as to whether evil is defined as something positive or as a mere privation is irrelevant to the formal question as to why God allowed something without which we would have all (God knows) been better off.[32]

On the one hand, if in the long run evil makes the universe better, then evil is a means to that better universe and so is really not evil. Evil is good. On the other hand, if evil does not make that contribution to the universe, why is it in the universe if the universe comes from an all-good and powerful deity? The first alternative expresses the denial of a genuine evil problem. And it nicely expresses an irritation many feel with best possible world theodicies. If the best possible world requires evils, are not the evils a means to the realization of that world and so not really evil? The problem also seems to make use of a Thomistic point. As noted when dis-

---

30. Griffin, *God, Power, and Evil*, 22.   31. Ibid., 180.
32. Ibid., 28.

cussing *ST* I, 19, 9, God wills the evils of natural corruption and punishment insofar as these evils appear as good in respect to the perfection of the universe. Moreover, if the end is appropriate, then the appearance of good is veridical. Hence, Aquinas also mentions that the ordering of the lower to the higher makes the evil of killing animals for food good. Returning to Griffin, if God deals with evil by placing it in relation to a good end, then is evil really evil? It seems not. But it also seems to be insufferable to say that to someone afflicted.

Griffin applies this thinking to Hick.

Finally, Hick's view that God ordains the actuality of sin, rather than simply its possibility, means that he must finally be seen, along with the previous traditional theists, as denying the reality of genuine evil. If he had held the former position, that God only wills a situation in which evil is possible, and that the creatures are really free to cause evil which God did not desire ... then the reality of genuine evil could be affirmed. For it could be maintained that while the freedom to cause evil is good, the actual exercise of this freedom has resulted in events not necessitated by this freedom, and without which the world would have been a better place, all things considered. However, once it is said that God wills the actual moral evil, that God foresaw it all and this because it all flowed from the divine decision, and that it can all be accounted for in the principle of "O felix culpa"—then it seems impossible to hold that any of the apparent evil is genuine.[33]

Again, "Hick even brings 'dysteleological' evil within the framework of those things that contribute to soul-making, thereby finally seeing them as teleologically (i.e., instrumentally) good."[34]

From my Thomistic perspective, I would second Griffin's critique. Hick reformulates the idea of original sin. In the traditional account of Aquinas, humans lost grace and returned to the state of nature. It is true that the natural state is intrinsically unstable and consequently fraught with *quandoque* evils. Nevertheless, it is

33. Ibid., 200.
34. Ibid.

also true that the natural state is good and willed by God. The state includes the implicit metaphysics, freedom, and obligation that I described in chapter 2. The *ratio entis* that entails these items is such a spontaneous abstraction that it forever marks human existence as a good that is reflective of the creator. This irremovable status in goodness allows God to will the natural state as an antecedent good. *Quandoque* evils emerge as evils that God permits and orders to a good. What Hick's reformulation of original sin lacks is Aquinas's antecedent good of nature. For Hick humans are initiated as "against" God.[35] Moreover, the basic features of man's divinely appointed situation make it "virtually inevitable" that humans exercise this freedom, not in a God-centered way, but in a self-centered way.[36] Hick does speak of the first humans as created in the "image" of God and in terms of freedom.[37] But there is no grounding of freedom in the cognitive presence of being as the good. Hence, Hick's basically evil starting point means that the good that God must first will is some consequent good for which

---

35. Hick, *Evil and the God of Love*, 287.
36. Ibid., 285.
37. "And so man, created as a personal being in the image of God, is only the raw material for a further and more difficult stage of God's creative work. This is the leading of men as relatively free and autonomous persons, through their own dealings with life in the world in which He has placed them." Ibid., 254. Elsewhere Hick indicates a more substantive view of the human as image of God, though it gets little play in his theodicy: "God has formed the free human person with a nature than can find its perfect fulfillment and happiness only in active enjoyment of the infinite goodness of the Creator. He is not, then, trying to force or entice His creatures against the grain of their nature, but to render them free to follow their own deepest desire, which can lead them only to Himself. For He has made them for Himself, and their hearts are restless until they find their rest in Him. He is not seeking to subjugate them but to liberate them, in order that they may find in Him their own deepest fulfillment and happiness." Ibid., 344–45. Hick then goes on to compare God to a psychotherapist. In my opinion, this point that the human is created with a fundamental orientation to God stands in tension both with Hick's stated position that humans are for God by being initiated "against" God (see above n. 18) and with Hick's subsequent theodicy. In fact here Hick sounds a very Thomistic note. A radical orientation to God is the linchpin in the transcendental Thomist interpretation of Aquinas, though it can also be glossed in an *a posteriori* manner. Hick must make a choice about how he wants to proceed. In any case I will stay with Hick's expressly developed theodicy in which we begin from the "fallenness" of human nature.

Personalist Theodicies 171

the evil is willed as a means. God's relation to humans is like a drill sergeant who intends to inflict suffering on the recruits in order to prepare them for battle. But in light of the good end of virtues appropriate for combat, I believe that all would agree that the suffering of the recruits is really good. That is why drill instructors are allowed to intend the suffering of the recruits. The same relation seems to be the case between God and human suffering in Hick's theodicy.

At this point a reader of Hick might object that given other things Hick says, the attribution to him of an instrumental view of evil in which God in some sense wills the evil is a gross misreading. For example in discussing the Holocaust, Hick seems to be quite clear that the Holocaust is not at all willed by God:

> What does that ultimate context of divine purpose and activity mean for Auschwitz and Belsen and the other camps in which, between 1942 and 1945, between four and six million Jewish men, women, and children were deliberately and scientifically murdered? Was this in any sense willed by God? The answer is obviously no. These events were utterly evil, wicked, devilish and, so far as the human mind can reach, unforgivable; they are wrongs that can never be righted, horrors which will disfigure the universe to the end of time, and in relation to which no condemnation can be strong enough, no revulsion adequate. It would have been better—much much better—if they had never happened. Most certainly God did not want those who committed these fearful crimes against humanity to act as they did. His purpose for the world was retarded by them and the power of evil within it increased. Undoubtedly he saw with anger and grief the sufferings so willfully inflicted upon the people of His ancient choice, through whom His Messiah had come into the world.[38]

But a reader should note a play of perspectives here.[39] There is the perspective of the universe or the world, and there is the perspective of the "ultimate context of divine purpose." I have noted Hick

---

38. Ibid., 361.
39. I am indebted to Griffin, *God, Power, and Evil*, 200–201, for this observation about the play of perspectives in Hick's theodicy.

to extend soul-making beyond death. Hence, the second perspective is different from the first as something much larger. But it is in terms of the perspective of the world or universe that Hick says the Holocaust is not willed by God and is called utterly evil. What is the case from the perspective of the divine purpose? The next paragraph provides three answers of which I quote the first. "Our Christian awareness of the universal divine purpose and activity does, however, affect our reaction even to these events. First, as regards the millions of men, women, and children who perished in the extermination programme, it gives the assurance that God's good purpose for each individual has not been defeated by the efforts of wicked men." Is one wrong to take the reference to God's good purpose as a reference to God's soul-making in which evil is a divine instrument and so something good? I do not believe that Hick's strong negative remarks about the Holocaust and God's attitude about it are truly ultimate. They are made from a limited context. This realization leaves the impression that in some weird way the Holocaust, like other sufferings, is God's "gracious disciplining of His people." In other words, it is good.

In sum, for Hick God in some fashion causes and is responsible for evil. The justification of God then lies in fashioning some good end for evil in the perspective of which evil is not evil. The evil God originally caused is really good. That is the bare bones outline of Hick's theodicy.[40]

Despite my agreement with Griffin that Hick's theodicy denies genuine evils, Griffin denies me my Thomism. Griffin criticizes Aquinas for the same reason that he criticizes Hick. In other words, both Aquinas and Hick end up denying genuine evil. Regarding Aquinas, Griffin disputes what I have called the order of nature. No appeal to the order of nature can be made because the order of nature has no power. God's omnipotence always gets in the way of creatures doing anything. In particular Griffin affirms that

---

40. See Hick, *Evil and the God of Love*, 351.

Aquinas's distinction between God's primary causality and the creature's secondary causality is "merely verbal."[41] The latter must collapse into the former.

The relation between the primary and secondary causation is not one of partly-partly, but of wholly-wholly. That is, the effect is not achieved partly by God and partly by the natural cause but wholly by God and wholly by the secondary cause (*SCG* III, I. 70. 8). This seems to mean that there are two *sufficient* causes for the effect ... Thomas concedes that it seems difficult to understand how there can be two agents for an action, that one or the other seems superfluous (*SCG* III. I. 70. 1–4). But he says that the idea is understandable if we distinguish between the thing that acts and the power by which it acts. The secondary causes are genuine causes; but they are able to produce their effects only by virtue of the power that God provides. An analogy is provided by comparing the secondary cause to an instrument and the primary cause to the artisan who gives motion to the instrument and is thereby the principal agent (*SCG* III. I. 70. 5–8).[42]

Griffin objects that the analogy with the agent and instrument fails to work with God and creatures. His objections are two. First, "the very analogy used by Thomas, that of the artisan and his instrument, suggests that all the activity is God's, while the so-called secondary causes are merely instruments employed by God."[43] I believe that Griffin is thinking of a situation in which the primary agent simply gives motion to an instrument. For example, a man swinging a sword in the air, or an artist doing likewise with a brush or a chisel. And there is some excuse in Aquinas's text for these thoughts. In *C.G.* III, 70, Aquinas says "as the artisan applies an instrument to its proper effect, though he neither gives the form whereby the instrument works, nor preserves it, but simply gives it motion." But a reader cannot forget the first part of the sentence expressing the application of the instrument. In other words, Aquinas is speaking about the artisan's moving the brush on the canvas

41. Griffin, *God, Power, and Evil*, 81.   42. Ibid., 80.
43. Ibid., 81.

or the chisel on the wood. In those cases there are clearly two activities—the movement of the brush and the painting, the movement of the chisel and the cutting. So correctly understood, the analogy with artisan and instrument does not suggest that "all" the activity is from God.

Second, Griffin maintains that only if the instrument offered some "passive resistance" could the analogy work. For example, the statue is poor because the chisel was dull. The detail of the painting was poor because the brush was fuzzy. But this passive resistance is precluded with God because the divine agent is a creator.

And, to the extent that the analogy does suggest that there is some given stuff with which God must do the best that is possible, this suggestiveness is due precisely to that aspect of the analogue which cannot be retained in regard to the relation between God and the secondary causes. There is nothing which is "given" with which God must work; the so-called secondary causes are themselves creatures which are created ex nihilo. Any "defects" in them are there because God willed them. Accordingly, it is illegitimate to suggest that any evil in the effects produced by means of these secondary causes can be attributed to any defects which are not themselves due to God's will and which therefore prevent God's will from being perfectly fulfilled.[44]

A reader can understand how this would lead to Griffin's charge of a denial of genuine evil. If evil has to arise from defects in things willed by God, then we can exonerate God from causing the defects only by some consequent good to which these defective creatures will lead. But cast in the future light, the defects take on the appearance of good.

But Griffin is too quick to criticize and too slow to understand. As I cited above in chapter 3, Aquinas trumpets at *De Malo* I, 3c: "the first cause of evil is not evil but good." What this means is that to get evil in creation, creatures do not have to arise as defective. Rather, as arising from the first cause that is goodness itself,

---

44. Ibid., 81.

creatures arise as integral and whole analogates of the good. For example, God creates both the lion and the human. One need not assume, and should not assume, that either has "defects," for example a disease or a physical impairment, willed by God. But from these integral analogates *quandoque* evil follows. *Quandoque* evil results when these integral analogates accidentally clash, as when the paths of the lion and the human happen to cross at a time when the lion is hungry. Then the human has an arm ripped off or worse. Instead of the lower being for the higher, the higher is for the lower. It is not necessary to reduce the clash to some preceding evil. Preceding the clash is no lack of something that ought to be there. We find only a healthy lion and a healthy human.

The above presupposes chance events, for that is what the meeting of the lion and the human is. But Griffin goes on to claim that since for Aquinas God is a universal cause, then there is no such thing as chance in the universe.[45] In other words, God cannot produce a material world with real contingency. Such a world must contain rogue factors. Those factors are eliminated, however, insofar as the world is reduced to God. *Quandoque* evils are again pinned on God. So, if Griffin seems too quick to criticize, I seem too quick to solve.

In truth what Aquinas says is that God's providence is not affected by chance. Since God's causality extends to all things, there is nothing outside of God's causality that could thwart it.[46] For God there is no chance. Yet God's providence is said to include or contain chance events. One of the things under divine providence is chance events.[47] The first is what Aquinas means when he claims

---

45. "[Aquinas] states that there is really no such thing as 'chance' in the universe, for nothing escapes the universal (divine) cause." Ibid., 81.
46. "But if these contingent events are traced back further to the highest, divine cause, it will be impossible to find anything that lies outside its sphere of influence, since its causality extends to all things insofar as they are beings [*omnia inquantum sunt entia*]." Aquinas, *In VI Meta.*, lect. III, n. 1215; John P. Rowan, trans., *Commentary on Aristotle's Metaphysics* (Notre Dame, Ind.: Dumb Ox Books, 1995), 417.
47. "It would appear that it was because of these two arguments to which we have

that there is no chance for divine providence. But how can that be? Chance events are the intersection of two unreduced lines of causality. But are the lines unreduced if they are caused by God? Rather, are not the lines reduced to one in their divine cause? *Prima facie* it seems so, and with that appearance real chance disappears. Chance is simply a phenomenon in a limited field of vision. How can the lines be regarded as novel and so productive of real chance?

Aquinas is quite cognizant of the problem. But he insists that God can cause the contingent because God is the cause of being as being. Aquinas says that as such a cause God produces the proper accidents of being, among which are the necessary and the contingent.[48] The mention of being as being means that Aquinas is speaking within the context of his metaphysics. "Being as being" is the formula for the subject of the science of metaphysics. In his commentary on the *Metaphysics*, Aquinas understands God to be a universal cause in virtue of the fact that his proper effect is *esse*. Also, in the commentary, he remarks that God is a cause of things insofar as they are beings because God is an agent giving being, *agens per modum dantis esse*.[49] So a reader can ask this question. What is it about a first cause whose proper effect is *esse* that saves real contingency by keeping the lines of causality unreduced? Answering this question requires taking seriously what Aquinas means by existence in the sense of *esse*, something from which Griffin unfortunately excuses himself.[50]

In my earlier summary of Aquinas's metaphysics of *esse*, I not-

---

just replied, that some were persuaded to consider corruptible things—i.e., things in which chance and evil are found—as removed from the care of divine providence." *ST* I, 22, 2c; Anton C. Pegis, ed., *The Basic Writings of St. Thomas Aquinas*, vol. II (New York: Random House, 1945), 233; *C.G.* III, 74.

48. "Now, as has been pointed out (n. 1215), being as being [*ens inquantum ens est*] has God himself as its cause. Hence just as being itself is subject to divine providence, so also are all the accidents of being, among which are found necessity and contingency." Aquinas, *In VI Meta*, lect. III, no. 1220; Rowan, *Aristotle's Metaphysics*, 418.

49. Aquinas, *In VI Meta*, lect. III, n. 1215.

50. Griffin, *God, Power, and Evil*, 74.

ed that for Aquinas the *esse* of the thing is the act of all form and as such is a nonformal act. As the first cause of *esse*, God instantiates this act. This point requires that in our minds we should try to poise creatures against God, as the finite and determinate against the infinite and indeterminate. Such an attempt might sound impossible for the human mind, but the human mind already does something like it with the nongeneric notion of being. As I mentioned in chapter 2, generic notions are diversified into their species by additions from without. Such diversification is impossible with the notion of being because everything if it is anything is a being. Hence, Aquinas says that addition is made to the notion of being by the category expressing what is implicit within being. After one has abstracted the notion of being, one returns to some category of being, for example, the category of substance or one of the accidental categories, by surfacing it from the depths of being. This mental move from analogon to analogate is some likeness of the transition from creator to creature. Likewise, Aquinas's reiteration of Damescene's description of God as an infinite ocean of substance, *pelagus substantiae infinitum*, should be remembered.[51] If, as Aquinas wants, the ocean is imagined as infinite, then there are no coasts. Hence, ships can appear on the ocean not by being launched from the shore but only by surfacing them from the depths. So the human mind is not without any likenesses to understand the transition from creator to creature.

But what has this to do with saving real contingency in the context of universal creative causality? To me the answer seems to be this. In terms of form and finitude, the creature is an end of a line. Beyond the creature is only the creator which as *esse subsistens* is not a form and is infinite. So the creature is a certain kind of terminus from which a true beginning can be made. Again, because the creature is unreduced to more form and finitude, it emerges from the creator with a certain novelty that can play a role in causing

---

51. *In I Sent.*, d.8, q.1, a.1, ad 4m.

the contingent. God has really done something, and so the something that God has done can go on to do something. So, if a material world, because of the key role of motion within that world, entails a world with rogue factors, then that is a world that God can create without violating its nature.

In conclusion, I do not think that under the weight of Griffin's criticisms Aquinas loses that antecedent good which is a material cosmos and from which God permits but then orders the many *quandoque* evils that result. Unlike Hick Aquinas has the advantage of a profound metaphysics that can provide *sufficient* insight into the transition from creator to creature such that creatures are really good also.

THE BROTHERS KARAMAZOV

Adams, Hick, Griffin, and Stump all acknowledge the force of Ivan Karamozov's disquisition "Rebellion" in Dostoevsky's *The Brothers Karamazov*.[52] And so it might be appropriate now to offer a Thomistic reflection upon this classic appeal for personalism in the philosophical discussion of evil.

"Rebellion" begins with Ivan informing his brother Alyosha, who he assumes to be naïve, of some unpleasant facts. They are culled from history books and current newspapers. They included: the Turkish atrocities against the Slavs, such as bayoneting unborn babies cut from the wombs of their mothers; blowing their heads in two by firing pistols at point-blank range after the child acquired an amusing interest in the shiny weapon; "modern" European Christians, to the tune of "Die in the Lord," guillotining repentant criminals with pasts full of suffered abuse; "educated" Russians savagely and with increasing pleasure and joy whipping their children, or consigning them on a winter's eve to an outhouse after forcing them to eat their excrement from an accidental defecation; or finally letting them be torn to pieces by hunting hounds after

---

52. Fyodor Dostoevsky, *The Brothers Karamazov*, translated by Andrew R. MacAndrew (New York: Bantam Books, 1970), "Rebellion," 284–97.

Personalist Theodicies 179

the child accidentally injured one of the master's dogs. It is no use to wonder if these incidents are fictional. We all know the truth of events like them. But focusing on the latter two, Ivan delivers a searing reflection that demands a presentation in its own right and not in summary:

> The day the mother embraces the man who had her son torn to pieces by the hounds, the day those three stand side by side and say, "You were right, O Lord," that day we will at last have attained the supreme knowledge and everything will be explained and accounted for. But that's just the hurdle I can't get over, because I cannot agree that it makes everything right. And while I am on this earth, I must act in my own way. You see, it's quite possible, if I'm still alive or am resurrected on the day the mother embraces her child's murderer, that I may join them all in their praises and shout with them, "You were right"; but as of now, I do not want to join them. And while there is still time, I want to dissociate myself from it all; I have no wish to be a part of their eternal harmony. It's not worth one single tear of the martyred little girl who beat her breast with her tiny fist, shedding her innocent tears and praying to "sweet Jesus" to rescue her in the stinking outhouse. It's not worth it, because that tear will have remained unatoned for. And those tears must be atoned for; otherwise there can be no harmony.[53]

With the references to "Lord" and to "Jesus," the reader knows that the discourse is on the level of Christian belief. This is an important point to bear in mind. What is the thought that Ivan "cannot get over?" As I take it, what offends Ivan is that an innocent human being is used as a means to an end. This is irredeemably offensive even if the end includes the human being. Also, since for Christians, humans by grace become children of God, Christians that offer theodicies in which the innocent become the means to an end, for example, eternal harmony, are crazy. You do not treat people as the means to an end even when the end is their own good. Such seems to be the case in the theodicies of Hick and of Stump.[54] If the end is going to redeem the evil suffered, as in Ad-

---

53. Ibid., 295.
54. "Rather, I am trying to avoid constructing the sort of explanation for evil which re-

ams's theodicy, it seems necessary that the evils suffered by the baptized be something like what Aquinas called *quandoque* evils, evils that God does not will but permits and then orders to some good. Can the examples of evils mentioned by Ivan be categorized as *quandoque* evils?

At *ST* I-II, 85, 5, ad 2m, Aquinas faced the objection that if grace removes the effects of original sin, why is it that the baptized still suffer a defect of nature like death? He replied this way:

> Both original and actual sin are removed by the same cause that removes these defects, according to the Apostle (Romans 8: 11): "He ... shall quicken ... your mortal bodies, because of His Spirit that dwelleth in you": but each is done according to the order of Divine wisdom, at a fitting time. Because it is right that we should first of all be conformed to Christ's sufferings, before attaining to the immortality and impassibility of glory, which was begun in Him, and by Him acquired for us. Hence, it behooves that our bodies should remain, for a time, subject to suffering, in order that we may merit the impassibility of glory, in conformity with Christ.[55]

By grace, the life of God within a human, a human achieves the exalted status of a whole in terms of which Ivan's difficulty becomes understandable. Aquinas's theological reason for the baptized remaining within the state of nature is to regain the immortality lost in original sin by way of imitation of Christ who won it back. This theological reason clears the way to reintroduce Aquinas's thinking about evils in the state of nature. Within that framework, I want to discuss two of Ivan's examples of evils: the girl severely whipped by her father and the boy thrown to the dogs. Clearly these two cases of evil are not willed by God. They follow the sins of the father and the landowner. As Aquinas said at *ST* I,

---

quires telling the sufferer that God lets him suffer just for the sake of some abstract general good for mankind.... It seems to me nonetheless that a perfectly good entity who was also omniscient and omnipotent must govern the evil resulting from the misuse of that significant freedom in such a way that the sufferings of any particular person are outweighed by the good which the suffering produces *for that person*." Stump, "The Problem of Evil," 411.

55. From Pegis, *Basic Writings of Thomas Aquinas*, vol. II, 702.

19, 9, God in no way wills the evil of sin. That conclusion leaves nature in some way to do the explaining. In particular, the explanation for the sins must lie within human nature. I have repeatedly mentioned *C.G.* IV 52, in which Aquinas notes that the light of the intellect is naturally weak in humans so that sense passions can occlude it. But to deal with Ivan's examples I wish to mention how the intellection of being itself can go askew. It can create faux epiphanies of itself that can prompt the atrocious acts under consideration. So, how could the human, understood as an intellector of being, be so perverse as the father and the landowner?

The play of being to create a faux epiphany of being is evidenced in the incidents described by Ivan. If the contemplation of the small takes the form of the contemplation of the vulnerable and unconnected, being can be drawn intensely to the instance. The more vulnerability the greater the intensity of being. Hence, in this weird way the Russian parent gets greater and greater joy the more he whips the innocent young daughter. As I mentioned in chapter 2, being produces joy and it is being that can be more present the more vulnerable the daughter becomes. Such is perhaps the tragic psychology that can befall the human mind in its natural workings. Other permutations are possible and so no evil of which we are aware is a surprise. For example, if one needs to exercise power to overcome feelings of inferiority, then striking out at a child might fill the bill. If being is intense in one's cognition of the defenseless child, then one's violence against the child in some way is violence against being itself. Otherwise why derive such satisfactions of power from incongruously dealing with a defenseless child? Perhaps this tragically twisted psychology explains the nobleman's decision to set the hounds upon the boy.

God could never target by his willing the torture of the girl or the death of the boy. Both are his adopted children by grace.[56] But left in the state of nature because of the theological reason men-

---

56. The Abraham and Isaac incident does not involved baptized persons. Hence, it does not fall within the present discussion.

tioned, both young individuals can become tragic targets of the human will. Not just the passions of sense can render the children this way, but the play of being in human psychology can do the same. This play, in my opinion, is part of the weakness of the human intellect, the same intellect that in other respects reflects the goodness of the creator. If what I am saying is correct, then Ivan's mental block is removed. God does not treat his supernaturally adopted children and their suffering as means to an end, even as means to their own end. That scenario is what Ivan says cannot be atoned for. And I agree. But where the sufferings are *quandoque* evils that are only permitted in the willing of some antecedent good, the suffering can also be ordered to a good and redeemed by that good.

THOMISTIC "NATURAL DESIRES" OF THE HUMAN PERSON

At first glance another personalist treatment of evil could be marshaled from Thomistic theses about various natural desires. For example, there are the natural desires to know God, for beatitude, and for immortality. A philosopher would appear to have the information relevant for dealing with the problem of evil when these are coupled with another Thomistic thesis that natural desires either could not be or are not in vain.[57] For instance, if God made us with these desires and they are so obviously unfulfilled in this life, what does that say? Would God not be as delinquent as a parent who brings a new human into existence but does not nourish it? Hence, maybe this life is not the only life. Perhaps

---

57. For the alternatives here and texts for both, William R. O'Connor explains, "The difference in expression is accounted for by considering the impediment as present or absent. When the impediment is present, the natural desire is in vain if it cannot reach its goal; when the impediment is absent, the natural desire is in vain if it does not reach its goal." *The Natural Desire for God* (Milwaukee: Marquette University Press, 1948), 189–90. Denis J. M. Bradley, *Aquinas on the Twofold Human Good: Reason and Human Happiness in Aquinas's Moral Science* (Washington, D.C.: The Catholic University of America Press, 1997), 468, acknowledges only one way to save the natural desire: "This conviction—that God has actually ordained man to supernatural end—and it alone, sustains Aquinas's unhesitating affirmation that the natural desire to see God is not in vain."

Personalist Theodicies 183

humans were originally brought into existence in a life in which these desires are divinely fulfilled but this earlier life was forfeited by something the first humans did. Or perhaps, in our present life we are ordered to another life in which these desires will be fulfilled. Is it plausible to believe that the creator would leave his most perfect creature in a state of deep frustration? So cannot a philosopher make a personalist appeal to these natural desires as a reason to believe that the problem of evil is somehow rectified for each human being?[58] I would like to take each of the three desires named above and to determine just what implications follow from them. I will try to show that God's not fulfilling these desires does not leave humans so destitute that a cosmological explanation of evil becomes hideous.

Aquinas describes the natural desire to know God at *ST* I, 12, 1, and at I-II, 3, 8. This natural desire is a natural desire to know the creator's essence. Citing scripture, 3 John 2, Aquinas also seems to understand the object here as the same as the object involved in what Christians call the beatific vision. Aquinas's response at I-II, 3, 8, is the more expansive presentation of the natural desire to know God. A selective quote is the following:

Now the object of the intellect is *what a thing is*, i.e., the essence of a thing .... Wherefore the intellect attains perfection, insofar as it knows the es-

---

58. Paul St. Amour, in his "The Scale-Wielding God and the Limits of Philosophical Theodicy," 264, indicates this approach from natural desire: "In the suffering of evil, what is contradicted is nothing less than the natural (and hence, at least on Thomistic grounds, normative) desire, which any rational creature experiences, not merely, for being, but for the fullness of being, for the perfection of one's human nature, for what Aquinas called well-being, *bene esse*." The thinking here hearkens back to the huge mid-twentieth-century debate on Henri DeLubac's thesis in *Surnatural*, that contrary to Renaissance Thomism no natural order with a complete end for the human existed. The standard complaint was that DeLubac's thesis threatened the gratuity of the supernatural order. For summaries of the positions, see P. J. Donnelly, "Discussion of the Supernatural Order," *Theological Studies*, 9 (1948), especially 241–49, and William R. O'Connor, *The Natural Desire for God* (Milwaukee: Marquette University Press, 1948). For some of the contemporary discussion see my *Being and Some Twentieth-Century Thomists* (New York: Fordham University Press, 2003), 295–306.

sence of a thing. If therefore an intellect knows the essence of some effect, whereby it is not possible to know the essence of the cause, i.e., to know of the cause *what it is*; that intellect cannot be said to reach that cause simply, although it may be able to gather from the effect the knowledge that the cause is. Consequently, when man knows an effect, and knows that it has a cause there naturally remains in man the desire to know about that cause, *what it is*. And this desire is one of wonder, and causes inquiry.... If therefore the human intellect, knowing the essence of some created effect, knows no more of God than *that He is*; the perfection of that intellect does not yet reach simply the First Cause, but there remains in it the natural desire to seek the cause. Wherefore it is not yet perfectly happy. Consequently, for perfect happiness the intellect needs to reach the very Essence of the First Cause.[59]

The natural desire to know God is an *a posteriori* desire. In other words, it is evoked subsequent to knowledge from experience. So we are not born with this desire. Such is not the sense of the word "natural." The knowledge to which this desire is subsequent is a proof or demonstration that God exists. Subsequent to the proof's conclusion is an application of the desire to know the natures of things. This applied desire seems to be the first operation of the intellect whose object is the essence or quiddity of things.

The key thought appears to be that from some effects knowledge that the cause exists is possible, but not knowledge of what the cause is. Hence, a desire to know remains. The issue for the reader is to understand how effects lead to causes that still raise the interest of the intellect. For if the effect does not give me knowledge of what the cause is, why is that not the end of desire rather than the beginning of wonder? Actually, the situation is not as black as the text appears to make it. In his *De Trinitate* commentary, Aquinas insists that "we cannot know that a thing is without knowing in some way what it is either perfectly or at least confusedly [*cognitio confusa*]." Hence, "we cannot know that God and other immaterial substances exist unless we know somehow

---

59. *Summa Theologica*, translated by Fathers of the English Dominican Province (N.Y.: Benziger Brothers, 1947), vol. I, 601–2.

in some confused way [*sub quadam confusione*], what they are."⁶⁰ Evidently, Aquinas's often mentioned analogy of the human intellect to the eye of the owl serves to deny a perfect knowledge of what God or a separate substance is. Room exists for a confused knowledge of the quiddities of both. Hence, in my opinion, I-II, 3, 8, needs the resources of analogical conceptualization understood as an intellectual grasp of sameness in difference. Any analogon will be a mysterious and far richer object that is only dimly and imperfectly portrayed through its analogates. Such an object keeps desire and wonder alive.

To connect analogy with the above text, some backward references are necessary. At I, 4, 3c, Aquinas describes three ways in which things can communicate in form. The first two are fairly simple. On the one hand, things can communicate in the same form according to the same formality and measure, as two things equally white. On the other hand, things can do the same but not according to the same measure, as two things unequally white. Aquinas then describes a third type of formal communication and applies it to how creator and creature communicate in *esse*.

In a third way some things are said to be alike which communicate in the same form, but not according to the same formality; as we see in non-univocal agents. For since every agent reproduces itself so far as it is an agent, and everything acts in accord with its form, the effect must in some way resemble the form of the agent. If therefore the agent is contained in the same species as its effect, there will be a likeness in form between that which makes and that which is made, according to the same formality of the species; as man reproduces man.... Therefore, if there is an agent not contained in any genus [nor in any species], its effects will still more distantly reproduce the form of the agent, not, that is, so as to participate in the likeness of the agent's form according to the same specific or generic formality, but only according to some sort of analogy; as being itself [*ipsum esse*] is common to all. In this way all created things, so far as they

60. Aquinas, *In de Trin.*, VI, 3c; Thomas Aquinas, *On The Division and Methods of the Sciences*, translated by Armand Maurer (Toronto: Pontifical Institute of Mediaeval Studies, 1963), 78.

are beings, are like God as the first and universal principle of all being [*totius esse*].[61]

The third communication in form—same form but not according to the same formality—seems to express the idea of sameness within difference. At the end of the quote, Aquinas explicitly connects the third way with analogy. He also connects it with how all things and God are alike in *esse*. In other words, *esse* as it is in the formality of creatures has some likeness to *esse* as it is in the formality of the universal principle of all being. Creaturely *esse* gives some insight into the nature of *esse* and so some insight into the first cause.

But this insight into creaturely *esse* is also analogous. In a number of texts Aquinas emphasizes that *esse* as an object of conceptualization, called *esse commune, esse formale,* and the *ratio essendi*, is not differentiated into individual *esses* by the addition of extrinsic factors as a genus is differentiated into its species by the addition of extrinsic differentiae. One reason that Aquinas gives is that apart from *esse* there is nothing.[62] Elsewhere he insists that *esse* is diversified as an act by a potency instead of a potency by an act, and that an individual *esse* stands to the thing that is its subject as received to receiver rather than as receiver to received.[63] So *esse commune* has to supply its own differentiation into individual *esses*. It, then, cannot stand apart from them as a genus stands apart from its differences. This leaves our intellectual insight into *esse commune* imperfect because it must be through different individual *esses*. There is intellectual success and achievement here but there is also failure and frustration. The nature of being both reveals itself and occludes itself.

61. Pegis, *Basic Writings of Thomas Aquinas*, vol. I, 4–41.
62. "Nothing which is extraneous from *esse* is able to be added to *esse* since there is nothing extraneous from it except non-being [*non-ens*]." Aquinas, *De Pot.* VII, 2c.
63. Ibid. and also *ST* I, 4, 1, ad 3m: "For nothing has actuality except so far as it is. Hence being [*esse*] is the actuality of all things, even of forms themselves. Therefore it is not compared to other things as the receiver is to the received but rather as the received to the receiver." Pegis, *Basic Writings of Thomas Aquinas*, vol. I, 38.

This dim insight into the nature of *esse* can be transformed into a dim insight into the divine quiddity, with suitable qualifications.[64] Since God the creator is *esse* in a subsistent configuration, then God is *esse* merged with its subject. But since a subject is in some respect common, then *esse* merged with the subject is *esse* made common. *Esse subsistens* would be the nature of *esse*. It would be an analogate that was the analogon.[65] In this respect and a few others, Aquinas concedes that Plato's doctrine of the ideas is correct. In the introduction to the commentary on the *De Divinis Nominibus* of Dionysius, Aquinas claims that though the Platonists are incorrect in ascribing a separate status to the species of natural things, they are not incorrect in doing the same for the most common things which are the good, the one, and being. In that respect, the Platonists hold for one first thing which is the essence itself of goodness, unity, and existence (*esse*). All other things are called good, or one, or beings by derivation from the first. In that latter respect the Platonists agree with the Christian faith and its teaching about God.

So what I am driving at is this. There is a desire to know more about God after knowing that his existence is connected with an already-existing desire to plumb the depths of analogical being. Our desire to know God is a specification of our desire to know the analogon of being. As an analogon, being, like any analogon, is an

---

64. Aquinas insists that *esse commune* is not *esse subsistens* because the former admits of addition while the latter does not. On how negation in the sense of a blotting or covering over can be wielded upon the *ratio entis* so that analogical *esse commune* can stand as a dim representation of God, see my *Being and Some Twentieth-Century Thomists*, 236–46.

65. At *In I Sent.* Prol. Q. 1, a. 2, ad 2m, while answering the objection that placing God and the creature in one science would place either a univocal or an analogical commonality prior and more simple to both, Aquinas places God and the creature in the second of two kinds of analogy in which the instances are not referred to a third but one to the other. This indicates that the analogon has been identified with the divine instance. Likewise, as mentioned above, remarks in the introduction to Aquinas's commentary on the *De Divinis Nominibus* of Dionysius indicate the same move. Aquinas claims that though Platonists are incorrect in ascribing a separate status to the species of natural things, they are correct in doing the same for the most common things which are the good, the one, and being. Our dim, negatively formed representation of *esse subsistens* from *esse commune* is the basis for the assertion of the second kind of analogy.

intrinsically fascinating intellectual object. It has a richness that is never fully conveyed by its analogates. But with the proof of God metaphysically understood as *esse subsistens*, our desire to know being transforms into a desire to know the analogon, not through knowing further analogates of it but, to know the analogon itself directly.

What does this interpretation of our natural desire to know God mean for the problem of evil? It means that we are not naturally totally destitute without a fulfillment of that desire. Prior to any fulfillment of the desire a tremendous accomplishment in the human mind occurs. That accomplishment is the analogical grasp of the nature of being. As analogical the grasp is dim and imperfect, but it is a grasp with a psychic effect. As it is used to know the higher substances, Aquinas is quite frank about the satisfaction that it provides. Aquinas agrees with Aristotle that the little we know of higher substances is loved and desired more than all the knowledge about less noble substances. Furthermore, this little and imperfect knowledge produces "intense joy" (*vehemens sit gaudium eius*) and brings the "greatest perfection to the soul" (*maximam perfectionem animae*).[66] He also expresses the matter in terms of intellectual vision and consideration, weak as they may be: "For to be able to see [*posse inspicere*] something of the loftiest realities, however thin and weak the sight may be [*parva et debili consideratio*], is, as our previous remarks indicate, a cause of greatest joy (*iucundissimum*)."[67] It is by looking back to this perfection naturally achieved in human nature that any absolute demands on the basis of natural desire are assuaged. Just as parents are not delinquent for not completely satisfying their child's desire for more food, so too God is not delinquent for not satisfying this natural desire to know the creator God directly.

Hence, it is no surprise that at I, 12, 1, Aquinas concludes only

---

66. *C.G.* I, 5, *Unde*; Thomas Aquinas, *Summa contra Gentiles*, vol. I, translated by Anton C. Pegis (Notre Dame, Ind.: Notre Dame Press, 1975), 71.
67. *C.G.* I, 8, *Utile*; Aquinas, *Summa contra Gentiles*, vol. I, 76.

the possibility of the beatific vision, not its actuality. The title of the article is: "Whether any created intellect can [*possit*] see the essence of God." The natural desire illustrates that the rational creature knowing the divine essence is not an absurdity like the eyes sensing sound or the ears sensing color.⁶⁸ This limited philosophical conclusion means that a cosmological account of evil is not excluded. It might well be the case that the rational creature is created without fulfillment of its natural desire to see God.

Does the natural desire for happiness impose personalist answers to the problem of evil? I do not think so. Since for Aquinas the will's desire for happiness is the will's desire for the good and the good is being, then the thoughts described above on the natural intellectual desire to know God apply to the natural volitional desire for happiness. At *ST* I, 82, 1c, Aquinas insists that natural necessity (*necessitas natualis*) is not repugnant to the will. For just as the intellect of necessity adheres to first principles, so too the will necessarily adheres to the last end, which is happiness (*ultimo fini, qui est beatitudo*). But "happiness" here is the *ratio boni*, for elsewhere the last end is the object of the will (*rationem finis, est obiectum voluntatis*, I-II, 9, 1), and the object of the will is the *ratio boni* (*ratio boni, quod est obiectum potentiae*, I-II, 8, 2c). Aquinas reiterates the point by saying that the will "tends naturally" (*naturaliter tendit*, I-II, 10, 1) to the *bonum in communi* which is its object and last end, just as the intellect knows naturally the first principles of demonstration. No empty or merely formal sense of the *ratio boni* could play these roles of igniting desire. Rather, it is the *ratio entis* that is playing the role of the *ratio boni*.⁶⁹

---

68. At *ST* I, 12, 4, ad 3m Aquinas claims that the ability, remote as it may be, of the created intellect to receive the divine essence is evinced by the created intellect's ability to apprehend the "concreted being in abstraction (*esse concretum in abstractione*)."

69. That the *ratio entis* understood as the *ratio boni* engenders willing is also expressed in this Thomistic argument for will in God: "From the fact that God is endowed with intellect it follows that He is endowed with will. For, since the understood good is the proper object of the will, the understood good is, as such, willed. Now that which is understood is by reference to one who understands. Hence, he who grasps the good by his intellect is, as

As so connected with being, the happiness that we can attain by our unaided powers should consist in the previously mentioned joy of metaphysical contemplation of God. Dim as it may be, that contemplation is some contact with the nature of being and with the nature of goodness. Other contacts with being in this life should also contribute to natural happiness. These contacts include everything because everything is an analogate of being, though a ranking of these analogates is obvious. As an intellector of being, the human analogate is chief among these analogates. Hence, the essence of human happiness, naturally considered, consists in metaphysical contemplation in a life lived according to Aquinas's natural law ethics.[70] And this is what Aquinas says when he describes the essence of imperfect happiness: "But imperfect happiness, such as can be had here, consists first and principally in contemplation, but secondarily, in an operation of the practical intellect directing human actions and passions."[71] That the contemplation is metaphysical is clear from another text on imperfect happiness. At *In de Trin.* VI, 4, ad 3m Aquinas says, "Man's happiness is twofold. One is the imperfect happiness found in this life, of which the Philosopher speaks; and this consists in contemplating the separate substances through the habit of wisdom."[72] At *C.G.* III, 44, "wisdom" is Aristotle's science of metaphysics: "And at the beginning of the *Metaphysics*, [Aristotle] calls the science he intends to treat in this work, wisdom."[73]

---

such, endowed with will. But God grasps the good by His intellect. For, since the activity of His intellect is perfect, as appears from what has been said, He understands being together with the qualification of good [*ens simul cum ratione boni*]. He is, therefore, endowed with will." *C.G.* I, 72, Ex hoc; Aquinas, *Summa contra Gentiles*, vol. I, 239–40. As Aquinas also remarks at *ST* I-II, 10, 2, ad 3m: "The last end moves the will necessarily, because it is the perfect good [*bonum perfectum*]."

70. On the integration of Aquinas's metaphysics with his natural law ethics, see my *Being and Some Twentieth-Century Thomists*, ch. 8.

71. *ST* I-II, 3, 5c; *Summa*, English Dominicans, I, 599.

72. Aquinas, *Division and Methods*, 84.

73. Aquinas, *Summa contra Gentiles*, vols. III–I, translated by Vernon J. Bourke (Notre Dame, Ind.: University of Notre Dame Press, 1975), 151. See also, "Philosophers, then, study these divine beings [God and the angels] only insofar [*nisi prout*] as they are the principles

Of course such a life does not satiate all volitional desire for the good. Metaphysically known as subsistent *esse*, the intelligible heart of the *ratio entis*, God is, as mentioned above in n. 64, not simply the realization of being as such but also the realization of the good itself. In other words, metaphysical knowledge of God engenders not only an intellectual desire for the divine essence but also a volitional desire for the same. The will would attain final and perfect happiness in the vision of the divine essence. Aquinas says: "final happiness consists in the vision of the Divine Essence, which is the very essence of goodness [*ipsa essentia bonitatis*]."[74]

Hence, just as our desire for knowledge transforms into a desire to know the divine essence, so too does our desire for happiness.[75] But just as the former is consequent upon an impressive intellectual achievement, so too is the latter. And so just as human nature is not naturally destitute of all knowledge of the divine quiddity, so too it is not the case that human nature is naturally destitute of all happiness. As quoted above, there is an intense joy in the little that we know of the higher substances. Analogical conceptualization of being makes this thinking understandable. Such natural perfection makes an existence without a call to the supernatural order a real possibility. Because of its own excellence, philosophy cannot eliminate it. And so the natural desire of happiness cannot be used as a surefire indication that the riddle of human existence has its solution in perfect happiness. Consequently one knows how to understand Aquinas when at *C.G.* III, 48, he argues as follows,

It is impossible for natural desire to be unfulfilled [*esse inane*], since 'nature does nothing in vain.' Now, natural desire would be in vain if it could never be [*numquam posset*] fulfilled. Therefore, man's natural desire is ca-

---

of all things. Consequently, they are the objects of the science that investigates what is common to all beings, which has for its subject being as being." Aquinas, *In de Trin.* V, 4c; Aquinas, *Division and Methods*, 44.

74. *ST* I-II, 4, 4c; *Summa*, English Dominicans, I, 604.

75. "Naturaliter desideratur non solum perfecta beatitude, sed etiam qualiscumque similtudo vel participatio ipsius." *ST* I-II, 3, 6, ad 2m.

pable of fulfillment [*implebile*], but not in this life, as we have shown. So, it must be fulfilled [*impleatur*] after this life. Therefore, man's ultimate felicity comes after this life.

Aquinas's use of "*numquam posset*" in the major premise of this reasoning shows that when he claims that an unfulfilled natural desire is in vain, he means a natural desire unfulfilled *in principle*, not in fact. Also, the last line should then read: "So, it must be fulfilled, if it is fulfilled, after this life."

Another natural desire is the intellectual desire to exist forever. Aquinas mentions it in the course of arguing for the human soul's incorruptibility at *ST* I, 75, 6.

Moreover we may take a sign of this from the fact that everything naturally aspires to being [*esse*] after its own manner. Now, in things that have knowledge, desire ensues upon knowledge. The senses indeed do not know being, except under the conditions of here and now, whereas the intellect apprehends being absolutely [*esse absolute*], and for all time; so that everything that has an intellect naturally desires always to exist. But a natural desire cannot be in vain. Therefore every intellectual substance is incorruptible.[76]

I do not think that the mentioned "*esse absolute*" is God metaphysically understood as *esse subsistens*. Rather the phrase suggests the absolute consideration of the *De Ente et Essentia*.[77] So understood, "*esse absolute*" would be referring to a conceptual grasp of a commonality within judgmentally grasped *esses*. Elsewhere Aquinas refers to such an intelligible object as *esse commune*, *esse formale*, *ratio essendi*, and the *perfectio essendi*.[78] Along with *essentia*, *esse commune* is a dimension of the analogon of the notion of being, the *ratio entis*. The analogous character of *esse absolute* is important for understanding Aquinas's argument for the

---

76. Pegis, *Basic Writings of Thomas Aquinas*, vol. I, 692.
77. See Thomas Aquinas, *On Being and Essence*, translated with introduction and notes by Armand Maurer (Toronto: Pontifical Institute of Mediaeval Studies, 1968), 46–47.
78. For these designations see respectively: *C.G.* I, 26; *De Pot.* 7, 2, ad 6m; *ST* I, 4, 2c.

soul's incorruptibility. As intellected through the differences of its instances, any analogon is appreciated as being far richer than it is portrayed through its analogates. Analogons are, then, intrinsically fascinating. This appreciation of analogons excites an intellectual interest to know more of them by knowing more of their analogates. Where the analogon is *esse absolute*, the interest in knowing more of its analogates would demand all time since the analogon of which *esse absolute* is a dimension is a transcendental. In other words, analogical knowledge produces a desire to live forever as an end produces a desire for the means. Such a natural intellectual desire would be absurd, and so in vain, if the intellectual soul were corruptible by nature.

In this argument Aquinas does not establish the truth of everlasting life. He establishes an intellectual desire for it and one condition for the desire not being in vain—the incorruptibility of the soul. Why is Aquinas so circumspect? Why does he not demand more on the basis of this desire? Again, the imperfect happiness of the intellector of being lies in the background. As elicited, our desire for more follows a certain fulfillment and accomplishment. We do succeed in knowing the analogon, although imperfectly and confusedly. That success is the basis for a desire for more that has been mentioned in the text. But the same success also establishes a borderline between the natural and the supernatural. As we saw Aquinas remark back in *De Malo* 5, 5c, "a certain natural aptitude to [immortality] belongs to man according the soul; however, its completion is from a supernatural power [*ex supernaturali virtute*]."[79]

79. See my section "Natural Corruption as Nondefinitive" in chapter 4.

7

The Thomist and the Contemporary Discussion

COSMOLOGICAL THEODICIES

In chapter 6 I critiqued personalist theodicy as possible but as nondefinitive. Its claim to be definitive was tied to an exaggerated philosophical view of the human person. Such a view was engendered by the play of the notion of being in respect to a consideration of the human person as isolated and fragile. Such a consideration of the person can enlist the notion of being so that the person acquires all the preciousness of being and a faux epiphany of being results. This endearing view of the human makes intractable any cosmological explanation for evil. The constant cosmological referencing of a human's suffering to a good brought about elsewhere always invites the query, "And what about the sufferer?" But considered from Aquinas's perspective, the human has a natural dignity but not a dignity so great that cosmological theodicy becomes impossible. Given that the human's intellection of being is analogical, that is, the grasp of a sameness within difference, being never so perfectly seats itself in the intellect that the human has the dignity of a whole. Naturally, human dignity consists in rising to the rank of the principle part of the whole.

I now wish to turn to the discussion of cosmological theodicy. Here too I argue that from the perspective of Aquinas's philosophy, theodicy of this kind is possible but not definitive. Hence, I will defend as possible some of the accounts of why evil exists in the world of a good and omnipotent creator; others I will critique insofar as they claim to be definitive accounts. Again, the ability of being to create faux epiphanies of itself will play a role.

DIOGENES ALLEN AND SUFFERING AS AN EXPERIENCE OF GOD

In his article "Natural Evil and the Love of God," Diogenes Allen presents an exceptionally strong and, in my opinion, attractive case for a cosmological morality. A reader will hear many apparent echoes of points from my chapter 5 summary of Aquinas's thoughts. But Allen takes a unique approach. He describes the experiences of suffering by three people: the Stoic Epictetus; a Protestant nun, Sister Basilea Schlink; and a mystic, Simone Weil. Common to all of them is the claim that one can find peace in the very experience of suffering. The existential perspective is now wielded by theists and not only by atheists like Camus and Flew. This twist on the perspective has received little or no acknowledgement among philosophers dealing with the problem of evil. The problem of evil has its solution not in our thinking about it but in our experience of it. In fact the experience of God in the experience of evil is so satisfying that a future good such as the resurrection "is not needed or used to make up for present adversities and thus allow one to maintain God's goodness in spite of present adversities."[1] I would like to re-

---

1. Diogenes Allen, "Natural Evils and the Love of God," in *The Problem of Evil*, edited by Marilyn McCord Adams and Robert Merrihew Adams (Oxford: Oxford University Press, 1990), 206.

late what Allen has to say about the above three personages and follow each summary with a Thomistic comment.

According to Epictetus, despite the adversity hurled at us by the universe, the universe is an ordered whole in which we are a small part, "a piece of matter." Hence, we can bear our illness as "a small sacrifice toward the rest of the universe."[2] The key idea here seems to be to identify with something larger than ourselves. The Stoic finds this something larger in the ordered universe with which he has connected by an act of humility.[3] By this act of humility the Stoic accepts himself as a part of that larger something, although Allen does mention that recognizing ourselves as parts of a whole ironically means the parts have somehow transcended that whole. The cognitional ability to reach this perspective means that as material as we are, we are also spiritual beings.[4] In sum,

> But to approach nature with the expectation that we ought to be better looked after, makes it unlikely that we will learn from suffering. Suffering can teach us that we are a very small part of the universe and that we are not to expect as much as we do from its workings. When this is learned, we can then see more soberly and accurately what it does provide for us. What it does provide gives us ample reason to be grateful, in spite of the tragedies its workings produce, whether for us or for others. Indeed in our humbled and more realistic condition we can see the glory of the entire world-order and be grateful for our capacity to yield ourselves to it courageously and magnanimously even when we are caught in its workings.[5]

There is much truth here. As I have pointed out repeatedly since chapter 1, an overly exalted view of the human—Allen calls it "egotism"—lies behind many quandaries with evil. For Aquinas as for Epictetus humans by nature are parts of something larger, and so a modicum of peace and satisfaction can be found in contributing to that whole despite our own demise. Nevertheless, a profound difference between the two exists. Epictetus identifies this whole with the material universe. For Aquinas the whole is being. Thomisti-

2. Ibid., 190.
3. Ibid., 195.
4. Ibid., 194.
5. Ibid., 192–93.

cally speaking, our natural satisfaction is found not in conforming ourselves to the rhythms of the cosmos but to the precepts of Aquinas's natural law ethics. In that ethics, respect and solicitude is owed to ourselves and our fellows in virtue of our intellection of being. Our lives should be led by contributing to an aggrandizement of being both in knowledge and in human behavior.

Yet Epictetus's confusion about the whole in which we live and move is not surprising to Thomistic psychology. One can ask Epictetus just what is so inspiring about the cosmos that a humble recognition of our status as a part of the cosmos gives a peace that can face the adversities of life? We are parts of many wholes, and that fact is the bane of our existence. Epictetus needs to explain why the membership in the universe is different. For the Thomist the explanation lies in the ability, mentioned in chapter 2, of the notion of being to produce faux epiphanies of itself. The cognitional presence of both the physically and temporally large and small can so engage the notion of being that the object takes on all the preciousness of being itself. Hence, as mentioned by Aquinas, some identified God with the heavens. Likewise, Kant admitted that he could not suppress the thought of God when he looked at the starry heavens. A confusion of the notion of being occasioned by the gargantuan size of the universe is what creates an endearment with the cosmos such that membership in it is considered a privilege. As understandable as this feeling of peace is, its basis is incorrect. Our life's compass is not calibrated on true north. Our intellection of being can play tricks in human psychology. In basic human awareness, humans as intellectors of being are the genuine epiphanies of being. Human happiness begins to form from fidelity to that point.

Allen next considers Sr. Basilea Schlink. Here, according to Schlink, we still consider ourselves as parts of the cosmos but now, unlike in Stoicism, the cosmos is understood to have transcendent cause. In other words, if you understand the world as created and then you have the previously described Stoic experience, you will interpret the Stoic experience of suffering differently. Instead of the experience being one of awe and praise of the cosmos, the experience will be one of the love of God. Allen remarks:

> Actually *belief* in a loving father is precisely what enables a person to perform, in the face of adversity, a second act. It is that action which enables a person *to experience* God's love in the midst of suffering. It can be performed only by a person who believes in a loving God and who also has the humility of the stoic. The first act is a necessary condition for the performance of the second.... Sister Basilea Schlink claims, "When you are in suffering say, 'Yes, Father,' and strength will flow into your heart." She offers this not as a theory but as what actually happens when you so act. There are others who make the same claim; a gracious presence is experienced.[6]

Allen is on the fence about this experience. For he admits, "To believe in God and to act on that belief in the face of adversity might make a person feel marvelous whether there is a God or not."[7] Yet Allen is sufficiently intrigued to say that "one would like to know more about this experience." I would say that Allen is correct to wonder about the veridicality of the experience and I would offer this observation. In light of Aquinas's understanding of human psychology, Sr. Schlink's experience can be viewed as a continuance of the trick played by being on Epictetus. What we are calling an experience of God's love is in truth the past experience of the cosmos as a faux epiphany of being. The Christian's strong belief in God leads the Christian to read the experience as an experience of God's love. What appears to be an experience of God's love is in truth something else. The most that a Thomist could concede is that since God is the nature of being, the notion of being has some likeness to God; hence a heightened experience of the copy is some experience of the original. Aquinas admits a similar confusion in the human desire for happiness which, some argued, implies a natural knowledge of God.[8] Aquinas is claiming that prop-

6. Ibid., 195–96.
7. Ibid., 197.
8. "Now, man naturally desires God in so far as he naturally desires beatitude, which is

erly speaking, there is no natural experience of God, though it is understandable why some people might think so.

Finally, Allen considers Simone Weil's discussion of a specific kind of suffering called "affliction." According to Weil, affliction succeeds in crushing or degrading us where other sufferings do not. Affliction is said to be caused by prolonged or frequent physical suffering, "but the source of affliction is primarily social. A person is uprooted from the fabric of social relations, so that he no longer counts for anything. There is social degradation, or at least fear of it."[9] With affliction one cannot find consolation in being part of a cosmos either created or not created by God. That membership is just what affliction has caused one to lose. Hence, if we are now to experience God, it will not be through suffering but within it. Also, affliction is said to fill one with "self-contempt, disgust and a sense of guilt and defilement."[10] And so those who bring on affliction are soul killers. But paradoxically for Weil affliction is the most perfect contact with God's love in this life. Here the distress itself is experienced as God's loving touch. So in affliction separation from membership in the world does not cause the world to be an insuperable obstacle to an experience of God's love. Distance can also be a form of nearness.[11] Just as Schlink brought her theism to bear on the experience of the Stoic, Weil brings her understanding of the crucifixion of Christ to bear upon the experience of affliction. Because Christ the Son became sin for us, his crucifixion was his greatest distance from the holiness of God the Father. In other words, the crucifixion is affliction. Hence, Weil is confident that the nearness experienced in the distance of affliction is a nearness to Christ.

---

a certain likeness of the divine goodness. On this basis, it is not necessary that God considered in Himself be naturally known to man, but only a likeness of God." *C.G.* I, 11, *Ad quartum*; Thomas Aquinas, *Summa contra Gentiles*, vol. I, translated by Anton C. Pegis (Notre Dame, Ind.: University of Notre Dame Press, 1975), 83

9. Allen, "Natural Evils and the Love of God," 199.
10. Ibid., 199.
11. Ibid., 202.

Again, one would like to know what is going on here. And again I believe that Aquinas's philosophical psychology is helpful in understanding how distance can be a form of nearness. As explained in chapter 2, not only is there a heightened presence of the notion of being in the contemplation of the gargantuan, but the same can be true in the contemplation of the minute. Consequently, the minute can evoke reactions of endearment. To contemplate the small, everything else must be put aside, cleared away. But to remove every *thing* else is not to remove the notion of being. It still is present with the small though everything else has gone. This remaining juxtaposition of the small and being thus calms the soul and can lead to a happiness in a solitary life. But to return to affliction, as mentioned, it effects an isolation of the person. The person loses membership in the world. Nevertheless, one experiences a comforting nearness. Why cannot this experienced nearness be the notion of being? As distant as the minute is from the gargantuan both can provoke the use of being for their consideration, and so both can be experienced as epiphanies of something. Moreover, because the something is being, which is also the good, not surprisingly to suffer dismissal is to encounter something consoling. This would in truth be the experience of affliction that Weil is interpreting through her understanding of Christ.

In conclusion, the three experiences that Allen relates are significant but not so significant as to be what Epictetus, Schlink, and Weil claim. We do not experience the divine itself in any of them. In truth, we are experiencing in a heightened way what is most like the divine in this life, the notion of being. Some intimation of the presence of intellection of being is Allen's noted remark that understanding ourselves as parts of a whole means that the parts somehow transcend the whole. This remark is reminiscent of Aquinas's remark that we are more like wholes than parts thereof because we understand being. Hence, in my opinion, the experiences of Epictetus, Schlink, and Weil are not in their own unique way solutions to the problem of evil, except perhaps as dreams are

Cosmological Theodicies   201

solutions to the troubles of wakefulness. Nevertheless, the experiences involve elements of truth. Being produces joy even when in a faux epiphany of itself. Also, rejection or ostracism does produce, as Simone Weil holds, the self-worthlessness of affliction. Since persons are intellectors of being, an intimation of this fact can make rejection feel like a consignment to nothingness.[12] But through correct reflection on being, as I believe is found in Aquinas, one can maintain joy even as the reflection extends into the lived world shot through as it is with contingency.

DAVID HUME AND *DIALOGUES CONCERNING NATURAL RELIGION*, X AND XI

For the impossibility of cosmological theodicy, there is no better place to begin than Parts X and XI of Hume's *Dialogues concerning Natural Religion*. Using a dialogue format Hume savages any theist who attempts to make sense of the present world. Hence, ironically, the attempt to ground the need for religion on human misery destroys religion. Part X begins with a litany of evils.[13] A perpetual war exists among all living creatures. Artifices of nature are causes of embitterment. Man's own psyche creates superstitions that blast every enjoyment from life. Human society offers no respite but creates new enemies so that one can truly say that man is the greatest enemy of man. Finally, there are woes that arise from the distempered condition of our mind and body so that all the goods of life together would still not make a very happy man. The purpose of this enumeration is to stymie any claim that on bal-

---

12. Consequently, I do not believe that G. K. Chesterton got it completely right when he described suicide as a rejection of being, "The suicide is ignoble because he has not this link with being: he is a mere destroyer; spiritually, he destroys the universe." *Orthodoxy* (New York: John Lane Company, 1914), 133. Such a destruction may be intended in some cases. But for some others suicide results from a loss of self-worth because the suicide experiences the rejection of his fellows as the rejection of being itself. Being has rejected him, he has not rejected being.

13. David Hume, *Dialogues Concerning Natural Religion and Other Writings*, edited by Dorothy Coleman (Cambridge: Cambridge University Press, 2007), 69–71.

ance the world is good. Hence, the world is too disordered to be the effect of an infinite being.

The weight of this description engenders a number of attempts at rejoinder. The first reply is to admit that it is bad here in this world but to insist that in some other locale and time of the universe conditions are or could be better.[14] Hume admits the reply as possible but criticizes it as pure speculation. The point is based upon the existence of an infinite being. But an infinite being is only an assumption. It would never occur to one from the above mentioned facts. Finally, even if the facts were not so discordant, good not mixed with so much evil, the facts would still be finite. But the finite does not suffice to prove the infinite.[15]

Part XI begins a second theistic rejoinder. Concede the irreconcilability of an infinite God with the present near total defeat of good in the world, but insist that both are reconciled if God is finite, though far exceeding mankind. Again Hume admits that reconciliation is possible but only if one is already convinced of a supreme being. If one has only the above litany of sad facts before one, the idea of a supreme but finite being would not arise. Hume drives the point home with the example of the badly built palace:

Did I show you a house or palace, where there was not one apartment convenient or agreeable; where the windows, doors, fires, passages, stairs, and the whole economy of the building were the source of noise, confusion, fatigue, darkness, and the extremes of heat and cold; you would certainly blame the contrivance, without any farther examination. The architect would in vain display his subtlety, and prove to you, that if this door or that window were altered, greater ills would ensue. What he says, may be strictly true: The alteration of one particular, while the other parts of

---

14. "This world is but a point in comparison of the universe: This life but a moment in comparison of eternity. The present evil phenomena, therefore, are rectified in other regions, and in some future period of existence." Ibid., 75.

15. "You must prove these pure, unmixed, and uncontrollable attributes from the present mixed and confused phenomena, and from these alone. A hopeful undertaking! Were the phenomena ever so pure and unmixed, yet being finite, they would be insufficient for that purpose. How much more, where they are also so jarring and discordant." Ibid., 77.

Cosmological Theodicies 203

the building remain, may only augment the inconveniences. But still you would assert in general, that, if the architect had had skill and good intentions, he might have formed such a plan of the whole, and might have adjusted the parts in such a manner, as would have remedied all or most of these inconveniences. His ignorance or even your own ignorance of such a plan, will never convince you of the impossibility of it. If you find any inconveniences and deformities in the building, you will always, without entering into any detail, condemn the architect.[16]

Hume claims that the world is like this badly built building that can obviously be corrected and so speaks ill of its architect.

Hume describes four circumstances that cause evil for sensible creatures and insists that none of them is necessary and in fact are easily rectified. First, our constitution is such that pleasures as well as pains excite animals to action.[17] For this purpose why not use pleasure alone? Second, pain is produced because the world proceeds by general laws.[18] For example, fire produces pain because fire burns. Yet God could abrogate these laws. Such abrogation would mean that man is unable to employ his reason to conduct himself, but such an inconvenience would be addressed by God immediately producing goods. For example, though we could no longer count on fire burning in the case of food preparation, we would not have to worry about that because God would create food in our bellies. Hume also observes that even now the good life is lived among many contingencies. If God added a few good ones, for example, a good fleet always meets a fair wind, good princes enjoy health and a long life, small touches to the brain of Caligula convert him into a Trajan, how would general laws and human conduct be confounded? Third, there would be less pain if we were better endowed.[19] Hume suggests that it would not be extravagant to insist that humans be endowed with a greater propensity to industry and labor. Such an endowment would go a long way to cure most of the ills of human life. Finally, fourth, there is the inexact workman-

16. Ibid., 80.
18. Ibid., 81–82.
17. Ibid., 81.
19. Ibid., 82–84.

ship in the springs and principles of the great machine of nature.[20] Winds are necessary to move clouds upon the earth which in turn are necessary for rain. But these winds often rise to hurricanes and the rains to floods. Would not a supreme being have left these parts of nature more finely adjusted so that they would keep within useful limits?

Hume finishes by claiming that the above four considerations, with little variation, apply to moral evil such that any vice at all in the universe will be a recalcitrant puzzle.[21] So in light of the facts, viz., natural and moral evil, even the idea of a finite supreme being would not arise. If one is to conclude anything, the conclusion would be expressed this way: "The whole presents nothing but the idea of a blind nature, impregnated by a great vivifying principle, and pouring forth from her lap, without discernment or parental care, her maimed and abortive children."[22]

To begin a Thomistic comment I would summarize Hume this way. Hume concedes the logical compatibility of an infinite being with the present universe. Yet if you epistemologically begin from the term that is the present universe, you would never be logically constrained to relate that term to an infinite term. In other words, though it is possible to relate the finite to the infinite, it will always suffice to relate the finite to the finite. Hume's use of the phenomenon of evil is really a modification of the more general claim that you cannot prove the infinite from the finite. What would a Thomist say? Because of the Aristotelian roots of his philosophical thought, Aquinas, like Hume, is an a posteriori thinker. Moreover, Aquinas, like Hume, has been quoted as admitting that in its natural workings the material universe is a messy and laborious affair. Moreover, Aquinas admits that those workings can be so messy, that God's effect of justice is not known. So what does Aquinas see that Hume does not? As noted, Aquinas sees evil as a privation.

20. Ibid., 84–85. 21. Ibid., 87.
22. Ibid., 86.

Hence, evil always presupposes a good from whose *esse* the infinite goodness of its cause is proved. As Aquinas remarked, "If evil exists, God exists."

Aquinas's philosophical psychology is another avenue to the infinity of the cause of *esse*. The infinity of the creator is reflected, albeit dimly, in the human creature understood as an intellector of being. As noted in chapter 2's discussion of Aquinas's natural law ethics, the human has the status of an intellector of being when correct and incorrect, when moral and immoral. In all of these Aquinas can see the play of the intellection of being. So when Aquinas looks out at human affairs, in his vision evil is like a veneer over the good which can be and is at times punctuated by success. The *esse* of that basic level of good that is the intellector of being suffices to prove an infinite cause.

The level of good marked by the intellector of being is also relevant to understand why Hume's four suggested ameliorations for evil are not remedies that the creator, even as infinite, is constrained to provide us. Since the creator is the realization of the intelligible heart of the *ratio entis*, then by motivating human psychology with the intellection of being, Aquinas makes human psychology at least always implicitly and sometimes explicitly a knowledge and love of the creator. In that minimal way at least Aquinas can view the present world as an expression of what is the case in its creative source. In other words, even this world acquits the creator of its responsibility in creating. Hence, in the consideration of a Thomist, Hume's four ameliorations appear as demands for miracles in the present world. But as above and beyond the natural order of things, miracles are things the creator can accomplish but is not morally constrained to accomplish.[23] So the appar-

---

23. It is interesting to note how similar Hume's four suggestions are to Aquinas's characterstics of the supernatural state of innocence, i.e., the state in which God created Adam. Hume's first two can be compared to the discussion of Adam's impassibility at *ST* I, 97, 2; Hume's third to question of whether Adam had all virtue at 95, 3; and Hume's fourth to the nature of Adam's abode of paradise at 102, 2.

ent lack of these ameliorations provides no ground to question the infinity of the creator. In reply Hume could say that God's infinity is not separate from God's other attributes, and so infinity in God should also mean infinite benevolence and goodness. Would not a requirement to reflect benevolence and goodness lead God to make the changes that Hume suggests? But Aquinas could say, as he does about God's infinite mercy, that God's infinite goodness and benevolence are reflected in the simple fact that God has brought the creature from nothing to existence.

So far a cosmological solution to the problem of evil remains a possibility.

WILLIAM ROWE AND "POINTLESS EVILS"

Another critic of a cosmological theodicy is William Rowe. In his "Evil and Theodicy" Rowe argues for the claim that there are no goods that would justify God permitting all evils.[24] Among recalcitrant evils are instances of intense animal and human suffering; for example, (E1) a fawn excruciatingly dying alone in the forest from burns and (E2) a five-year-old rape and murder victim. Rowe can envisage no good that could not be realized without these evils and so claims that the evils are pointless. Rowe admits that he does not have a complete list of intrinsic goods.[25] Nevertheless, he is confident that no good exists to justify permitting these evils. He describes the basis for his confidence this way:

Given the high degree of intrinsic badness of E1 and E2, we do know that the justifying goods would be very significant goods. But this, by itself, is no good reason to think that the goods would be ones we don't know of. For we do know of very significant goods. Consider, for example, the state consisting of a vast number of conscious beings deeply enjoying the admi-

---

24. From *William L. Rowe on Philosophy of Religion: Selected Writings*, edited by Nick Trakakis (Burlington, Vt.: Ashgate Publishing Company, 2007), 91–104.

25. Ibid., 95. Among intrinsic goods of which Rowe is aware are pleasure, happiness, love, the exercise of virtue, good intentions, and knowledge. Unlike Aquinas, Rowe does not mention the *ratio entis* as the *ratio boni*.

Cosmological Theodicies 207

rable qualities exhibited by one another. This is a very significant good we know of. So the mere fact that the goods must be significant is not, of itself, good reason to think that the goods that might justify an omnipotent, omniscient being in permitting E1 or E2 would be goods we do not know.[26]

Since a moral being, if able, would prevent pointless evils, then the existence of pointless evils is a reason to deny the existence of God who by definition is moral.

Rowe goes on to analyze the theodicy of John Hick. Rowe's critique of Hick is useful to better understand Rowe's own position. According to Hick, haphazard and unordered evils are necessary because they are necessary for moral development, soul-making. The claim is clarified by a consideration of the opposite. If evils occurred in an orderly way, then we would do good out of fear of punishment, and out of fear of interfering in soul-making, we would refrain from helping others. Rowe's criticism is that this rationale does not justify permitting E1 and E2. Rowe observes that nature will still be lawlike enough for human providence if the fawn were put out of its misery earlier and the rapist and murderer could still have developed virtue without his heinous deeds.[27]

So, the crucial claim in Rowe's thinking seems to be that there is something inadequate in a theodicy that has animals and humans experiencing horrendous evils for goods, even very significant ones, that could be realized otherwise. If it is conceded that the good could exist without the suffering, then the concession produces the impression that I suffer "pointlessly" or needlessly. But I do not believe that it follows that since a good, even a significant one, can be independently realized, then it is independently realized. In other words, granted that virtue can be realized in the murderer without his having to murder, it does not follow that when virtue is realized with murder, then the murder has nothing to do with the realization of the virtue. For example, reflection

---

26. Ibid., 97.
27. Ibid., 101–2.

on what the murderer has done is a real prompt for his remorse and his recommitment to the good of his fellows. In other words, Rowe's criterion for pointlessness, viz., the ability of the good to be realized without the evil, fails to establish pointlessness. Hence, in the light of the murderer's return to virtue, why would the victim, if the victim could know about it, not derive satisfaction, and profoundly so, even joy? Again, if we understand ourselves as parts of a larger whole, then why should we not derive satisfaction from goods that happen not only to us but also to our fellows, even as a result of evils happening to us? In sum, Rowe is claiming that if the good could be realized without the suffering, then I suffer needlessly. I say no, because when I am suffering I could be contributing to the good of another. The very goods, viz., the realization of virtue in the murderer and the laws of nature, that Rowe claims make sufferings E_1 and E_2 pointless verify my claim; though, given an infinite creator, one may not know to what other goods one contributes. Here I recall Aquinas's point about the amorphous nature of our knowledge of the consequent good to which the creator orders the *quandoque* evils that the creator permits. To say it Thomistically, by utilizing previous material on the relation of *quandoque* evils to consequent goods, even though the evil is an *accidental* cause, the evil is an accidental *cause*. Aquinas's category of a *per accidens* material cause seems to accommodate Rowe's examples of pointless evils but in a manner that does not leave one with a problem.

Rowe might reply that even if he grants the above criticism, it remains simply intuitive that if a good can be realized without enlisting an evil, then a moral being realizes the good in that way. Aquinas would beg to differ. What God is "obliged" to do is to reflect his goodness. Since metaphysically understood God is the unique *esse subsistens*, then this reflecting will reflect the *ratio entis*, that is, some way of possessing *esse*. But as I explained in chapter 2, that object is reflected in a created situation that contains both things that are necessary in *esse* and things that can fail in *esse*. Such a created situation fulfills a reflection of the divine goodness as does a situation like the supernatural state of innocence of Adam and Eve in which the lion lies down with the lamb. Even though the supernatural situation can be said to reflect the divine goodness more clearly, the other situation does in its way also reflect the divine goodness. Both a flickering candle and a steady light illuminate. Even a created world in its natural state will reflect the divine perfection, even to the point of including a knowledge and love of the creator, though it will do this intermittently and imperfectly. It is a creative option. God's fidelity to the morality of being does not entail that God create the better. It entails that God create what reflects his goodness.

J. L. MACKIE AND FURTHER OBJECTIONS TO A COSMOLOGICAL THEODICY

In a famous article, "Evil and Omnipotence," J. L. Mackie uses the problem of evil to support his claim that religious belief is not simply false but is also irrational.[28] He accomplishes this by critiquing four theistic defenses. His opinion is that the four are "fallacious." Their summary and my Thomistic comment follow.

The first theistic defense claims that evil is necessary because it is a "counterpart" to the good.[29] Mackie considers two ways in which evil could be good's counterpart and finds them wanting. First, just as you cannot have the large without the small, so too you cannot have good without evil. Two problems exist with this analogy. On the one hand, the large is not an intrinsic feature of a thing while the good is. On the other hand, you would kill any motivation to eliminate evil; for just as increasing the large increases the small, so too the more you increase the good the more you increase evil.

Second, evil might be good's counterpart as its logical opposite

---

28. J. L. Mackie, "Evil and Omnipotence," in Adams and Adams, *The Problem of Evil*, 25–37.
29. Ibid., 28–30.

just as nonred is the counterpart of red. Since it is a metaphysical principle that a quality must have a real opposite, for example, redness can occur only if nonredness also occurs, then good cannot exist without evil. Mackie claims that this second understanding of "counterpart" confuses an epistemological principle with an ontological one. To be perceived, a quality requires a contrast to its opposite. So, if everything were red, I would not perceive redness. But simply in order to be, a quality does not require the existence of its opposite. So, reality could be all red.

Because of an inability to elaborate a sense of "counterpart" for evil that is not problematic, the first defense fails. I do not believe that you can find this first defense in Aquinas, and so a Thomist can exempt himself from answering Mackie. The closest thinking in Aquinas to the first defense is Aquinas's already mentioned thesis about privation as a condition for change.[30] Any changeable thing involves privation. For example, water is changeable to air because water as water lacks what constitutes air. But this condition of change sense of privation is not the sense of the word used when Aquinas means to speak about evil.

A more Thomistically appropriate theistic defense is Mackie's second: evil is a necessary means to the good.[31] Mackie objects that this thesis restricts God's power and subjects God to causal laws. In some instances Aquinas would propose this thesis. If the world is considered in its natural workings, then natural corruption is a means to an end, viz., the perfection of the universe. A cycling of matter from the lowest to the highest species and back again permits the multitude of species to remain in existence and so makes the world a reflection of the creator's perfection. According to Aquinas, God and other designated agents intend this evil for the perfection of the whole. The second defense would not apply to *quandoque* evils, since of themselves these wreck the perfec-

---

30. See "*C.G.* III, 71: 'If Evil Exits, God Exists'" in chapter 5.
31. Mackie, "Evil and Omnipotence," 30.

tion of the universe. As mentioned, God only permits them. They are not intended as means or as ends. When Aquinas says that God orders *quandoque* evils to good, this ordering should not be taken as a means to end situation.[32]

Again, the Thomistic comment above comes from the perspective of the world in its natural structures. A Thomistic metaphysician sufficiently imaginative or whose intellect is prompted by Christian revelation would discern, for example, the possibility that the world is actually in a supernatural structure. Hence, for example, death is not simply a natural corruption but a punishment for an original human transgression that caused the demise of a graced condition. In other words, a Thomist would not take Mackie's second theistic defense as a definitive one. For a Thomist, *contra* Mackie, the thesis is not fallacious but it is not proven. Hence, by restricting the second defense to a natural order, Aquinas does not run afoul of Mackie's criticism that the second defense restricts God's power and subjects God to causal laws. At this point Mackie might respond that if God is not subject to the natural order such that God could have created a world without evil, then God should have done so. But this remark forgets the gratuity of any supernatural order. The gratuity of the supernatural is not an ad hoc device. Philosophically speaking, the gratuity of the supernatural is based upon: (1) God's obligation, not to do what is better, but to reflect his perfection, and (2) a world with evil can reflect that perfection as does a world without evil. It should be added that Aquinas does not leave the second point in the abstract. His elaboration of natural and *quandoque* evils shows how the second point can hold true in the present world. In particular, human nature is not so much a victim to physical evils and vices that over time no one achieves, albeit imperfectly, a knowledge and love of the creator.

Mackie says that the third theistic defense is a variant of the second, and so, I assume, that we are still speaking of evil as a

---

32. See "Bracketing *Quandoque* Evils between Goods" in chapter 3.

means. The third defense claims that the universe is better with some evil than with none.³³ The claim is elaborated in two ways. The first uses an aesthetic analogy. Just as a silent pause in a musical performance can add beauty to the music, so too the lack of good, for example, the evil of pain, can add to our appreciation of the good of health. Second, evils provide for opportunities to overcome evil, for example, the exercise of virtue, and the universe is better for this. Mackie has three criticisms of the third defense. First, the goods about which the third defense speaks are not really goods but means to what is really good, viz., pleasure and happiness. Hence, God could immediately create happiness; it is absurd for God to keep misery in existence to make possible virtue and heroism. Second, God is not concerned to minimize evil but to maximize evil to promote virtue. This seems strange. The third criticism is called "fatal."³⁴ Beside the evils of pain and disease, there are the evils corresponding to the goods of virtue, for example, the vices of malevolence, cruelty, cowardice, and others. If the third defense is to address vices, then it would seem to engender an infinite regress. Physical evils will terminate at death, but vices can be increased to infinity. Hence, especially for this criticism the third defense is fallacious.

Again, insofar as the third defense is referring to what Aquinas would call *quandoque* evils, then we cannot be speaking in terms of evil as a means to good. In the natural order, *quandoque* evils cannot be used as a means to good, because of themselves they are geared to wreck the universe, not to contribute to it. God's basic relation to them is one of permission in the course of willing something else. The something else that God is willing is the preservation of the specific natures of material substances that *in toto* constitute a reflection of the divine perfection. God's subsequent ordering of *quandoque* evils to some good does not render the evils a means to an end. So Mackie's second criticism does not ring true

33. Mackie, "Evil and Omnipotence," 30–32.
34. Ibid., 32.

Cosmological Theodicies 213

for Aquinas. God would not be concerned to maximize evil to maximize good, because the evil in question is *quandoque*.

Aquinas would concede Mackie's first criticism. As mentioned when discussing Rowe's pointless evils, virtue can be realized apart from evil. For example, Adam and Eve were created chaste without having to go through a period of struggle with concupiscence. This situation is a supernatural one and is not one that God owes to us. But it is true that even in the natural order, virtue can be realized without going through a crucible of evil. I admitted that Rowe's murderer could have come to a respect for life without going through the killing of the young girl and suffering remorse. The murderer could have come from a family that taught him that value from a young age. But for Aquinas none of these concessions implies a divine delinquency for not having created us in a better state. Aquinas's ethics of a respect and solicitude for the intellector of being would lead one to understand that in God's case the respect and solicitude is for God himself. So, if God creates, God is obliged to create something that reflects a knowledge and love of himself. Such is a universe like the present one in which humans slowly, and admittedly with great aberration, come to a knowledge of the truth. As Aquinas says at I, 44, 2c: "antiqui philosophi paulatim et quasi pedetentim intraverunt in cognitionem veritatis." Likewise, at *C.G.* I, 4, Aquinas expresses tempered optimism concerning natural reason's ability to know God: "Non nisi quibusdam pauci, et his etiam post temporis longitudinem proveniret."

Finally, that God is obliged only to create a universe that reflects his perfection, not obliged to create a better universe, means that Mackie's third criticism does not apply. God is not driven into an infinite regress. Rather, God can stop at any point in the regress because any point in the regress is a responsible option for the creator.

In sum, insofar as the third theistic defense appears to treat what Aquinas calls *quandoque* evils as a means to the good, Aquinas would not make the third defense. If one corrects that misunderstanding of the third defense, then of course Aquinas would make the third defense. I have noted that Aquinas explains in a second way why God permits *quandoque* evils. Following Augustine, Aquinas says that God is so powerful that God can make good out of evil. Also as mentioned earlier, though as a philosopher one could be confident of the previous explanation, as a philosopher one would be unable to pin down the identity of this redeeming good. Too many unresolved possibilities would remain in the philosopher's mind. So, again, the theistic defense is not fallacious as Mackie claims but is nondefinitive.

MACKIE'S FOURTH CRITICISM AND AQUINAS ON THE CAUSALITY OF HUMAN CHOICES

Mackie criticizes a fourth theistic defense. Because of the large discussion which it has spawned, the fourth defense merits for its discussion a separate section in this chapter. Mackie introduces the fourth defense as a way in which the theist might deal with his "fatal" third criticism of the third defense.[35] The fourth defense maintains that God is not responsible for evil because God creates humans with free will. Through the exercise of their own free will, humans, not God, introduce evil into the world. Mackie expresses two objections and then, as the *coup de grace,* the paradox of omnipotence. Mackie first notes that if God can cause humans who are good some of the time, why cannot God cause humans who are good all of the time. If the theist replies that God cannot do the latter because humans are "really free" in the sense that their choices are not determined by their characters, then Mackie rejoins secondly that real freedom is sheer randomness and is hardly worth being the great good for which God creates the world.

These comments suffice to show the fallaciousness of the fourth theistic defense. Mackie, though, concludes his article with his omnipotence paradox which shows that traditional theists must give up the standard way of understanding omnipotence if the problem

---

35. Ibid., 33–36.

of evil is to be solved. The paradox can be expressed as follows. If God cannot cause us to be really free, then God is not omnipotent. If God can cause us to be really free, then before causing us to be really free God may have been omnipotent but not after.

Would Aquinas make the fourth theistic defense? I do not believe so. My reason is that implicit in the fourth defense is an understanding of the human creature as a first cause, at least of its free actions. In an early, important text discussing whether God is a cause of the act of sin, Aquinas opposes such an understanding.

> First, because from this [that the act of sin as an act is not from God] it seems to follow that many first principles exist: for this is the nature of a first principle—that it is able to act without the help of a prior agent and its influence. Whence if the human will were able to produce some action whose author was not God, the human will would have the nature of a first principle. Yet proponents of this view attempt to solve this problem saying that the will *per se* is able to produce an action without the influence of a prior agent, nevertheless it does not have being [*esse*] from itself but from another, which also is required for the nature of a first principle. But this [reply] seems inappropriate, viz., that what does not have being [*esse*] from itself is able to act from itself; also what is not from itself is not able to last through itself. Also every power proceeds from an essence and every operation from a power. Whence that whose essence is from another requires that the power and operation is from another. Moreover, although through this response [the problem] is avoided because [the will] would not be first simply, nevertheless [the problem] would not be able to be avoided that [the will] would be a first agent if its action were not reduced to some prior agent just as to a cause. Second, because the action of sinning is a certain kind of being [*quoddam ens*], not only insofar as privations and negations are called beings, but also insofar as a thing existing in a genus is a being because actions themselves are ordered to a genus, it would follow, if the actions of sinning are not from God, that some being having an essence would not be from God, and so God would not be the universal cause of all beings, which is against the perfection of the first being.[36]

36. *In II Sent.* d. 37, q. 2, a. 2c; Thomas Aquinas, *Scriptum super Libros Sententiarum Magistri Petri Lombardi Episcopi Parisensis*, vol. II, edited by Pierre Mandonnet (Paris: P. Lethielleux, 1929), 952.

In the context of efficient causality, Aquinas gives two arguments against the view that the action of sinning is not from God. First, the view appears to accept either (1) the thesis that there are many first causes, or (2) the thesis that a power with a cause of its *esse* can be the first cause of its operation. Second, the sinful action is a certain kind of being, *quoddam ens*; it is an *ens* in the sense of having an essence capable of extra-mental existence. As such, the action stands in contrast to privations and negations. Now earlier in his commentary on Lombard's *Sentences*, Aquinas has already asserted *esse* to be the defining note of the *ratio entis*.[37] Consequently, God should be the cause of the *quoddam ens* that is the act of sin insofar as God causes the act's *esse*. Some years later Aquinas will describe God as a cause of *ens inquantum ens* by being a cause of *esse*. At *In VI Meta.*, lect. 3, n. 1215, God's causality is said to extend to all things insofar as they are beings, *omnia inquantum sunt entia*, because God is the agent who gives things their being, *agens per modum dantis esse*.

Unlike Aquinas's first approach which is from the *esse* of the will, his second approach is from the *esse* of the sinful action itself. Any action is treated as a being because it has its own *esse*; but it can have *esse* only because God causes the *esse*. Not only does a substance have an *esse* but the accident that is its action also has an *esse*.[38] In this context God is the first mover by causing the *esse* that actuates the action. In other words, since the action is

37. "Since in the thing there is its quiddity and its being [*esse*], truth is based on the being of the thing more than on the quiddity, just as the name of being [*nomen entis*] is imposed from the being [*esse*]." *In I Sent.*, d. 19, q. 5, a. 1c. "Just as motion [*motus*] is the act of the mobile insomuch as it is mobile; so too being [*esse*] is the act of the existing thing [*actus existentis*], insomuch as it is a being [*ens*]." *In I Sent.*, d. 19, q. 2, a. 2c.

38. In Aquinas's metaphysics not only do things like a human have *esse*, what I called the standard attributes also have an *esse*. At *De Ver.* I, 1, Aquinas says that the notion of being, *ratio entis*, that is divided into the Aristotelian categories of substance and accidents is itself divided into a nature plus *esse*. In his *De Ente et Essentia*, ch. 6, Aquinas mentions for the accident a secondary being (*quoddam secundum esse*) different from the *esse* that causes the thing to subsist as a being (*ens*). The same distinction between types of *esse* is found in the *Summa contra Gentiles* I, 22, and 26. For apparently contrary texts and a discussion, see Joseph Owens, *An Elementary Christian Metaphysics* (Houston: Center for

Cosmological Theodicies 217

the actuality of the power and God actuates the action by causing its *esse*, then in the same stroke God is the mover of the power. God does this for all actions or operations, including those that are our choosings. In Aquinas's eyes his opponent's position that God is not the cause of our choices is victim to a certain metaphysical naivety. For Aquinas, outside of God there is not the least shred of existing that is not traced back to God.

A later parallel text confirms the metaphysical context of *esse*:

Attending to the essence itself of the act, others have said that the action of sinning is from God, which is necessary by a twofold argument. First, by a common argument, because since God is a being through his essence, because his essence is his being [*esse*], it is necessary that what in whatever way exists, is derived from him, for nothing other exists which is its being. But all things are called beings through a certain participation. Yet everything that is called such by participation is derived from that which exists through its essence, just as all ignited things are derived from that which is fire through its essence. It is clear, however, that the action of sinning is a certain kind of being [*quoddam ens*], and it posited in a category of being. Hence, it is necessary to say that it is from God.[39]

Only God has *esse* essentially. Every other being, then, has *esse* by participation and from God. Among such beings that participate *esse* is an action. Hence, all actions qua actions, even sinful actions, are from God. The context of participation presupposes a metaphysics in which God has been reached as the one and only subsistent *esse*. Hence, it can be concluded *a priori* that every being other than God is a being only by having *esse* other than itself

---

Thomistic Studies, 1985), 160, n. 5. It should be again pointed out that as actuating both things and their categorical accidents, these kinds of *esse* present *esse* itself as the act of all form both substantial and accidental. Hence, *esse* is a nonformal act. It is an act without finitude and determination. This is some explanation of Kant's observation in *The Critique of Pure Reason* that there is no difference between one hundred possible dollars and one hundred actual dollars. *Esse* adds, but *esse* does not add a further determination. This thinking about *esse* will become a key point in what seems to be Aquinas's explanation of how God can infallibly act in the created will without determining the will.

39. Aquinas, *De Malo*, 3, 2c; in Thomas Aquinas, *Quaestiones Disputatae*, edited by Raymundus Spiazzi, vol. 2 (Rome: Marietti, 1965), 498.

and so is dependent upon God. This metaphysical understanding of an existing action as a composition of itself and its *esse* can also be reached more directly by submitting it to the twofold operation of the intellect—conceptualization and judgment. Just as Tom exists both really and cognitionally when I perceive him, so too do the accidents of Tom. The two operations would commence from that data.

Finally at *ST* I, 22, 2, ad 4m, Aquinas remarks:

> When it is said that God left man to himself, this does not mean that man is exempt from divine providence, but merely that he has not a prefixed operating power determined to only the one effect; as in the case of natural things, which are only acted upon as though directed by another towards an end: for they do not act of themselves, as if they directed themselves towards an end, like rational creatures, through the possession of free choice, by which those are able to take counsel and make choices. Hence it is significantly said: In the hand of his own counsel. But since the very act of free choice is traced to God as a cause, it necessarily follows that everything happening from the exercise of free choice must be subject to divine providence.[40]

Two comments. Note that the power of free choice is a power not understood to be directed to only one effect. This echoes Mackie's "real freedom" that he dismisses as sheer randomness. Second, the *responsio* of the article explains how God is a cause.

> The causality of God, Who is the first agent, extends to all beings [*omnia entia*] not only as to the constituent principles of the species, but also as to the individualizing principles; not only of things incorruptible, but also of things corruptible. Hence all things that have being in whatever manner [*omnia quae habent quocumque modo esse*] are necessarily directed by God towards the end; ... it necessarily follows that all things, inasmuch as they participate being [*esse*] must to that extent be subject to divine providence.

Again note the context of the divine efficient causality of *esse* in which all things other than God participate.

---

40. Anton C. Pegis, ed., *The Basic Writings of St. Thomas Aquinas*, vol. I (New York: Random House, 1945), 233–34.

Cosmological Theodicies

In conclusion, the relation of God to our choosings is one of efficient causality that produces the choosing itself by giving an *esse*, an act of existing, to the choosing. So, in the light of his metaphysics Aquinas understands God's efficient causality to bear directly on the free choosing itself. God's causality does not stop when his causality produces the power of choice. God's causality continues and goes on to make the power operate. Aquinas does not consider his position determinist, and so Aquinas is not similar to Mackie who expresses a determinism of character. Aquinas remarks that God so works in the will that the will's ability to do otherwise is not impaired. For example:

The will is said to have dominion of its acts not through the exclusion of the first cause, but because the first cause does not act in the will so that it from necessity determines the will to one thing just as it determines nature. And so the determination of the act remains in the power of reason and will.[41]

Also:

God is not said to have left man in the hands of his own counsel without God operating in the will, but because God gives to the will of man dominion of its acts so that the will is not obligated to some part of a contradiction, which dominion God does not give to nature since through its form it is determined to one.[42]

Also:

When it is said that God left man to himself, this does not mean that man is exempt from divine providence, but merely that he has not a prefixed operating power determined to only one effect; as in the case of natural things, which are only acted upon as though directed by another towards an end: for they do not act of themselves, as if they directed themselves towards an end, like rational creatures, through the possession of free choice, by which these are able to take counsel and make choices.[43]

Finally:

---

41. *De Pot.* 3, 7, ad 13m; in Aquinas, *Quaestiones Disputatae*, II, 59.
42. Ibid.
43. *ST* I, 22, 2, ad 4m; Pegis, *Basic Writings of Thomas Aquinas*, vol. I, 233.

Although the non-being of the effect of the divine will is not able to simultaneously stand with the divine will, nevertheless the effect's ability of failing [*potentia deficiendi effectum*] stands simultaneously with the divine will. For these are not incompatible: God wills someone to be saved and this person is able to be damned. But these are incompossible: God wills someone to be saved and the person is damned.[44]

Aquinas says that God so works in the will that God does not determine the will to one thing. In other words, God's working in the will is not to the detriment of the will's ability to do otherwise. As the last text above says, under God's causality, that something *will not* happen does not mean that it *cannot* happen. It is simply a modal confusion to think that *will not* equals *cannot*. So under the divine causality, the will acts freely. For to act with the real ability to do otherwise is to act freely. The fact that the will does not do otherwise does not mean that the will cannot do otherwise.

As controlling, if not determining, as God is in Aquinas's position, God is not obliged to cause us always to do good. God can confirm a rational being in doing good. In fact God did just such a thing with Jesus and Mary.[45] But it should be noted that such situations involved supernatural means. Hence, if God did the same for all, it would again be supernatural, and there is no divine obligation to do the supernatural. Unlike Mackie, Aquinas sees no divine delinquency in God not creating an all-good world.

AQUINAS AND PLANTINGA

Hence, one can say, in my opinion, that a lack of engagement exists between Aquinas and a theist like Alvin Plantinga. Plantinga is within the paradigm of the fourth free will explanation for evil because Plantinga holds that the creature is a first cause of its choices. In describing "Liebniz's lapse," which claims that God can create any possible world, Plantinga differs and points out:

---

44. *De Ver.* XXIII, 5, ad 3m; Thomas Aquinas, *The Disputed Questions on Truth*, vol. III, translated by Robert W. Schmidt (Chicago: Regnery, 1954), 118.

45. See *De Ver.* XXIV, 9c.

Cosmological Theodicies 221

If we consider a world in which *GT* [God actualizing *T*. *T* is the state of affairs that includes all the states of affairs that God strongly actualizes] obtains and in which Curley [a fictitious mayor Boston] freely rejects the bribe, we see that whether it was within God's power to actualize it depends in part upon what Curley would have done if God had strongly actualized *T*. Accordingly, there are possible worlds such that it is partly up to Curley whether or not God can actualize them. It is of course up to God whether or not to create Curley, and also up to God whether or not to make him free with respect to the action of taking the bribe at *T*. But if he creates him, and creates him free with respect to this action, then whether or not he takes it is up to Curley—not God.[46]

Yet Plantinga defends the truth of counterfactuals and so includes them within God's omniscience.[47] Why does not God actualize only those possible worlds in which God sees that we do good, as Mackie claims God should do if God is good? Plantinga's clever answer is the possibility of the "sad truth" that what God sees is that for any

---

46. Alvin Plantinga, "God, Evil, and the Metaphysics of Freedom," in Adams and Adams, *The Problem of Evil*, 100. Also, "If a person S is free with respect to a given action, then he is free to perform that action and free to refrain; no causal laws and antecedent conditions determine either that he will perform the action, or that he will not. It is within his power, at the time in question, to perform the action, and within his power to refrain." Ibid., 84. "What God thought good, on this view, was the existence of creatures whose activity is not causally determined—who, like himself, are centres of creative activity." Ibid., 89. Though Plantinga does not mention Mackie's omnipotence paradox, Plantinga could nullify the paradox as Bruce Reichenbach does by asserting that God causing our free actions is contradictory and contradictions do not count against omnipotence: "There are 'limits' to what an omnipotent being can do in the sense that an omnipotent being cannot bring about a state of affairs whose description contains or entails a contradiction; it cannot bring about logically necessary truths or the logically impossible, not because it lacks some ability, but because logically necessary truths and the logically impossible cannot be brought about. The former hold true in all possible worlds and the latter in none. But this 'limit' would not reasonably be held to count against a being's being omnipotent. Indeed, the latter 'limit' is critical to the atheologian's own case. Unless it is inconsistent with God's nature to do that which involves or entails a contradiction, the problem of evil is no problem at all, for in that case the presence of a contradiction between God's goodness and the existence of evil would not mean that one would have to be sacrificed. God could allow or even bring about evil and still be good." Bruce R. Reichenbach, *Evil and a Good God* (New York: Fordham University Press, 1982), 3–4.

47. Plantinga, "God, Evil, and the Metaphysics of Freedom," 92–97.

possible world Curley sins in that world. Plantinga expresses it this way:

> Significant freedom, obviously, does not entail wrongdoing; so there are possible worlds in which God and Curley both exist and in which the latter is significantly free but never goes wrong. But consider W, any one of these worlds. There is a state of affairs T such that God strongly actualizes T in W and T includes every state of affairs God strongly actualizes in W. Furthermore, since Curley is significantly free in W, there are some actions that are morally significant for him in W and with respect to which he is free in W. The sad truth however, may be this: among these actions there is one—call it A—such that if God had actualized T, Curley would have gone wrong with respect to A. But then it follows (by the argument of Section 6) that God could not have actualized W. Now W was just any of the worlds in which Curley is significantly free but always does only what is right. It therefore follows that it was not within God's power to actualize a world in which Curley produces moral good but no moral evil. Every world God could have actualized is such that if Curley is significantly free in it, he takes at least one wrong action.[48]

What Plantinga describes for Curley, Plantinga calls "transworld depravity." For Plantinga it is possible that all free creatures are infected with transworld depravity. So it is possible that what God sees is that free creatures have limited God's creative options, so that God cannot create a world without evil. Plantinga expands upon this possibility to include worlds with less evil than this actual one.[49] Hence, it is possible that this world is in fact the best world that can be.

Interestingly, theists who continue to make the free will defense and who criticize Plantinga criticize the divine omniscience. In other words, God does not have, as claimed by Plantinga, a knowledge of counterfactuals. Such critique leaves God only with a knowledge of what free creatures would probably do and so excuses God from evil even more obviously than in Plantinga's theodicy. Any complaint that these theists attack God's omniscience might be met in the same way as Reichenbach met Mackie's omnipotence

---

48. Ibid., 101–2.   49. Ibid., 106–7.

Cosmological Theodicies 223

paradox—an antecedent cause for a creature's free act is a contradiction, hence it is not an obstacle to omnipotence; likewise certain knowledge of future free acts is a contradiction, hence it is not within God's power. But an admitted remaining problem for these theists is that despite God's good efforts, the created order may spiral out of control. Evil as a conceptual problem would have a solution, but evil as a real problem may well lack a solution.

Robert Merrihew Adams expresses well the issue with Plantinga's thesis on the truth of counterfactuals. For example, "If I lived in Boston, I would have been a mailman like my father." According to Plantinga, those counterfactuals are true whose consequents are true in a possible world most similar to the actual world and in which is the counterfactual's antecedent. Being an expert on the Counter-Reformation debate between the Dominican Bañez and the Jesuit Molina on predestination, Adams applies many of the difficulties in Molina's doctrine of God's middle knowledge to claims about the truth of counterfactuals. But an additional problem with consistency emerges with Plantinga's attempt to combine the counterfactual thesis with an understanding of a creator God. For God's creative activity is supposedly guided by his knowledge of the truth of counterfactuals. But knowledge of the latter is determined by the actual world. So evidently God acts without a knowledge of counterfactuals in order to know the counterfactuals that should guide God's action. Here is how Adams puts it concerning how I know if I did x, y would happen:

> According to the possible worlds explanation, that depends on whether the actual world is more similar to some world in which I do x and y happens than to any world in which I do x and y does not happen. That in turn seems to depend on which world is the actual world. And which world is the actual world? That depends in part on whether I do x.[50]

The only apparent way out of the circle is to say that God does not act before he knows the actual world. Instead, before God knows

---

50. Robert Merrihew Adams, "Middle Knowledge and the Problem of Evil," in Adams and Adams, *The Problem of Evil*, 118. Likewise, Reichenbach, "If counterfactuals of free

the actual world, the actual world acts on God. There is an *a posteriori* moment in the divine knowledge. As far as a Thomist is concerned this passivity in the divine knowledge is another objection to omniscience. In line with his metaphysical understanding of God as *ipsum esse* and *actus purus*, Aquinas not only marks God's knowledge by certitude, he makes God's knowledge a priori. That is, God knows others by knowing himself, lest potency be placed in pure act.[51]

---

choice are to be items of God's knowledge and if they are to be used in the selection of agents who always freely do the right, God must know them *before* there was an actual world and *before* he decided which possible world to actualize. But he cannot *know* them before this, since it is yet indeterminate which world he will actualize and which counterfactuals are true, for their truth depends upon the actual world in respect to similarity of relevant states of affairs." *Evil and a Good God*, 70.

51. "The intelligible species is to the intellect, therefore, as act to potency. If, then, the divine intellect understood through some intelligible species other than itself, it would be in potency with respect to something." *C.G.* I, 46, *Adhuc. Per*; Aquinas, *Summa contra Gentiles*, vol. I, 175. Adams raises a second issue. He concedes that transworld depravity is possible but objects that it is not probable in a context of God's knowledge of counterfactuals. Speaking from a context of Suarez's doctrine of God's middle knowledge, which Adams considers equivalent to Plantinga's doctrine of God's knowledge of counterfactuals, Adams observes, "God uses His middle knowledge to make such predeterminations effective, choosing conditions and helps of grace that He knows will elicit a favorable response, and avoiding those under which He knows that the creature would not act according to the divine purpose. This presupposes, of course, that for every possible honorable free act of every possible free creature, in any possible outward circumstances, there are some incentives or helps of grace that God could supply, to which the creature would respond favorably though he could have responded unfavorably. But this is a very plausible presupposition if we assume, as Suarez does, that the theory of middle knowledge is correct, and that there is an infinite variety of natural and supernatural ways in which God can work on us inwardly, assisting our reasoning, affecting our feelings and perhaps our beliefs and desires, without causally determining our response." Adams, "Middle Knowledge and the Problem of Evil," 123–24. For other helpful discussions of Molina from a Thomistic viewpoint, see Anton Pegis, "Molina and Human Freedom" in *Jesuit Thinkers of the Renaissance*, edited by Gerard Smith (Milwaukee: Marquette University Press, 1939), 75–131, and Reginald Garrigou-Lagrange, *God: His Existence and His Nature*, translated by Bede Rose (St. Louis: B. Herder Book Co., 1949), II, 465–87. A good description of Augustine as precursor to Molina is Eugène Portalié, *A Guide to the Thought of Saint Augustine*, translated by Ralph J. Bastian (Chicago: H. Regnery Co., 1960), 198–201. In his *Freedom in Molina* (Chicago: Loyola University Press, 1966), 47–48, Gerard Smith conducts a textual survey that confirms Aquinas's causal approach for God's knowledge of our free acts.

So, again, Aquinas would not be making the fourth theistic defense mentioned by Mackie. For, not only does Aquinas metaphysically have God the creator dispensing *esse* to rational substances, Aquinas has God doing the same for their free acts of will. Also, the fourth defense would trap Aquinas into denying both the infallibility of God's providence and God as pure act. Hence, the free choice of the rational creature is neither a necessary effect nor an uncontrolled effect. How can this be? How can the choice be controlled but not necessary? Now the Thomist must face the great issue of explaining the relation between the creator and human choices. But if the Thomist overcomes that hurdle, the Thomist quickly confronts another. Many of those divinely caused choices are evil, and monstrously so. If Aquinas keeps God involved in causing the choice, do we not make God responsible for evil? For example, if a human decides to commit murder, and so morally is already a murderer, and if the creator is related to all choices both good and bad, then do we not have two murderers, viz., the creature and the creator?

Before I begin my remarks on these two issues, I wish to make one comment regarding Mackie's dismissal of "really free" as sheer randomness. As should be clear from chapter 2, in Aquinas real freedom is a great good because it is one of the psychic effects of the intellection of being. In turn the intellection of being is the basis of obligation in Aquinas's natural law ethics. Because of that deep connection with the *ratio entis*, aka the *ratio boni*, freedom is a great good that renders humans "principle parts" of material creation.

THE AVOIDANCE OF DETERMINISM

I have quoted Aquinas to the effect that God so works in the human will that God does not determine the will to one thing. In other words, God's working in the will is not to the detriment of the will's ability to do otherwise. Under God's causality, that something *will not* happen does not mean that it *cannot* happen. It is simply a modal confusion to think that will not equals cannot. So under the divine causality, the will acts freely. For to act with the real ability to do otherwise is to act freely. The fact that the will does not do otherwise does not mean that the will cannot do otherwise.

Yet how can God so act in the created will that the will's ability to do otherwise is left unimpaired? Aquinas's answer needs to be carefully set out. Yet before doing so, I want to insist that Aquinas does not have to answer this question. The question asks how something is so. But questions of how something is so do not necessarily have to be answered in order to assert that something is so. For example, a native from the jungles of New Guinea placed on the sidewalks of New York City would know perfectly well that automobiles are moving down the avenue. But being ignorant of the workings of the internal combustion engine and being informed that automobiles are not living things, our native would have no understanding of how the motion is taking place. The same would be true if he spotted an airplane passing above him. The point is that one can be absolutely sure *that* something is so while being perfectly ignorant about *how* it is so. Ignorance of the *how* fails to mean ignorance of the *that*.

Aquinas can claim that he knows perfectly well that we are truly free and that our choices are caused by God. Aquinas's basis for the first assertion is his philosophical psychology of the intellection of being. As a nongeneric intelligibility, being contains the differences of all things and as such can be called the good, the *ratio boni*. Up and against being everything else shrivels and becomes one good among others. This cognitive situation leaves us indeterminate. We can choose because any thing is a *good*, but we are not compelled to choose because anything is only *a* good. Fears that this cognitive situation is an illusion are met by sense realism. The intelligibility of being is drawn from realities given in sense cognition. Hence, we are confident that implications of intelligibility are real and genuine. Aquinas's basis for the second assertion is the extrapolation just described of his metaphysics of *esse* to the Aristotelian categories beyond that of substance.

Now it can be true that sometimes contradictions are produced by faulty analysis and reasoning. Yet reflection upon the philosophical analysis behind Aquinas's two assertions shows the analysis to be probing and accurate. Hence, the Thomist is in a situation similar to the New Guinea native. Just as the native knows that the auto is self-moving and that this is compatible with the auto being nonliving, so too the Thomist knows both that a human is really free and that this is compatible with human choices being caused by God. Aquinas could rest content with establishing the truths of human freedom and the extent of God's causality and concede ignorance about know how these truths are compatible.

But to his credit, Aquinas does not leave the situation by simply acknowledging that. He attempts to move on the how question. Aquinas's answer needs to be carefully set forth, and I take pains in the following to present it in five points.

First, as can be read from *De Ver.* XXIII, 5, *sed contra* and *ST* I, 19, 8, *sed contra*, another way Aquinas speaks of the will's ability to do otherwise is to speak of the will's contingency. The will's freedom is a particular case of the contingent. The contingent is what happens but need not happen, for example, the crop of apples that comes in but could have been destroyed earlier by a late spring frost. Hence, Aquinas's account of how divine providence does not destroy contingency is relevant for our purposes.

Second, in these two texts, Aquinas insists that God's immutable and indefectible will does not exclude contingency.[52] Why does God's indefectible will not exclude contingency? The reason given is always the same—God is the most efficacious agent. Aquinas says "*agens fortissimum*" in the *De Veritate* and "*efficacissima*" in the *Summa Theologiae*. For example, Aquinas says, "The divine

---

52. Obviously presupposed here is the freedom of God's will regarding creation. For a presentation of Aquinas's thesis, especially as elaborated in the *Contra Gentiles*, that in the same act of will by which God necessarily wills himself God freely wills creatures, again see my "*Contra* Spinoza: Aquinas on God's Free Will," *American Catholic Philosophical Quarterly*, 76 (2002), 417–29.

will is the most strong [*fortissimum*] agent. Whence it is necessary that its effect be assimilated to it in all ways. So not only does it happens that what God wills is made, which is as if to be assimilated to the species; but it happens that it is made in the way that God wills, either as necessary or contingently."[53] At first thought, God's most efficacious causality only seems to intensify the determinism problem. In other words, as most efficacious, why is not God the most determining? To begin to make sense of Aquinas's reason, consider the billiard balls in the next point.

Third, because billiard A is bearing down upon ball B with a definite and determinate trajectory, velocity, weight, spin, and so forth, ball B can move only in one way. Because of A's character, A erases from B any real ability to act in any other way when A strikes B. A study of the billiard balls enables us to become clear about what kind of preceding causality excludes freedom from the will. Preceding causality *as determinate and finite* excludes any ability to be otherwise.

Fourth, the question arises: "Is God bearing down on the created will like ball A bearing down on ball B?" I believe that Aquinas's repeated references to God's most efficacious causality intend to give a negative answer. How so? Recalling the sketch of Aquinas's metaphysics, one sees an identity between being the most efficacious agent and being a creator. A creator is the most efficacious agent because its causality requires no preexisting material cause. But in Aquinas's metaphysics, God is a creator because God is subsistent *esse*. Why does realizing that being the most efficacious agent is synonymous with being subsistent *esse* ruin any analogy between God and ball A? As known from things in our experience, *esse* is the act of all form. This insight requires understanding *esse* to be an act that is not a form. As such, *esse* is not like form which of itself is finite and determinate. As a nonformal act in a subsistent configuration, the divine *esse* should be without limit and de-

---

53. *De Ver.* XXIII, 5c.

termination. God, then, is unlike ball A. Looking from B to A, one sees finitude and determination bearing down on B. Looking from the created will to God, one sees only the infinite.

Fifth, hence, understood as subsistent *esse*, God does not move the will like ball A moves ball B. Because A is finite and determinate, A imposes a determinism upon what it impacts; because God is infinite, God moves without erasing any ability to do otherwise. It is true that because God is intelligent, God works with a plan and a design. But a providential God still does not mean God is like ball A. Because of God's simplicity, order and design are in God *as identified with his infinite subsistent esse*. Order and design are not present in God *as finite and determinate*. Hence, divine providence is compatible with human freedom. One of God's effects can be precisely my choosing this with a real ability to choose that instead.[54]

54. In his *Evil Revisited: Responses and Reconsiderations* (Albany: State University of New York Press, 1991), ch. 4, David Ray Griffin criticizes my earlier presentation of Aquinas's position. In "Super God: Divine Infinity and Human Self-Determination," *Proceedings of the American Catholic Philosophical Association*, 55 (1981), 197–209, I emphasized the infinity of subsistent existence and at the same time insisted that we had no positive concept of the infinite. To Griffin this seemed to be contradictory; I was claiming both an insight into the infinite and no insight into the infinite. To avoid the appearance of self-contradiction, I should have at least indicated in that early article Aquinas's material on the nongeneric character of the notion of being. As I explained above in chapter 2, for Aquinas (and Aristotle whom Aquinas is echoing), even before the human gets to God, the human has a sense of the infinite—the concrescence of all possible perfections and all degrees thereof. The human has that sense of the infinite in what Aquinas calls the notion of being. Aquinas advances the infinity of the notion of being in the thesis that unlike a generic notion, the notion of being cannot be divided by receiving addition from the outside. See *De Ver.* I, 1c; XXI, 1c; *C.G.* I, 25. For example, animal is divided into the species man by the addition of the intelligible note "rational." Rational must come from outside what is meant by "animal" under pain of including it in the meaning of "animal" and so making all animals rational. Being cannot undergo division into the Aristotelian categories of substance and the various accidents in exactly the same manner. The reason is that outside of being there is only nonbeing. So placing differentiating notes outside of being is to consign them to oblivion. Hence, in some way being includes everything, even what will differentiate it. However, this appreciation of being as infinite is not a clear and distinct one. Since the differences remain within the notion of being, then we intellect the notion but we intellect it dimly and in a veiled manner. It is a sameness in difference, or as the Scholastics say, an analogous concept. As analogous being, the

Parenthetically, I want to make two observations. First, Aquinas's position that God is the cause of our free acts does not lead to quietism—that is, I do nothing but wait upon God to act in my will. Knowing that God moves my will, without detriment to the will's ability to do otherwise, means that I also know that I am placed in an environment that confronts me with true and genuine incentives, or final causes. Far from numbing me into inactivity, Aquinas's claim that God's causality is involved in our free acts places us in a context that really calls forth from us our actions. That context genuinely bids me to act. Only a determinism would make illusions of the experienced incentives to do this or to do that. Hence, my sole concern should be to apply myself to those true incentives for good that I know my experience presents. In short, thought through, Aquinas's position does not lead to inactivity on our part but to fervor for action.

Second, since God causes the free act without detriment to its freedom, we can boldly petition the creator to cause in us the free acts by which we live the moral life. In the very exercise of the will, we are not alone and left to our weaknesses. The creator's causality is there, and it can unfailingly direct our wills to the morally good without introducing any determinism.

The centrality of Aquinas's metaphysics of the act of being, *actus essendi*, is evident here. The ability of this existential metaphysics to handle what some consider to be an intractable problem presents this metaphysics as a high water mark in human thought. But before a Thomist celebrates, others would insist that another problem remains.

---

infinite both reveals itself and hides itself. We see enough of it to be entranced by it. But we are condemned to know it only through its differences and so never know it directly or in itself. When I wrote, drawing from Owens, that we are unable to form any proper concept of the infinite, what I meant was that we had no direct knowledge of the infinite, as we have a direct knowledge of generic notions (also called "univocal") from which we are able to clear away the differences. We have no direct knowledge of the infinite, because in Aquinas the infinite is being and we do not conceptualize being apart from the differences of things. But we do conceptualize it imperfectly as we do, and that suffices for us to employ it in philosophy, especially in a metaphysics in which the first cause is the very nature of being.

THE AVOIDANCE OF DIVINE CULPABILITY

If as subsistent *esse* God causes our free acts of will, is not God a cause of evil? Because some of our choices are horrendously evil, even if we never get to carry them out, it appears that God is a cause of evil. For example, Hitler's decision to kill the Jews was horrendous, and, morally speaking, the decision already made Hitler a murderer, even if his plan never materialized because of some impediment. But as a cause of Hitler's choosing, is not Aquinas's God also a murderer? Are there not two murderers here—the creator and the creature?

Again, Aquinas faces the issue directly. Continuing the above line of metaphysical reflection, Aquinas now makes a distinction. At *In II Sent.* d. 37, q. 2, a. 2c, Aquinas says that God is the cause of the act of sin *as an act* but God is not the cause of the act of sin *as a sin*.

Second, because the action of sinning is a certain kind of being [*quoddam ens*], not only insofar as privations and negations are called beings, but also insofar as a thing existing in a genus is a being because actions themselves are ordered to a genus, it would follow, if the actions of sinning are not from God, that some being having an essence would not be from God, and so God would not be the universal cause of all beings, which is against the perfection of the first being... whence it is not able to be said absolutely that sin is from God, as homicide, or something of this kind, unless with this addition—insofar as it is an act and insofar as it is a being [*unde non potest dici absolute quod peccatum sit a Deo, ut homicidium, aut aliquid hujusmodi, nisi cum hac additione, inquantum est actus et inquantum est ens*].

So, along previously described metaphysical lines, Aquinas explains that God is the cause of the act of sin as an act. Why is God not the cause of sin as sin? Let us begin by turning our focus to *ST* I, 19, 9:

Now the evil that accompanies one good is the privation of another good. Never therefore would evil be sought after, not even accidentally, unless the good that accompanies the evil were more desired than the good of which the evil is the privation. Now God wills no good more than He wills His own goodness; yet He wills one good more than another. Hence He in no way wills the evil of sin, which is the privation of right order towards the divine good.

God in no way wills the evil of sin. For example, fornication is mentioned in the above paragraph. Why? No one would will an evil unless he willed the good to which the evil is attached more than the moral good. So the pleasure to which the evil of fornication is attached, in light of which the fornication appears as good, the fornicator values more. Yet God cannot prefer some good to himself, which he evidently should do anyway, hence God cannot will the evil of sin. So, God cannot join the fornicator in the willing of the evil. For all of God's willing the act of sin as an act, God does not join in willing the merely apparent good. The willing of the merely apparent good appears to be the prerogative of the creature alone.

Now there are a number of issues here. First, what is it about the human that allows the human's will to target the merely apparent good, the good not in line with the moral good? Second, how is God the moral norm? Do all who act morally have God as their moral norm? Some people do not even know that God exists, yet they appear to act morally. Even if God does exist, why should he be the moral norm?

The classic text for Aquinas's treatment of the first issue is *De Malo* I, 3, with parallel passages at *In II Sent.* d. 37, q. 2, a. 2; *De Veritate*, XXIV, 8; *Summa contra Gentiles* III, 10; and *Summa Theologiae* I, 63, 1. I want to begin with *De Malo* I, 3, and we will see where it leads us. The question at *De Malo* I, 3, is whether good is the cause of evil. As ironic as it sounds, Aquinas argues that good is the cause of evil. In the *De Malo* text, he says that this point is most obvious in natural things, things apart from human agency. Defects in natural things come about through the impact of stronger and more perfect things. The more perfect things do not principally aim to introduce the defect but aim to introduce their own qualities. That introduction can necessarily so compromise the

Cosmological Theodicies 233

natural thing that evil follows in the action of the natural thing. An example is the seed that produces stunted plants because of the impact of too much water. The moistening of the seed by the water necessarily compromises the seed so that improper growth results. The technical way of expressing Aquinas's point is to say that evil is basically the *per accidens* effect of integral and good things pursuing some good. The reader will recall that earlier, in chapter 4, I discussed this framework. In order to understand the meaning of *per accidens* intention at I, 19, 9, I consulted *C.G.* III, 6.

Before moving to evil in voluntary matters, I want to note that this explanation has a presupposition. The presupposition is that every being is initially integral and good. This is so because everything is an instance of the good. In other words, nothing afflicted by privation proceeds from the good. Evil appears later when integrally good things clash. This understanding of the genesis of natural defect leaves the identity between the *ratio entis* and the *ratio boni* uncompromised.

Moving to voluntary matters, that is, human choices or decisions, Aquinas says that a partial similarity to natural things exists. There is some similarity because we have a clash. For example, this time the clash is between the will and something pleasurable outside the rule of reason. Aquinas mentions adultery. Here the pleasurable hits the will like the above mentioned water hits the seed. But a dissimilarity also exists. The seed is affected by the water necessarily, but the will is not carried away by the pleasure. Rather, the will itself retains some responsibility for introducing the defect. The will wounds itself. But how can the will wound itself without already being defective and so disproving the thesis that good is the cause of evil? The remainder of the article is an astounding case of philosophical phenomenology as Aquinas describes the original condition of the human will.

In all things of which one thing ought to be the rule and measure of the other, good in the ruled and measured thing is from the fact that it is regulated and conformed to the rule and measure; evil is from the fact that it is not ruled or measured. So, if there is some carpenter who ought to cut rightly according to some rule and if he does not cut directly, which is to cut badly, the bad cutting will be caused by this defect, viz., that the carpenter was without the rule and measure. Similarly, pleasure and each other thing in human affairs must be measured and ruled according to reason and divine law. Whence, the non-use of the rule of reason and of divine law must be understood in the will before the evil choice.

For a thing of this sort, viz., not to consider the above rule, it is not necessary to search for some cause, because for this the freedom of the will suffices, through which the will is able to act and not to act; and not actually considering the rule, taken in itself, is not an evil, fault, or punishment. For the soul does not hold nor is it able to actually hold always the rule. But from [not actually considering the rule taken in itself] is taken in the first place the reason of fault, because without an actual consideration of the rule, [the will] proceeds to some choice; just as the carpenter does not do wrong in this that he does not always hold the measure, but from this that not holding the measure he proceeds to cutting; and similarly the fault of the will is not in this that it does not actually consider the rule of reason and of divine law; but from this that not having the rule or measure it proceeds to choose; and so it is that Augustine says that the will is the cause of sin insofar as it is deficient; but that defect he compares to a silence or shadow, because namely the defect is only a negation.

The key idea for understanding how the will introduces evil into its choices is the will's "nonconsideration of the rule" (*non consideratio regulae*). What is this? First, the nonconsideration cannot be a total and complete cognitive absence of the rule. If the nonconsideration were a complete absence, then the will would do evil without any awareness that it was doing evil. This unawareness would mean that the will's act was not a fault or a sin. Why? To sin means to do evil voluntarily. But voluntary action means action both with knowledge and with will.[55] Hence, to sin the will must have some awareness of the object as evil, and this awareness requires some recognition of the rule.

---

55. For Aquinas sin is a voluntary act, and a voluntary act is one performed with knowledge and will. See *ST* I–II, 6, 2c.

Second, neither can the rule be completely present in our awareness. A complete cognitive presence of the rule would extinguish from the object of an evil choice any and all appearance of good, with the result that the object is impossible to choose. For Aquinas, a minimal condition for our willing anything, even something evil, is that the thing at least "appears" as good. His reason refers to the psychology of willing that I sketched in chapter 2: "The will naturally tends to good as its object. That it sometimes tends to evil happens only because the evil is presented to it under the aspect of good."[56] In contrast to us in this life, the blessed in heaven in the beatific vision have the rule of the good completely present in their consciousness. Consequently, the blessed apprehend all other things as they should be apprehended. Evil appears as the evil that it is, and good appears as the good that it is. Because evil always appears as it is, evil never exercises any attraction over the wills of the blessed. In short, for the blessed evil is never a possible object of choice.

So, the nonconsideration of the rule must mean an incomplete cognitive presence of the rule in virtue of which evil can *appear* as good though still be *known* as evil. In sum, Aquinas says, "consequently there cannot be any sin in the motion of the will so that it tends to evil unless there previously exists some deficiency in the apprehensive power, as a result of which something evil is presented as good."[57] Now, what is the rule? This question should return us to my interpretation of I-II, 94, 2, for the first practical principle: "Do good and avoid evil." In chapter 2, I argued that the subject of this proposition concerned understanding ourselves and others as intellectors of being. Before such a presentation of the nongeneric notion of being our will is not left simply free but it is left also morally necessitated or obliged. Presuming my interpretation, how would the moral rule suffer an eclipse such that the merely apparently good emerges as a possible target of willing?

At *De Ver.* XXIV, 8, Aquinas provides two reasons for the imper-

---

56. *De Ver.* XXIV, 8c; Aquinas, *Truth*, vol. III, 169. Also *ST* I, 19, 9c.
57. *De Ver.* XXIV, 8c; Aquinas, *Truth*, vol. III, 169.

fect cognitive presence of the rule. The first reason is our passions or sense appetites. The passions can arise so that what we saw as evil only becomes known as evil while taking on the appearance of good. For example, in my calm deliberation in the doctor's office and in light of the norm of respect and solicitude for the human, my continual self-abuse of stuffing myself with refined carbohydrates appears as the evil that it is. Yet when I pass a bakery and smell the wonderful confections inside, there is a rush of sense appetite for what I intellectually know is bad for me. In the context of that passion, what I know from memory to be bad for me at least "appears" as good and this is sufficient for me to possibly choose it and so bring about a moral evil. I can do what I know to be wrong. The passion never obliterates my previous knowledge of the baked goods as evil even while they are appearing as good. Their *appearance* as good is the erroneous judgment that Aquinas says is necessary for the evil act.[58]

For humans the passions are a huge source of evil acts. Because passions follow sense apprehension, we can be bombarded by things that incite all kinds of passions that invest something bad—because it is not in line with the first practical precept—with the appearance of good. This is especially the case for us who live in a media culture.

But passion cannot provide the complete explanation for the nonconsideration of the rule. Besides committing crimes of passion, we also commit cold-blooded murder. Moreover, for the theologian Thomas Aquinas not only humans are sinners but also the angels are sinners. But angels are incorporeal beings and so lack the sense appetites that are the passions. In other words, what is the form of the nonconsideration of the rule that applies to intellectual creatures as intellectual? Aquinas presents another way sin

---

58. "The fact that something appears good in the particular to the reason, which yet is not good, is due to a passion; and yet this particular judgment [*iudicium*] is contrary to the universal knowledge of reason." *ST* I–II, 77, 2, ad 2m; Pegis, *Basic Writings of Thomas Aquinas*, vol. II, 634.

Cosmological Theodicies 237

can take place. Since this way is more common, shared by us and by the angels, it offers the more profound explanation of how evil acts of will can take place.

Aquinas says that in this second case "sin does not presuppose ignorance but merely absence of consideration of the things which ought to be considered."[59] And earlier in *De Malo* I, 3c, he says that for this mere absence of consideration the freedom of the creature suffices: "ad hoc sufficit ipsa libertas voluntatis." By mentioning the creature's freedom, Aquinas is referencing the will's state of indifference to all finite things, thanks to their cognitional juxtaposition to being as the good. Above in chapter 2, I discussed this state. I mentioned the state's absence of obligation, or moral necessity. In this state, before all things I am with complete indifference. I am in this state before I become aware of obligation, and I fall back into it after becoming aware of obligation. To use some terminology from computer programming, this state is my "default position."

The appearance of moral necessity as expressed in the first practical precept requires further concentration. This is understandable in terms of Aquinas's epistemology. To initially grasp obligation, we have to grasp as the good ourselves as intellectors of being. But our cognitive attention is first directed to things. The knower is known subsequently by a reflection from things to the knower.[60] This reflec-

---

59. *ST* I, 63, 1, ad 4m; Pegis, *Basic Writings of Thomas Aquinas*, vol. I, 587.

60. See Aquinas's *Commentary on the Metaphysics* XII, lect. 11, no. 2608, on Aristotle's remark "But science, perception, opinion and thought always seem to be about something else and only indirectly about themselves." Of course, as subsistent forms angels know in the opposite manner. They first know themselves and their ideas and then other things. Hence, the "default" position of their awareness is different. It is a knowledge of creation that does not include the creator's decisions about supernatural elevation. The divine announcement of those decisions is over and above the angel's natural knowledge. Hence, things can appear as good to the angel while still being known as possibly out of line with the creator's *de facto* providence. The angel would sin by choosing without regard and deference for the creator's designs. See, *ST* I, 63, 1. For commentary see "Appendix 2" in Blackfriars's translation of the *Summa Theologiae* (New York: McGraw-Hill Book Company, 1968), 311–20 and Jacques Maritain, *The Sin of the Angel* (Westminster, Md.: The Newman Press, 1959).

tion is a mental effort over and beyond our original knowledge of things and the presence of the notion of being in them.

So it is not strange for Aquinas to say that the "soul does not hold nor is it able to actually hold always the rule." We can let the thought of the rational creature as an epiphany of being slip out of focus. When that happens, we revert to the prior state of freedom. In that state things are no longer seen against the rule but seen only against the *ratio entis*. This will mean that things not good in relation to the rule will still appear as good in relation to being. As such they are possible objects of choice, and if chosen, evil will be done.

At this point, a reader could consider John Crosby. While honestly trying to be more phenomenlogically accurate than the Thomist tradition on the willing of evil, Crosby misses this default position of the will. He argues that the will possesses a scope wider than the *ratio boni*. The will also acts under another *ratio*: the *ratio* of the merely subjectively satisfying.[61] Crosby argues for the presence of the second *ratio* based on a case study that reveals the usual analysis of the relation between the will and the good to be "phenomenologically very deficient."[62] The case is Cain's murder of Abel. By the usual analysis, Cain's act is the result of a misconception about "what threatens the integrity of his being."[63] Cain perceives God's acceptance of Abel as such a threat. In other words, the will is still fundamentally ordered to the objective good, what is "really perfective of me."[64] Cain, however, misunderstands that order insofar as Cain sees Abel as a threat to Cain's integrity. Crosby objects that if the usual analysis were true, then it would be easy to straighten out Cain. But all explanations of why God's acceptance of Abel is not threatening "would talk right past him."[65] The disconnect shows

61. "The will, then, has an alternative to the *ratio boni*, namely the *ratio* of the merely subjectively satisfying." John Crosby, "Is All Evil Really Only Privation?" *Proceedings of the American Catholic Philosophical Association*, 75 (2002), 206. For another presentation of Crosby, see his "How Is It Possible Knowingly to Do Wrong?" *Proceedings of the American Catholic Philosophical Association* 74 (2001), 325–33.

62. Crosby, "Is All Evil," 205. 63. Ibid., 204.
64. Ibid., 206. 65. Ibid., 205.

that Cain is fascinated with his own integrity in a manner that falls outside the good. Crosby says that Cain regards himself as the only one who should find acceptance with God.

In replying to Crosby I do not want to be taken as defending the traditional position of which Crosby speaks. Rather, I wish to reply on the basis of my understanding of Aquinas's psychology that I have been describing. Hence, I would maintain that Crosby is failing to realize that the *ratio boni* that is the first object of the will is not the *ratio boni* as it plays a role in the first moral norm: do good and avoid evil. In the first sense, the *ratio boni* leaves us simply free before any being which as *a* good is not *the* good and so does not have to be willed. It is no surprise that in such a situation the will might choose a good that is not really perfective of me. For the moral good to appear, a reflective knowledge of being is necessary, aka the good, within one's own intellection. Then one is confronted by a good that leaves one both free and morally necessitated.

So in his focus on the *ratio* of the subjectively satisfying, Crosby is still at the first psychic stage only and is failing to realize the presence of the *ratio boni* that is the object of the will and whose first effect is the will's simple freedom before all finite goods. Moreover, the ability of the *ratio boni*, at this stage, to play its second trick of engendering faux epiphanies of being easily accommodates Crosby's case study. Cain's estimate of himself is another case of a faux epiphany of being. Like Rachel who, as I explained in chapter 2, so values her children that she cannot tolerate good brought about somewhere else, Cain so values himself that he cannot tolerate a divine favor showered on another. Cain's estimate of himself as "the apple of God's eye" is understandable. It derives from the singularity of his labor which is conveyed to its fruits that Cain offers in sacrifice to God. That singularity, like the minute, is what usurps being in Cain's mind so that to him his sacrifice possesses a worth out of all proportion to the truth. That exalted worth is what is offended by a good brought about elsewhere. The drama of the incident is fully within the ambit of the *ratio boni* understood as the *ratio entis*.

Crosby may have scored a point against the traditional position insofar as the traditional position appears to understand the *ratio boni* very narrowly as "what really perfects me." But what Crosby calls the *ratio* of the subjectively satisfying falls under that *ratio boni* as it is convertible with the *ratio entis*. In that larger sense, the *ratio boni* also has a role in our psychology of willing. I fail to see a deficiency of phenomenology in Aquinas's psychology, at least as I understand that psychology.

So the "defect" here is an absence of consideration of the rule. This "defect" is not so much a defect that it is an evil. A true evil is a lack of something that should be there, for example, lack of sight in a man, but not lack of sight in a rock. But the absence of consideration of the rule should be there so that the creature is free and freedom is a good. Yet the absence is not so natural that it escapes the will, for the will acts in this state with the knowledge that it could, and should, act with a consideration of the rule.

So from reading I, 19, 9c, the answer to our first question is that passions and the default state of human freedom enable the human to entertain the merely apparent good. Both of these points enable human psychology to be in a state of seeing something as good that it knows to be evil. As Aquinas says at *De Malo* I, 3c and *C.G.* IV, 52 (on the existence of original sin), there is nothing defective or evil about this psychology. We are not always able to carry around the rule, and naturally our soul does not so dominate the body that sense appetites contrary to reason are impossible. In these states, the absence of consideration of the rule is not a defect in the sense of a privation, that is, something that ought to be there, even though the absence enables evils to appear as good. In other words, for all of its being a condition for evil choice, the absence of consideration of the rule is not itself an evil. As noted, Aquinas calls it a mere negation, not a privation. Hence, Aquinas maintains that evil only comes from good. Only in the context of an actual choosing does the absence take on the character of a privation.

The carpenter analogy mentioned above in *De Malo* I, 3, illustrates this point. If you have ever tried, freehand, to cut a line perpendicular to the edge of a board, you will know that it is almost impossible. You may get lucky and do it, but usually you will be off, plus or minus, the ninety degrees. Hence, a norm in carpentry is to use the ruler. A variation of this rule is "Measure twice, cut once." But unfortunately, my arm is not the ruler, and so I am not always able to carry around the ruler. Also, by laziness, lack of time, false confidence (it's a small board), cutting without the ruler looks good. Hence, I can choose to cut freehand. Even if I am lucky and cut straight, I still did something wrong and am a bad carpenter. The wrong was choosing apart from the norm to use the ruler. Here the absence of the norm is a defect in the craft of carpentry. Good carpenters should not make a choice with that absence.

The presentation of what is evil as something good is a prerogative of human psychology, for only the created will in its natural state can sometimes be in the condition of nonconsideration of the rule.[66] The psychology fails to apply to God. That is why Aquinas says that God cannot will the act of sin as sin. Obviously, as a spiritual being God lacks a sensitive nature, and so the passions play no role in the divine psychology. What about the second reason for the rule's nonconsideration, namely, the rule's reflexive presence in our awareness? The order in the divine knowledge precludes this reason. God knows and knows himself first and foremost.[67] But as *esse subsistens*, the intelligible heart of the *ratio entis*, what God is is not just an epiphany of being but an analogate of being that is the analogon. Hence, by using points known in the psychol-

---

66. This psychology is the context for appreciating Maritain's enigmatic expression that in the line of evil the creature is a first cause and its effect is to "nihilate." See Jacques Maritain, *St. Thomas and the Problem of Evil* (Milwaukee: Marquette University Press, 1942), 33–35. This nihilation is the introduction of deficiency into the act of will subsequent to being able to entertain the merely apparently good.

67. See *C.G.* I, 48.

ogy of human morality, one can claim that the moral norm to be respectful and solicitous of epiphanies of being is front and center in the divine consciousness and that the norm takes the particular form of God's necessarily being faithful to himself. In other words, God sees everything in and through the moral norm that is himself. For example, God sees fornication, that is, willful sex outside of marriage, for the evil that it is. By targeting the pleasure of an essentially procreative act outside of marriage, the fornicator acts against the good of the human species which in turn is meant to be a special reflection of the creator. For God to join in this willing would be for God to prefer something more than himself, as Aquinas claims at I, 19, 9.

Hence, the creature alone makes it possible for God to dispense *esse* that actuates the act of sin. When God dispenses the *esse* that actuates the act of sin, any defect in that act has its origin from the created will. The existence of the created will in its natural state allows *esse* to be given in such a way that a defective act will result. Because of the created will to which the *esse* is going, *esse* can be specified in a way not possible otherwise. In sum, *esse* is rendered the act of a defective act not because of God from whom it comes but from the creature to which it is going.

How, then, does the analogy with the bent leg and the created will go? Aquinas mentions this analogy throughout his career. He mentions it early at *In II Sent.* d. 37, q. 2, a. 3c, and late at *ST* I, 49, 2, ad 2m. A translation of the first, that continues Aquinas's noted thesis that God is the cause of the act of sin as a *quoddam ens*, is:

> For in all things in which a defect happens from the second cause but not the first cause, it is necessary that whatever is in the deficient effect of essence and goodness proceeds wholly from the first. That the defect is reduced to the second deficient cause is evident from limping which is from the walking power, by the mediation of the tibia, through which, viz., the curvature of the tibia, slanting in the walking of the limper results; whence, whatever is there of walking, is wholly from the walking power; but defect, or slanting of the walking, is not from the walking power, but

from the tibia alone. Similarly also is the order of God to the created will just as a first cause to a second cause. So from the part of God no defect is able to happen; the created will, however, is able to defect. And so whatever is in the deficient act, namely of a sin, of the nature of act, and of being, and of good [*de ratione actus, et entis, et boni*], this wholly from the first agent, namely God, proceeds by the mediating will; but the defect itself which is in the act, in this way is from the will that it does not proceed from God. And so whatever name signifies deformity at the same time with the act, either in general or in particular, it is not able to be said that it is simply from God. Whence it is not able to be said absolutely that sin is from God, as homicide, or something of this kind, unless with this addition, insomuch as it is an act and insomuch as it is a being.

Just as the causality of the motive power is rendered defective because of the curvature in the leg, so too God's causing of the act of will can be rendered defective because of the will's nonconsideration of the rule through which what is actually evil can at least appear as good. Note that the analogy between the bent leg and the created will is also inexact. The leg cannot but limp, cannot but do something defective. The will, though, can do good. All of its choices do not have to be defective. When they are defective, however, the source of the defect is traced to the will itself.

Finally, the second question posed to us by I, 19, 9c, was why does Aquinas say that the evil of sin is the privation of right order toward the divine good. Some sinners would find this ridiculous. God is not even on their radar screens. But does not even my gloss of 94, 2, indicate the same puzzle? How is the moral norm of the human understood as an intellector of being congruent with moral rectitude being an order toward the divine good? The first is a creature, the second is the creator. But the integration appears when one recalls that for Aquinas the nature of the creator is the *ratio essendi*, the key component of the *ratio entis*. So fidelity to our fellows as intellectors of being is at bottom, though we may not recognize it, a fidelity to God himself. By orientating our moral compass to being, we are orientating ourselves to God, though we may not be aware of this for quite a while. Certainly if our fellows demand respect and solicitude as intellectors of being, then *a fortiori* as the instantiation of being God demands from us the same. So the two are congruent.

Returning to I, 19, 9c, God in no way wills the evil of sin. Only the creature can will the act of sin as sin. Without joining in the willing of the evil of sin, God can cause the act of sin as an act. But the act of sin as a sin, God can only will to *permit* for some good, for example, freedom in the natural state, or will to *order* to some good, for example, the manifestation of the patience of the martyrs. In the end the philosopher has only a guess as to what the goods are for which God both permits and orders the evil of sin.

A THOMISTIC FREE WILL DEFENSE?

I have argued that Aquinas's understanding of God's relation to the created free act would not allow Aquinas to make the free will defense described by Mackie. But would Aquinas, nevertheless, make some kind of free will defense? Yes, and my previous pages have already noted Aquinas doing so. But the recent material above makes Aquinas's thinking stand out. In particular, if God moves our wills without detriment to the will's ability to do otherwise, then final causes remain real and genuine prompts and incentives. Unfortunately, man's natural state surrounds humans with prompts against right reason. Hence, it is no surprise that the choices that God causes are choices in which he permits evil to be done. In other words, in the natural order, human free will is bombarded by lures or final causes that dispose it to vice rather than to virtue. As I quoted Aquinas at *C.G.* IV, 54, because of the "frailty of reason" we arrive at truth with difficulty and are easily overcome again and again by our "beastly appetites." As I also mentioned, this same frailty explains Aquinas's claim at *De Ver.* V, 5, that this same human providence explains the greater number of failures in human affairs than those in natural nonhuman affairs. My point is, again, that since God acts on the human will without introducing a determinism, then promptings for ignorance and vice remain alive and genuine. It should be no surprise, then, that the free acts that God realizes in creatures reflect this situation. So only with effort and much wandering in circles is an advance to virtue precariously made. From the viewpoint of human nature as such, you would not expect anything else.

It cannot be said too often that we are now in a different metaphysical universe from Mackie's fourth theistic defense. Aquinas's metaphysics has only one first cause, the fourth defense has two. Before a theist selects a free will defense, a theist should select a metaphysics. By investigating Aquinas's thinking behind his claims that God works in our will without detriment to the will's ability to do otherwise, and that God causes the act of sin only as an act and not as sin, I have tried to open the reader's mind to the truth of the Thomistic metaphysical alternative.

RICHARD SWINBURNE: NATURE AS A NECESSARY DISPLAY CASE FOR OUR KNOWLEDGE OF GOOD AND EVIL

In his *The Existence of God* and while discussing the problem of evil in chapter 11, Richard Swinburne argues that a moral choice for God occurs in a world where, among other things to be mentioned below, "the sufferers are not always those who benefit."[68] This remark locates Swinburne's handling of evil in the cosmological category. His handling of the problem of evil unfolds as follows. God has good reason to create beings with a free will able to be exercised on weighty matters of good and evil. Swinburne describes such a will as having a choice of destiny. For Swinburne we can become aware of these matters only *a posteriori*. As he says, "It is a very deep philosophical truth that by and large all knowledge comes from experience."[69] What is the experience for our knowledge of weighty matters of good and evil? The experience is an inductive knowledge of natural effects. Nature and its workings pro-

---

68. Richard Swinburne, *The Existence of God* (Oxford: at the Clarendon Press, 1979), 218.
69. Ibid., 214.

vide us with an acquaintance with objects that will determine our choices as good or bad ones. For example, tragic results for sheep that encounter tigers indicate what would be a good or a bad choice for us. Likewise, cows that perish from walking into bogs indicate another.

But since there might be some doubt about whether humans are included in this inductive knowledge arrived at from an observation of sheep and cows, nature must do two things. First it must instruct us with examples of humans meeting tigers and humans walking into bogs. Swinburne remarks, "If men are to have knowledge of the evil which will result from their actions or negligence, laws of nature must operate regularly; and that means that there will be what I may call 'victims of the system.'"[70] Second, to produce sure inductive knowledge in us, these victims must be "many."[71]

Swinburne asks whether God could avoid these evils by giving us knowledge of the effects of our actions outside of normal inductive inference. The entertained alternative is God directly giving us this knowledge by "saying out loud" not to do this. Swinburne says that this approach would make God so immediate to us that we would have "little temptation" to do wrong. We would know that God is watching our every choice and so we would lack a motive for doing evil, and thus lose a choice of destiny.[72]

To this reasoning Swinburne adds two arguments. A world without natural evils would deprive humans of the opportunity to show themselves at their noblest and also deprive them of a certain "gladness" derived from watching or participating in a tragedy. This last reason is not elaborated. But perhaps Swinburne is referring to how an experience with tragedy makes us appreciate the good. For example, after fighting through the Pacific battles of Peleliu and Okinawa, E. B. Sledge admitted that he gained a lasting appreciation of the simple goods of clean socks and dry shoes.[73]

70. Ibid., 210.
71. Ibid., 207.
72. Ibid., 212.
73. E. B. Sledge, *China Marine: An Infantryman's Life after World War II* (Oxford: Oxford University Press, 2002), 150.

Cosmological Theodicies 247

Subsequent to these three arguments Swinburne clarifies God's relation to natural evil by arguing that God has the right to inflict harm on some so that others may realize a choice of destiny. Swinburne does this by providing three reasons for denying a similarity of God to creatures through the example of a doctor who employs patients as involuntary guinea pigs. First, unlike the doctor's situation, prior to God's creating there are no "patients" to ask for their consent. Second, as partial causes of their children, parents can let one child suffer for the sake of another. But God is the total cause of our existence, hence God can intend much more. Third, our hesitancy with inflicting suffering derives from ignorance. But God knows exactly how much men will suffer, and what the effects of that suffering will be. Hence, God possesses the right to inflict harm. By these arguments Swinburne reveals that for him God is very much in control of natural evils. In fact God is intending them for good results at least in some.

Finally, in light of choices for destiny, aposteriorism, and the need for repetitive personal experience with natural evil so that inductive knowledge of evil is certain, Swinburne believes that the present quantity of evil is not an objection against God's existence. A last remark indicates a partial basis in philosophical psychology for this claim: "The argument against this from the existence of such evil as we find in our world, I have claimed, stems from a failure to appreciate the deepest needs of men and other conscious beings, and a failure to appreciate the strength of the logical constraints on the kinds of world which God can make."[74]

There have been worthy intrinsic criticisms of Swinburne. Among these criticisms Eleonore Stump incisively wonders if natural evils like cancer, tornadoes, and droughts are necessary in order to have significant free choices, like Belsen and Hiroshima.[75] I will not repeat this criticism but there is something to it, and some-

---

74. Ibid., 224.
75. From a Thomistic perspective, one could add concerns with Swinburne conceiving free creatures as first causes and having God will, instead of permit, *quandoque* evils.

thing like it can be elaborated from the perspective of Aquinas. In short, being in the state of innocence with all of its supernatural gifts still left our first parents with choices of destiny. This fact suggests that from a Thomistic angle Swinburne is missing something.

But before I make a critical engagement of Aquinas and Swinburne, I want to say that a reader of Swinburne would hear many apparent echoes of Aquinas.[76] Both Swinburne and Aquinas share a strong a posteriori view of human knowledge. Yet perhaps because of the empiricist bias of the British philosophical tradition, Swinburne never explicitly mentions what for Aquinas is the fruit of that knowledge, the *ratio entis*. Also, Swinburne's insistence on the reasonableness of God's intention to create beings with a choice of destiny sounds like *C.G.* III, 112, which argues for a providential ordering of things for the sake of the rational creature. Moreover, Swinburne's claim that part of man's end lies in a knowledge and worship of God seems to reiterate the fourth primary precept of natural law at *ST* I-II, 94, 2. Even God's right to inflict punishment seems to have a semblance to Aquinas on the Abraham and Isaac case. Also, the need for reasonable motives for choice, both human and divine, expresses the basic priority of intellect to will in Aquinas's psychology. Finally, the good of helping one another expresses the Aristotelian or Thomistic idea of the good of society and Aquinas's third primary precept in particular.

Yet scratching the surface reveals significant differences. As mentioned, Swinburne says that he finds all of the above congruent with our "deepest desires." For a Thomist these desires are not deep enough. Swinburne's psychology never crosses into the intellection of being, and the will's love of the same, with the subsequent linkage to freedom and obligation. In other words, Swinburne's description of the human is excellent topography but woeful geology. The importance of this superficiality means that

---

76. The following list comes from characteristics of Swinburne's World IV, the world God has a reason to create. See Swinburne, *The Existence of God*, 195.

Cosmological Theodicies 249

other than nature and its laws Swinburne misses a more fundamental basis for ethics and so compromises his treatment of the problem of evil.

Even before we know the relation between tigers and other higher mammals, buildings and fault zones, cows and bogs, we are aware of an obligation to be respectful and solicitous to ourselves and others. This fact of obligation is *a posteriori* but not *a posteriori* upon nature and its laws as Swinburne describes. Rather, the obligation is *a posteriori* upon our mental life. Obligation arises as the response to a heightened presence of being as the good within us and our fellows thanks to our intellectual capacity. Intellection of the analogon draws the analogon more intensely to those analogates who are intellectors. This insight demands that freedom in respect to those analogates be exercised in a respectful manner. Does not this human psychology already provide enough ethical material to confront us with choices of destiny? Am I going to hate my colleague or love him? If the former, then am I going lie to him or to slander him? And what does the hate, the lying, and the slandering do to me and the respect that I should have for myself? The drama in these choices seems to be substantial enough to qualify as choices of destiny. Yet the inductive knowledge of the consequences of our actions has not yet appeared on the scene. In other words, I seem to think that lying about others, for example, is wrong and significantly so, but that this has nothing to do with an inductive knowledge of nature and the results of my actions within it. I agree that this inductive knowledge can be utilized, but when it is utilized, it will be incorporated into an ethical concern that has already been established on other grounds. So what Swinburne describes is not so much false as incomplete. Aquinas's approach to morality does not require that natural evils be forced to play this exclusive role in human decision making beyond good reason. Also, *quandoque* evils can be basically understood as incidental effects of a natural world that reflects the goodness of the creator, even though it is full of contingency because the agents are all movers. Hence, not all of these *quandoque* evils need be ordered to human decision making.

Another indication of the above lacuna is a remark that Swinburne makes about the knowledge of an afterlife in World IV. Such a world is the one Swinburne thinks God has good reason to create and is most like our own world. Such a world involves death, but Swinburne says that God would have good reason to preserve us in some part of the world after we have ceased to exist in our part. Nevertheless, "if the advantages of a world with death are to remain ... the future existence must in no way be foreknown for certain by agents (else there would be no opportunity in our part of the world for choices of great seriousness)."[77] The idea is that since I know that both you and I will survive, then it is of small significance how I treat you and myself. What a blindness results to the good in the person right now! Even if we will survive, we are presently of precious value and that fact makes its own demands. It is a fact not threatened even by a certain knowledge of the afterlife. To believe that it is so threatened indicates a weak grasp of the current value of the person.

My point has been that Aquinas, who is like Swinburne an aposteriorist, has a more fundamental basis for the drama of morality. That basis is the life of the mind understood as an intellection of being. Unlike Swinburne (and I could also refer back to Hick), Aquinas is not led to tragically overplay the soul-making purpose of natural evils. But there is another way of expressing this difference. Aquinas sees human development properly occurring not within the sound and fury of *quandoque* evils but within the peace and tranquility of an ordered society. Speaking of securing the primary good of contemplation of God, Aquinas says:

> In fact, all other human operations seem to be ordered to this one, as to an end. For, there is needed for the perfection of contemplation a soundness of body, to which all the products of art that are necessary for life are di-

---

77. Swinburne, *The Existence of God*, 196.

rected. Also required are freedom from the disturbances of the passions—this is achieved through the moral virtues and prudence—and freedom from external disorders, to which the whole program of government in civil life is directed. And so, if they are rightly considered, all human functions may be seen to subserve the contemplation of truth.[78]

Aquinas presents the norm of human life and that for which we should strive as one free of disturbances. Philosophers like Swinburne and Hick would probably regard such a social state as too "bourgeois."[79] Such a society is too peaceful to be the hothouse necessary for the growth of the "higher-order goods." But if they did so react, they would betray their superficiality. Yes, there is the heroism of the soldier, fireman, policeman, and others; but there is also the heroism of the person who chooses against the motives for jealousy, character assassination, infidelity, blasphemy, and so forth that exist even in Aquinas's scenario.

Finally, because of this more fundamental drama of the life of the mind, it is not impossible to conceive a sufficiently imaginative metaphysician, perhaps encouraged by Biblical revelation, discerning the possibility of the creator establishing humans in a supernatural state that exempts them from natural evils yet nevertheless includes a moral challenge that is a choice of destiny.[80] Discerning that possibility would mean, however, that even if a theodicy like Swinburne's was comprehensive and did not leave some evil unexplained, the theodicy could not be definitive. This possibility would create the further possibilities that now the truth about human life is that it is a fall from an initial supernatural state and perhaps aimed to a restoration. There is no answer because there are too many possible answers.

---

78. *C.G.* III, 37, *Ad hanc etiam omnes*; Thomas Aquinas, *Summa contra Gentiles*, vol. III, translated by Vernon J. Bourke (Notre Dame, Ind.: University of Notre Dame Press, 1975), pt. I, 124.

79. Swinburne, *The Existence of God*, 195 and 215.

80. On the created state of the first humans, *ST* I, 94–102.

BRUCE REICHENBACH: DEVELOPING PLANTINGA AND SWINBURNE

In his *Evil and a Good God*, Bruce Reichenbach constructs theodicies both for moral evil and natural evil. These theodicies draw upon many of the theses of the above cosmological theodicists. For example, Reichenbach more radically employs Plantinga's free will defense since Reichenbach will not include a divine knowledge of counterfactuals. For natural evil, he appears to create a twist on Swinburne's thesis that the exercise of creaturely free will demands a world functioning according to natural laws. I would like to look at each of Reichenbach's theodicies and engage Aquinas's thinking with them.

Chapter 4 presents Reichenbach's theodicy for moral evil. Reichenbach understands moral evil to be "all the instances of pain and suffering—physical and mental—and all states of affairs significantly disadvantageous to the organism which are caused by actions for which human agents can be held morally blameworthy."[81] The theodicy is quite simple and direct. Reichenbach provides it on the opening page. In sum, since a world with free persons is superior to one without free persons, God creates such a world, and so God cannot be held responsible for the evils persons may choose to do.

One objection mentioned is the following. It is logically possible that a free agent will always choose the good. Since God's omnipotence includes the logically possible, then God could have realized only free agents that always choose the good. Finally, God's goodness would have motivated God to do so. Hence, Reichenbach's theodicy fails to explain why there must be moral evil.

In reply, Reichenbach points out that the reader has seen this

---

81. Bruce R. Reichenbach, *Evil and a Good God* (New York: Fordham University Press, 1982), xi. A Thomist would insist that the will's interior act of choice is also a locus of great moral evil. Accordingly, even if Hitler never got to carry out his plans for the Holocaust, his decision to do so was already a great moral evil. In sum, from a Thomist perspective, it is not only wrong to commit murder, for example; it is also wrong to intend to commit murder.

Cosmological Theodicies 253

objection in chapter 1. At that time Reichenbach asserted that the realization of free agents always choosing good is *ultimately* up to the free agents, not to God their creator. To say otherwise is to say that God causes the choice. But since causation equals determination, the choice is not able to be otherwise, that is, not able to be free. Reichenbach finishes by noting that his rejoinder does not diminish God's omnipotence because for God to be the cause of our free act involves a contradiction.

Reichenbach says that his objector might concede the above rejoinder but insist that through his omniscience, God can actualize beings that are always good. Reichenbach reminds the reader that this scenario was also discussed and rejected in chapter 1. Here he reminds us that the omniscience that his objector is ascribing to God includes counterfactuals of free will, viz., what I would be doing if I were not living in Houston or not teaching philosophy. Reiterating reasoning from his chapter 1, Reichenbach sees no way to explain how omniscience could include counterfactuals. He explains that God's omniscience means that God knows all true propositions But there seems to be no way counterfactual propositions could be true. First, they cannot be true by correspondence to their actual existence for there is never any such existence. Second they cannot be true by correspondence to the actual existence of the cause of the situation. But the cause *as free* does not contain the counterfactual in a way that could produce certain knowledge. In short, no matter how well you knew me, you could not tell with certitude what I would choose to do if I were not living in Houston and not teaching philosophy.[82]

---

82. Reichenbach does add one further reply to the omniscience scenario. His reply begins by granting God's foreknowledge of counterfactuals of free will. He then compares God's realization of only morally good agents with my selecting a xerox machine that produces only 11 by 14 inch size copies. Just as it is inappropriate to say that the machine has a freedom to do this, so too Reichenbach thinks that it is inappropriate to say that the divinely selected moral agents freely do good. Reichenbach acknowledges that the moral agents are not *causally* required to do good acts as the machine is causally required to produce copies

Reichenbach's theodicy for moral evil presents an opportunity for Aquinas to offer a critique of an assumption also present in a number of other previously considered theodicies like those of Plantinga, Hick, Stump, and Swinburne. Most basically expressed this assumption is that there can be an effect higher than its cause. In particular, the assumption is that God can cause a creature that he cannot control. Such a creature is one that is free. As so creating, it is maintained, God limits himself.

It is generally maintained by theists that God can limit himself in various ways without at the same time sacrificing his omnipotence. In particular, God limits himself in the creation of human persons who possess free will, for if human persons truly are free with respect to a particular state of affairs, then it cannot be the case that God can control them so that they will choose to bring about or will bring about that state of affairs. Put another way, God's causing them to do action A seems to be incompatible with their freely doing A. Thus it might be claimed that in creating persons who perform a very significant number of free acts and who thus might be appropriately termed free persons, God has made things which he subsequently cannot control.[83]

Echoing Reichbach's own critique of S. Paul Schilling who, unlike Reichenbach, holds for a God finite in power,[84] Aquinas could ask Reichenbach how creatures end up having an ability to act completely independent of the creator. In other words, how can crea-

---

of one size. But he insists that because of the *preselection* in both cases, the difference is not significant. The preselection, not the copier, necessitates the 11 by 14 inch copies. Likewise, the result which is the morally good action is necessitated by God's preselection of the agent that will perform it. In other words, because of the preselection, neither the machine nor the moral agent "could do otherwise." Consequently, the actual results are all necessary. Hence, omniscience, as it would involve knowledge of counterfactuals, is incompatible with free moral agents. I wish to make a comment here. This is an interesting example but in the end, in my opinion, it contains a modal confusion. Granting a divine preselection based on a knowledge of counterfactuals, the conclusion is not that all things *could* not be otherwise but rather *will* not be otherwise. "Will not" does not equal "can not." So the merely *de facto* necessity here leaves room for a possibility to be otherwise in human acts.

83. Reichenbach, *Evil and a Good God*, 165.
84. Ibid., 170–71.

tures be anything other than secondary causes? Again, according to Reichenbach's position creatures seem to rise to the status of opposing gods. Does this make sense? Can the dependent be what is independent? Reichenbach cannot appeal to one human producing another with their own freedom. There is no analogy here to the creator and creature. The creature is constantly dependent upon the creator, while the produced human is not constantly dependent upon its parent.

My point is similar to Aquinas's first argument at *In II Sent.* d. 37, q. 2, a. 2c that I quoted above in my discussion of Mackie's fourth criticism. Aquinas is dealing with those who claim that God is not the cause of the act of sin insofar as it is an act. Aquinas first counters that such a position is wrong because it would assert that many first principles exist. To avoid this result the proponents readjust their position: "the will through itself is able to produce action without the influence of a prior agent, nevertheless it has being [*esse*] from another." Strictly speaking, then, the will is not a first cause. The proponents' modified position seems to be exactly that of the free creature envisaged by Reichenbach and other theodicists. Aquinas's final counter is that it is contradictory [*inconveniens*] to say that what does not have being from itself is able to act by itself. The contradiction appears by reductions of the action to the power and then of the power to the thing's essence. Hence, if the essence is caused, then the action is caused. To say otherwise is a contradiction. In other words, how can a creature jump out of the divine causality and act on its own? In terms of what ability to act would the creature act on its own? An effect seems to rise higher than its cause here.

A few lines later in the text Aquinas drives the point home again by utilizing his metaphysics of *esse*. As a certain kind of being, a *quoddam ens*, the free act must also be caused by the first cause of existence. The created free agent cannot be the first cause of its free action. Rather, the created free agent proceeds to that action subsequent to the first cause of existence, providing the existence (*esse*) that actuates the action. Of metaphysical necessity, the creature is a secondary cause of its act, even the free acts that are its choices.

If Aquinas is considered to be, as he usually is, a classical theist, then he is at odds with many current classical theists on the issue of God's causality of the creature's free act. The latter believe it to be self-evident that God can exert no causality here. That assumption is packaged into what is called the "free-will" defense of theism from the problem of evil. For metaphysical reasons Aquinas would not adopt this strategy. It is important to note that even the Augustine and Molina understanding has God causing the free act itself. Instead of appealing to a divine efficient causality, it appeals to the final causality of divinely known *de facto* efficacious motives. Augustine, Aquinas, and Molina, would all agree with the condemnation of semi-Pelagianism at the Second Council of Orange in 529.[85] I would argue that under the pressure of that extrinsic norm, Christian theologians developed extremely interesting and profound philosophical explanations of the relation between the creator and the created free will. The current discussion of the truth of counterfactuals has given new life to the Augustine and Molina approaches, though not without serious criticism. Perhaps a renewed interest in the existence of things as a *sui generis* attribute[86] will spur interest in Aquinas's metaphysics of *esse* and his approach on God's causing of the creature's free choices.

---

85. "If anyone asserts that without the grace of God mercy is divinely given to us when we believe, will, desire, try, labor, pray, watch, study, seek, ask, urge, but does not confess that through the infusion and the inspiration of the Holy Spirit in us, it is brought about that we believe, wish, or are able to do all these things as we ought, and does not join either to human humility or obedience the help of grace, nor agree that it is by the gift of His grace that we are obedient and humble, he opposes the Apostle who says: What have you, that you have not received? [1 Cor 4:70]; and: By the grace of God I am that which I am [1 Cor 15:10; cf. St. Augustine and St. Prosper of Aquitaine]." From Heinrich Denzinger, *The Sources of Catholic Dogma*, translated by R. J. Deferrari (St. Louis: Herder, 1957), 76. The Council's point can be seen in Aquinas's position on whether our merits precede our predestination, e.g., *ST* I, 23, 5.

86. See Barry Miller, *The Fullness of Being: A New Paradigm for Existence* (Notre Dame, Ind.: University of Notre Dame Press, 2002).

Cosmological Theodicies   257

Reichenbach considers a theodicy for natural evils a more difficult task than the theodicy for moral evils. With natural evils there is no intermediary of free beings upon whom we can shift responsibility. God is the creator and sustainer of nature, and so God seems to bear the responsibility for natural evils. In chapter 5 of *Evil and a Good God*, Reichenbach argues that natural evils are not willed by God but are the unintended consequences of something he does will—a world operating according to natural laws: "In general what I want to argue is that the natural evils which human persons (and animals) experience (by and large) are not willed by God, but are the consequences of the outworking upon sentient creatures of the natural laws according to which God's creation operates."[87] Finally, God wills such a world because it is necessary for the existence of free moral agents.

Reichenbach elaborates this theodicy by asking us to consider the alternative—a world operating by miracle. Why is this the alternative? The answer is that in a world operating by natural laws, the actions of things would end up producing evils. To avoid these evils, the alternative is to have God himself do everything. God alone would be acting, just as happens in a miracle. Significantly, a miracle is defined as "a special act of God whereby for a moral or spiritual purpose he produces in nature a new being or mode of being."[88] It has been noted that this definition of miracle appears to preclude God from doing the same miracle twice.[89] That interpretation of Reichenbach goes a long way to making clear his problems with a world working by miracle.

Reichenbach sees three problems with a conception of a miraculous world. The first problem is the elimination of free moral

---

87. Reichenbach, *Evil and a Good God*, 101. "Natural Evils" are "all the instances of pain and suffering—physical and mental—and all states of affairs significantly disadvantageous to the organism which are caused by actions for which human agents cannot be held morally blameworthy." Ibid., xi.

88. Ibid., 102.

89. "On a plausible interpretation of this definition God could never perform the same miracle twice since on the second time around he would not be creating a *new* being or mode of being." Michael Martin, "Reichenbach on Natural Evil," *Religious Studies* 24 (1988), 92.

agents.⁹⁰ Reichenbach explains that since God is doing everything, God's causality overrides any causal connection between things in the world. Hence, God can have anything that he wants at any time that he wants. Fruit can grow on trees in winter, snow could fall in Houston in the summer, rivers could flow uphill, living things could emerge from fires. A veritable Alice's wonderland becomes possible. A rational agent could not exist in such a world because a rational agent plans and calculates. But planning and calculating in these circumstances is impossible. Finally, since being rational is part of being moral, then a moral agent is also incompatible with such a world. In a miraculous world, a moral agent would not know what to do to attain certain moral ends.

The second problem is that a miraculous world is incompatible with significantly free beings, that is, beings that could do wrong as well as right.⁹¹ In such a world evil could not be done because God would override the neurological processes necessary to entertain evil thoughts. So the attempt to remove natural evils by miracle leads to a denial of moral evil which amounts to a denial of significantly free beings.

Finally, a third problem is that a miraculous world entails that God perform contradictions.⁹² If God causes an object to become physically inseparable from another, then a thief is unhappy and the victim happy. If God causes the object to be separable, then the thief is happy and the victim unhappy. The only way God could avoid the natural evil of mental suffering is for the object to be both separable and inseparable.

For the above three reasons Reichenbach concludes that a miraculous world is not preferable to a world operating by natural laws. Natural evils are the result of the operation of natural laws. Since a world operating by natural laws is provided for the benefit of ourselves understood as significantly free, we should blame

90. Reichenbach, *Evil and a Good God*, 103–4.
91. Ibid., 104–5.
92. Ibid., 106–7.

Cosmological Theodicies   259

ourselves more than God if we are dissatisfied with the natural evils in the world.

What would be the Thomistic reaction to Reichenbach's theodicy for natural evils? The reaction would be far less severe than the Thomist reaction to Reichenbach's theodicy for moral evil. In my opinion, Aquinas would admit that Reichenbach's present theodicy is a possible one. First, recall Reichenbach's definition of natural evil: all instances of pain and suffering both physical and mental, and all states of affairs significantly disadvantageous to the organism which are caused by actions for which human agents cannot be held morally blameworthy. By this definition "natural evil" is wider than "natural corruptions" at *ST* I, 19, 9c, which are willed by God, although indirectly. "Natural evil" would seem to include what are for Aquinas unnatural evils. Unnatural evils are not willed by God at all. But as Reichenbach develops his theodicy, natural evil appears to be used only for unnatural corruptions, for example, the death of the fawn from burns. So both thinkers agree that evils exist in the natural world that are unintended effects of something that God does intend. Aquinas says that God does not will the evil of unnatural corruption. The relation of God's will to unnatural corruption is to will to permit it because of some antecedent good, viz., a creation inclusive of things that can fail in goodness. Second, just as the order of nature is meant for free moral agents in Reichenbach's theodicy, so too in the view of Aquinas corruptible things are meant for man and the perfection of his intellectual capacities.

But Aquinas would beg to differ by way of addition with Reichenbach's theodicy. First, Aquinas would note that natural evil is something more pervasive and regular than is suggested by Reichenbach's theodicy. Not only do some men drown, get consumed in fires, or get crushed by earthquakes. All other men grow old and die. Not only do some crops get diseased; all crops have their time and then wither away. To deal with these more pervasive and regular natural evils, Reichenbach needs to further develop his theodicy. Aquinas is prepared to offer as aid his doctrine of a universal equivocal cause of generation and corruption, for example, God as God indirectly intends and wills corruption for the order and perfection of the material cosmos.

Second, Aquinas would relate unnatural corruption not only to some antecedent good but to some consequent good also. Reichenbach does not locate his natural evils within these two kinds of goods. Natural evils are treated only as the incidental by-products of some good that God is intending. But in Aquinas's eyes these evils do not contribute to the perfection of the universe but tend to wreck that perfection. Hence, they are abominations not only to us but to God as well. That is why Aquinas has God willing to order them to some consequent good. As Aquinas said at *ST* I, 2, 3, God permits evil only because he can draw good from it. So Aquinas would insist on these two supplements to Reichenbach's natural evil theodicy.

Finally, in my opinion, Aquinas would insist upon further possibilities for explaining natural evils. In other words, Aquinas would dispute the definitiveness of Reichenbach's account. Just as I argued, contra Swinburne, that a supernaturally graced world without natural evils would still leave room for moral acts, so too, contra Reichenbach, would a miraculous world. In other words, even an environment exempt from natural and unnatural corruption leaves opportunity for significantly free acts. This possibility is related to Aquinas's thesis at *De Ver.* XXIV, 9, that apart from the beatific vision, the best that God can do, even speaking supernaturally, is to bestow only a relative indefectibility in the rational creature. The text reiterates the two causes of sin discussed in my chapter 2. First, there is the inability to always consider the rule; second, there is the play of the passions. Here, though, the rule that we are unable to always consider is God himself and not the human as intellector of being. I believe that the theological context in which Aquinas is working explains this shift in the rule. Certainly on the philosophical level an obligation exists to orient ourselves to God the creator who metaphysically speaking is the preeminent epiphany

Cosmological Theodicies 261

of being. "Know the truth about God" is the primary precept of Aquinas's fourth natural law at *ST* I-II, 94, 2. But absent a divine revelation, the only way that we can acquit ourselves of that responsibility is by faithfulness to created epiphanies of being, viz., ourselves and our fellows. If the creator does break into human history with a communication, or revelation, then that fact takes precedence and allows the moral rule to become the creator directly. Nevertheless, this religious rule, like the moral rule, still fights against the mind's tendency to default to the intellection of being in sensible things.[93] Hence, here too even though the contemplation of God can be made more continuous by the infused virtues, "it is impossible for reason in this life here below to be always in the act of correct contemplation so that the reason for everything we do is God."[94]

What is my point for Reichenbach? If the Thomistic metaphysician is imaginative enough or is prompted by revelation, the Thomistic metaphysician could envisage on purely philosophical grounds a creation of humans in a supernatural state. Such a state need not be so supernatural that the capacity to sin is absolutely removed. Hence, the metaphysician would conclude that where we are now could be a subsequent state owing to the sinful loss of a supernatural instauration. In other words, the truth about natural evils may not be their explanation as *quandoque* evils but as a

---

93. As mentioned, Reichenbach ventures that God could effect our brain states such that brain states necessary for bad thoughts do not arise. Appealing back to Aquinas's philosophical psychology and its use in Aquinas's ethics, I do not believe that what Reichenbach suggests is possible. The thought of being is abstracted from any brain state. Being's transcendental character assures us of that. In other words, not everything is a triangle, so the thought of triangle could be avoided by brain states productive of thoughts only of squares or circles. But everything is at least a being. So as ineluctably inhabiting the human mind, being cannot but give everyone some sense of their and their fellows' dignity and a sense of an obligation to respect that dignity. This situation would set the stage for significant freedom—freedom to do both good or evil. The exercise of that freedom would consist at least in choices to be faithful to the above obligation or disrespectful of it. The fact that one may not yet know how to carry out these choices because the world is operating by miracle does not count against this moral fact.

94. *De Ver.* XXIV, 9c; Aquinas, *Truth*, vol. III, 173.

punishment or a loss. Moreover, in light of the providential ordering of natural evils to good and the creator's capacity for supernatural effects, the same metaphysician would conclude that the meaning of present natural evils could lie in future supernatural states and not be confined to realizing goods somewhere in the here and now. These possibilities all preclude a definitive account for natural evils.

In conclusion, Reichenbach's theodicy for natural evil is one with which a Thomist could work, though a Thomist would insist upon developing it further, and, for all that, the Thomist would not regard the theodicy as definitive.

8

Conclusion and Comparison to Brian Davies and Eleonore Stump

As I began with Rachel, it is appropriate that I conclude with her. But before doing that I wish to comment on two recent Thomistic treatments of evil. The first treatment is *The Reality of God and the Problem of Evil* by Brian Davies.[1] Both Davies and I hold that the philosopher cannot definitively answer the question about why evil exists. But while I have claimed that the philosopher has no answer because the philosopher discerns too many possible answers, Davies claims that the philosopher has no answer because the God term in the statement of the evil problem escapes human conception. For Davies both the theist and the atheist are working with all too human categories of thought. Hence, evil cannot be used to explain God nor to critique God.

During my treatment of Hick's personalist solution to the prob-

---

1. Brian Davies, *The Reality of God and the Problem of Evil* (London: Continuum, 2006).

lem of evil, I briefly engaged Eleonore Stump's strategy for dealing with the evil problem. Since that sketch of her own thinking on the evil problem in her 1985 article, "The Problem of Evil," Stump has recently gone on to amplify substantially the ideas in that earlier sketched strategy and to connect her thinking with that of Aquinas. This much more robust version of her strategy is detailed in her *Wandering in Darkness: Narrative and the Problem of Suffering*.[2] Because of her connection with Aquinas, it is appropriate and incumbent upon me to comment also on Stump in the light of my own findings. Like Davies and myself, Stump appears to back away from giving *the* morally sufficient reason for God allowing evil. Instead, she offers Aquinas's theodicy simply as a "defense," viz., a description of "a possible world that contains God and suffering and that is similar to the actual world, at least in the sense that it contains human beings, natural laws, and evils much like those in our world."[3] Stump starts her defense from a loving God who, as such, would intend everlasting union with him. Evil is allowed because of its contribution to that end. Whether a fellow theist would accept her description as only a defense will be a question necessary to ask.

BRIAN DAVIES'S APOPHATIC TREATMENT OF THE EVIL PROBLEM

Brian Davies describes his position as a variation of the "I know God exists" solution of the problem of evil.[4] According to this type of solution, we have grounds that are independent of evil for philosophically asserting God's existence. My reader will recall that we found Aquinas asserting this position at *C.G.* III, 71, and *De Ver.* X, 12, ad 10m. In fact, borrowing from Boethius, Aquinas was more dramatic about it. Aquinas claimed that if evil exists, God exists. Aquinas reiterated Boethius in the context of his metaphysics

---

2. Eleonore Stump, *Wandering in Darkness: Narrative and the Problem of Suffering* (Oxford: Clarendon Press, 2010).

3. Ibid., 19. 4. Davies, *The Reality of God*, 17.

of *esse*. As a privation, evil presupposes substances whose *esse* is philosophically reducible to *esse subsistens*. This metaphysics of *esse* is the ground independent of evil for knowing God to exist. What is the ground for Davies?

As I mentioned in my chapter 5, nn. 36 and 46, Davies's ground for asserting God's existence is the distinction between individual and quiddity. Since the knowledge of the quiddity does not imply knowledge of any one individual, then something must explain the individuals that we have. Characteristic of the God, the explainer, is the lack of the individual and quiddity distinction. Importantly for his remarks on the evil problem, Davies insists that the understanding of God as a simple existent makes God "seriously odd" and "incomprehensible." Davies explains himself this way:

> Here, of course, one might ask "How can an individual be identical with its nature?" or "What would it be for something to be identical with its nature?" My answer to these questions is "I do not know." I can make sense of the suggestion that individuals in the material universe are not identical with their natures, for, as I have said, I think that we may, for example, understand and accept the claim that Mary is not humanity. But I have no idea what it would be to be something not like Mary in that respect.[5]

Also,

> We can get our minds around Smokey [the cat]. We can examine him, compare and contrast him with other things, note his progress and character, and even note how well or badly he is doing (considered as a cat). Can we do the same when it comes to God? Not if what I have been saying above is correct. There can be no laying hands on the source of the universe's being, and no way of comparing and contrasting it with other things on which hands can be laid (i.e. God, as I have argued, is not remotely subject to scientific analysis, as Smokey is).[6]

Davies's insistence in this second quote that we cannot compare and contrast God with other things seems to deny any common-

---

5. Ibid., 65.   6. Ibid., 92–93.

ality between God and creatures. Hence, it is not surprising that elsewhere even existence is equivocal between God and creatures: "Yet these reasons do not give us an understanding of what God is. In the sense that I can know what it is for a human being to exist, I cannot know what it is for God to exist."[7] Likewise, Davies admits that "We can make true statements about something without understanding what it is that (what reality it is that) makes those statements true."[8]

Davies blames creatures for our inability to get our minds around God: "[God] is not like anything we know (or think we know). Indeed, it makes sense to regard him as incomprehensible. For what we primarily know are things in the universe and truths about them expressed in propositions."[9] Behind this thinking about creatures is a fairly liberal interpretation of Aquinas's thesis that causes are like their effects:

> And when [Aquinas] says that causes are *like their effects* he simply means that seeing why the effects spring from their causes is seeing how the nature of the cause explains the effect and renders its effect necessary, and therefore unsurprising. He means that though, when drunk, I cannot be described as looking like alcohol, I am, when drunk, certainly showing forth what alcohol is. In this sense, so he thinks, I resemble alcohol. For him, the drunken man is, when properly understood, alcohol *in action*, alcohol expressing its nature in something—something which is, therefore, "like" alcohol.[10]

Davies does not seem to realize that he has rendered the like from like thesis from the perspective of *per accidens* causes. In other words, what he says would be perfectly accommodated by the rubbing hands causing heat that I mentioned in the first section of chapter 5. Davies misses the point that the like from like thesis is made from the context of *per se* causality. Hence, in the rubbing hands example, the thesis is verified in the already in place shoulders causing motion to a place in the hands.

7. Ibid., 228.
9. Ibid., 78.
8. Ibid., 227.
10. Ibid., 207.

Finally, to sum up his position Davies recalls some of Aquinas's many remarks that we can know that God is but not what God is.

> Aquinas makes the point by saying that when it comes to God we cannot know what he is (quid est). Aquinas does not mean that we cannot take ourselves to be able to make many true statements with God as their subject. As is well known, of course, he claims to be able to establish the truth of many statements of the form "God is ___." He does not, however, think that we are able to develop a science of God as, for example, we have already developed a science of cats, which is what he has in mind in saying that we cannot know what God is. We can, Aquinas, thinks, know what Smokey is, for Smokey belongs to the universe and is something we can single out while going on to compare and contrast him with things of this kind and with things of other kinds. Yet God, thinks Aquinas, is not like Smokey in any of these respects.[11]

Again one can only wonder if an inability to compare and contrast God with things will generate sheer equivocity between God and creatures.

This apparently strident negativity in our knowledge of the creator is the wand to make the evil problem disappear. Both the theist and the atheist are left with little material to explain *how* evil is compatible or incompatible with God. Since any ideas about God are drawn from creatures which are like their cause in only the most tenuous way, the God term in the evil problem inevitably gets construed too anthropomorphically. For example, Davies takes a point by point exception to God "as literally being a passionately committed and morally commendable combatant in the fight against evil in all its varieties." First, as good, God is at the peak of perfection and so not in time and not anxious about anything. Likewise, God cannot be thought as subject to standards of behavior. Also, as nontemporal God cannot be acted upon by others and so God suffers no passions. Finally, neither is God in a fight. Fighters are trying to conquer others "who are in some sense their peers."[12] But God is the maker of all things.

11. Ibid., 79.   12. Ibid., 251.

Davies acknowledges that his own position is so negative about our knowledge of God that the position might seem to identify God with a tennis ball. A tennis ball also is not a passionately committed and morally commendable combatant in a fight against evil.[13] But God is not "sub-moral" like a tennis ball. Why? Davies explains,

> [God] positively (and freely) calls into being the world in which we have moral values by which to live. In that case, however, it would be odd to suggest that he must be morally indifferent. That which freely calls into being the world in which we make moral distinctions can hardly be thought as positively indifferent when it comes to morality, or as being positively unconcerned with the moral values by which we live.[14]

I cannot find Davies providing the argument that God has will and that this will is free in regard to creatures. Granting him those points, however, has Davies avoided comparing God to a tennis ball?

I do not think so. What gets in Davies's way is his cosmological reasoning. The key to that reasoning is the gap between essence and individual, or essence and designated matter. In other words, the thought of man does not imply any particular human, say Tom; hence, that Tom is a man requires an explanation. Granting the thinking so far, a question now arises. How do we know that the explainer or cause is like the effect so that we can say that the cause in some sense intends the effect? In other words, how do we exclude the possibility that the cause for form in this matter is not like the rubbing hands that are the cause for the heat? In the latter situation, in which the heat is simply an accidental effect of the stationary shoulders, we have in the cause no intention at all for the effect. The answer to my question does not seem available from pure reason. Rather the answer is provided simply by experience. We notice that humans are produced by humans. But since we have no experience of God causing the universe, then there is always the possibility that the universe is a sideshow of God's

---

13. Ibid., 253.   14. Ibid., 253.

intending to produce something else. Human morality would not necessarily be something intended. And so the tennis ball possibility for the first cause still seems to be in play.

It is interesting to note that Davies's interpretation of the like from like thesis skirts dangerously close to *per accidens* causality. In fact, Davies's example of the like from like thesis is a case of a *per se* cause vis-à-vis a *per accidens* effect. The drunkenness is a side effect of chemical reactions just as much as the heat is a side effect of the rubbing of the hands. So, given that the divine cause is so unlike its effects, why may it not be the case that the effects are just *per accidens* to the divine cause? That possibility would still leave God seriously indifferent to our moral values.

To overcome the indifference criticism, Davies requires, in my opinion, a cosmological proof that begins from an effect that cannot be construed as an accidental effect of another line of causality. As noted, quiddity in an individual, or form in designated matter, is not that kind of effect. Some forms in matter are accidental effects of things that are *per se* causes of quite different effects. How do we know for sure that is not true of the form before us? If we cannot be sure, then it is possible that the cause does not intend this form at all. And there is the indifference.

If my interpretation of Aquinas's metaphysics is correct, then I can say that Aquinas transcends this problem. The effect from which Aquinas's philosophy of God begins is the *esse* of sensible things. Since without *esse* the thing is a mere possible, then *esse* possesses a priority and fundamentality to the thing that it actuates. This fundamental status is also behind the impossibility of *esse* being the *per accidens* effect of a prior line of causality. I believe it is in accord with this metaphysics that Aquinas insists that *esse* in created things "... cannot be understood except as derived from divine being [*esse divino*], just as a proper effect [*proprius effectus*] cannot be understood except as derived from its proper cause [*causa propria*]."[15]

15. Aquinas, *De Pot.* III, 5, ad 1m.

Does this metaphysics, then, just shore up Davies's position on the evil problem so that the position is left substantially intact or does it lead in another direction? In other words, does it lead to no answer because of a paucity of theodicy or to no answer because of an abundance of theodicy? Davies probably would insist upon the former. *Esse subsistens* is a case of an instance in which the distinction between individual and nature is absent. But as noted, Davies admitted that since sensible things basically determine his knowledge, he has no idea of that simple existent. Our ignorance of the divine quiddity explains, then, our ignorance of a theodicy. We cannot picture the God term so as to accurately explain how God and evil are compatible.

Davies could cite some eminent neo-Thomists in regard to this ignorance of the divine quiddity.[16] But other eminent Thomists, like Maritain and Wippel, ameliorate Aquinas's mantra that we know that God is but not what God is by citing other texts.[17] Hence,

---

16. "To say that *quid est Deus* is something *omnino ignotum* for man in this life, is to affirm that all knowledge, perfect or imperfect, of the essence of God is radically inaccessible here below. To every interpretation of St. Thomas to the contrary, the deservedly famous text of the *Contra Gentiles* presents an insuperable obstacle: 'We cannot grasp what God is, but what He is not, and the relation other things have with Him.'" Etienne Gilson, *The Christian Philosophy of St. Thomas Aquinas*, translated by L. K. Shook, (Notre Dame, Ind.: University of Notre Dame Press, 1994), 107. Focusing upon *C.G.* III, 49, para. 9, Anton Pegis says, "Now the purpose of the present paragraph is to characterize the most perfect knowledge of God that we have in this life, and the point is precisely that we do not know what this eminent and transcendent God is. Hence the further point about Moses is not his ignorance of any sublime knowledge, but the sublimity of the ignorance itself." Anton Pegis, "Penitus Manet Ignotum," *Mediaeval Studies* 27 (1965), n. 3. "Accordingly the divine *existence*, though a quiddity, remains utterly unknown to the human intellect in quidditative terms. Solely in terms of existential act, as a conclusion from the existential act attained in sensible things through judgment, is it reached by the human intellect. Correspondingly, the divine essence is utterly unknown in its own manner, that is, in the manner of essence." Joseph Owens, *An Elementary Christian Metaphysics* (Houston: Center for Thomistic Studies, 1985), 353. Also from Owens's "Aquinas: 'Darkness of Ignorance' in the Most Refined Notion of God," *The Southwestern Journal of Philosophy* 5 (1974): 93–110.

17. "To render ... 'de Deo quid sit penitus manet ignotum' (*Cont. Gent.*, lib. III, c. 49) by translating 'We do not know God in any way, in any thing, in any degree,' is to expose the reader to serious misconceptions." Jacques Maritain, *The Degrees of Knowledge*, translated by Gerald B. Phelan (New York: Charles Scribner's Sons, 1959), 425. "[O]ne should define

Conclusion and Comparison 271

in contrast to Davies's above cited claim that "... we can make true statements about something without understanding what it is that (what reality it is that) makes those statements true," Aquinas insists in his commentary on Boethius's *De Trinitate* that "we cannot know *that* God and other immaterial substances exist unless we know somehow in some confused way, what they are."[18] Both earlier and later in the *De Trinitate* commentary this confused knowledge is in virtue of the form or quiddity of the effect from which the causal reasoning proceeds. At I, 2, ad 5m Aquinas says that "When something is not known through its form but through its effect, the form of the effect takes the place of the form of the thing itself." Later at VI, 4, ad 2m, he also remarks,

If the effect is proportionate to its cause, we take the quiddity itself of the effect as our starting point to prove that the cause exists and to investigate its quiddity, from which in turn its properties are demonstrated. But if the effect is not proportionate to its cause, we take the effect as the starting point to prove only the existence of the cause and some of its properties while the quiddity of the cause remains unknown. This is what happens in the case of the separate substances.[19]

That in the second case we know "some of its properties" indicates that Aquinas does not mean that the quiddity of the cause is totally or completely unknown. But now what is the effect from which Aquinas reaches both God and some confused and imperfect knowledge of God's quiddity?

Again, if my interpretation of Aquinas's metaphysics is correct,

---

quidditative knowledge or knowledge of what God is very strictly, even as Thomas himself has done. He has made it clear, for instance, in the *De Potentia* and in the First Part of the *Summa Theologiae*, that when he agrees with John Damascene that we cannot know what God is, what he is thereby excluding is comprehensive and defining knowledge of God." John Wippel, "Quidditative Knowledge of God According to Thomas Aquinas," in *Graceful Reason: Essays Presented to Joseph Owens*, edited by Lloyd P. Gerson (Toronto: Pontifical Institute of Mediaeval Studies, 1983), 298.

18. *In de Trin.* VI, 3c; Thomas Aquinas, *On the Division and Methods of the Sciences*, translated by Armand Maurer (Toronto: Pontifical Institute of Mediaeval Studies, 1963), 77.

19. Aquinas, *Division and Methods*, 84.

the answer is the *esse* of sensible things. This created *esse* is originally grasped by the human intellect in its second operation. Traditionally the second operation is called judgment.[20] As so grasped, *esse* appears as radically particular. Judgmentally grasped *esse* is the *esse* of this thing or of that thing. Once portrayed to us by our various judgments, these particular *esses* are submitted to a case of the first intellectual operation. Characteristic of the first operation is the grasp of a commonality in a multiplicity. When the data are the judgmentally grasped *esses* of various things, the spied commonality is what Aquinas refers to as *esse formale*, *esse commune*, and the *ratio essendi*. It is the central portion of a larger commonality. This larger commonality is the *ratio entis* whose sameness in difference analogical character I have described. Hence, as a part of that whole, *esse commune* will be analogical also. Also, since any analogon is only dimly perceived, then the analogous character of *esse commune* should verify the confused and imperfect character of the quidditative knowledge about which we are speaking.

I have already noted a case in which Aquinas uses what he knows of *esse commune* to say something about the divine quiddity. In the final section of chapter 6, I described how Aquinas uses our abstractive knowledge of *esse* to establish within human nature a remote condition for the possibility of the beatific vision. Our intellects are not to the divine quiddity as our eyes are to sound. The beatific vision is not an incongruity for the human intellect, because the human intellect is already in some possession of the nature of *esse*. We discover the same thinking in other places. At *ST* I, 4, 2c, Aquinas argues that God has the perfections of all things. In his second argument, he says that since all perfections pertain to the *perfectio essendi* and since God is *esse subsistens*, then God has the perfections of all things. This syllogism can work only if there is some reflection between the *esse* we know in things and *esse* as it is in God.

---

20. For a delineation of this intellectual operation, see my *Being and Some Twentieth-Century Thomists* (New York: Fordham University Press, 2003), 189–96.

A reader of Aquinas can ask how Aquinas employs *esse commune* to think of God. Since *esse commune* is not a reality but an *abstractum* drawn from the individual judgmentally grasped *esses* of various things, how can *esse commune* be used to represent a reality? In fact a reader will point out that Aquinas himself makes this argument to distinguish *esse commune* from the divine *esse*. At *C.G.* I, 26, Aquinas argues,

> Moreover, that which is common to many is not outside the many except by the reason alone. Thus, animal is not something outside Socrates and Plato and the other animals except in the intellect that apprehends the form of animal stripped of all its individuating and specifying characteristics. For man is that which truly is animal; otherwise, it would follow that in Socrates and Plato there are several animals, namely, common animal itself, common man, and Plato himself. Much less, then, is common being [*esse commune*] itself something outside all existing things, save only for being in the intellect. Hence, if God is common being the only thing that will exist is that which exists solely in the intellect. But we showed above that God is something not only in the intellect but also in reality. Therefore, God is not the common being of all things.[21]

What is a reader to do? On the one hand, Aquinas takes various points about God from what he knows of *esse commune*; on the other hand, *esse commune* is only an idea while the divine *esse* is a reality. If the contradiction is to be removed, obviously Aquinas must be considering *esse commune* in different respects. Is there any evidence of that?

Back in question six of the *De Trinitate* commentary, Aquinas says that our confused cognition of the divine quiddity and of the quiddity of separate substance is attained "by negations; for example by understanding that they are immaterial, incorporeal, without

---

21. Thomas Aquinas, *Summa contra Gentiles*, vol. I, translated by Anton C. Pegis (Notre Dame, Ind.: University of Notre Dame Press, 1975), I, 129–30. In this passage Aquinas seems to reiterate a thesis about our mode of signifying perfections. We can conceive the simple only as nonexistent, and the existent only as composite. See *C.G.* I, 30 and *ST* I, 13, 1, ad 2m and 3c. The thesis echoes Davies's claim that he has no idea of a simple that is an existent.

shapes, and so on."²² Earlier negating is identified with separating: "Nevertheless, we reach a knowledge of [God and separate substances] ... by way of negation (as when we separate from such beings whatever sense or imagination apprehends)."²³ Finally, separation is explained as another capacity of the intellect's second act.²⁴ Not only can the second act compose, but it can divide or separate in the sense of negating.

Can negation be wielded on the *ratio entis*, of which *esse commune* is a portion, so that *esse commune* stands forth less as an abstraction and more as a reality? I believe so. As noted from the previous *Contra Gentiles* text, to be taken from data is characteristic of an abstraction. Hence, to remove the abstractive status from an intelligible object, the data must in some sense be removed while the object remains. In this case, the individual judgmentally grasped *esses*, in which the intellect spies the *abstractum* of *esse commune*, must somehow be dumbed down. According to Aquinas, these analogates of *esse commune* proceed from the analogon of *esse commune* in the light of the essences to be realized. As he has remarked, *esse* is "not determined through another just as potency through an act but more as an act through a potency," and is "not compared to others just as receiver to received but more as received to receiver."²⁵ Hence, by negating, or blotting out, the non-*esse* portion of the *ratio entis*, the mind removes from *esse commune* its capacity for addition in individual *esses*. In a sense the *esses* are dumbed down. The situation in which the data are in a sense removed should allow *ipsum esse* to stand forth, now less as an *abstractum* and more as a thing itself. The play of negation allows *ipsum esse* to remain an object without the appearance of

---

22. *In de Trin.* VI, 3c; Aquinas, *Division and Methods*, 78.
23. *In de Trin.* VI, 2c; Aquinas, *Division and Methods*, 70.
24. "[A]nd another [intellectual operation] by which it joins and divides, that is to say, by forming affirmative and negative statements." Aquinas, *In de Trin.* V, 3c; Maurer, trans., *Division and Methods*, 28.
25. Respectively *De Pot.* VII, 2c and *ST* I, 4, 1, ad 3m.

an abstraction. In sum, despite the sense origin of our concepts, *separatio* allows some of our concepts to shed their inappropriate *modus significandi* and to be used to think of God.

This ability to use *esse commune* to form a confused representation of the divine quiddity of *esse subsistens* is a major requirement in argumentation for the key divine attributes of knowledge and will. Only if we can represent in some fashion the divine quiddity can we notice a similarity between it as subsistent *esse* and a separate substance as subsistent form. Hence, we can transfer what we know of subsistent form, namely knowledge at the intellectual degree, to God. If I have no idea of the divine quiddity, as insisted upon by Davies, then I cannot catch that similarity between God and things and so lack a middle term for my arguments. Finally, since knowledge of the good is crucial for the presence of willing, then without the conclusion that knowledge is present in God the argument for volition in God cannot even begin.

To underline my point, consider Davies's argument that God is essentially good.[26] First, looking to creatures Davies formulates an idea of goodness in terms of succeeding. Something is good if it succeeds in being what it is, if it achieves the form it is meant to have. Second, turning to God as reached from creatures, Davies reminds us that as the first changer God is not changing. In other words, since God lacks the distinction between individual and nature, God is simply a form or nature. Hence God is at the peak of success, or is essentially good. But for Davies to catch the stretch of goodness between success in creatures and success in God, he has to form some picture, dim as it may be, of the God term. The data is crucial. Consider how we stretch our concept of human to animal. To Tom, Dick, and Harry, we juxtapose Fido, Flicka, and Flossy. Davies's negative theology cannot be left so negative that it lacks what Aquinas calls a confused and imperfect knowledge of the divine quiddity.

---

26. Davies, *The Reality of God*, 202–3.

That confused knowledge has been presumed operative throughout my presentation of Aquinas on evil. An insight into being, dim as it may be, gave us some idea of God's singular perfection as *esse subsistens*. Hence, if we were to have *esse* other than the divine *esse*, that *esse* had to be nonsubsistent and finitized by what it was with. So, there was no best possible world. Furthermore, like *esse* in being an act, the finitizing principle of form could be both subsistent or nonsubsistent. These alternatives engendered the basic division of created being into the necessary and the contingent. The latter alternative entailed two things. First, for the natural functioning of the contingent order, God wills, albeit indirectly, an arrangement in which each contingent thing will perish. Second, since the contingent order involves movers that act on something presupposed, a material always perfectly disposed to the action of the mover cannot be naturally guaranteed. Hence, unnatural corruptions will occur. God permits these for the good of the whole and somehow orders them to a good. Likewise, in human affairs bodily affections in line with morality cannot always naturally be the case. Here, too, God permits the evil and orders it.

The above points constitute a philosophical baseline. The same insight into being that generates the above account also relativizes the account. As noted, a created intellect cannot naturally know analogical being without establishing at least a remote disposition to an encounter with being itself in the creator. With the creator's gratuitous assistance that encounter is possible. Does it occur? The philosopher cannot say for sure. Before the manifold possibilities engendered by the philosopher's insight into being and its instantiation in the creator, the philosopher stops, pauses, and dreams.

ELEONORE STUMP AND THE LOVE OF GOD

With apologies to Eleonore Stump for this summary of her well-wrought thoughts in her mammoth *Wandering in Darkness*, I would dare to describe her mature position this way. Stump wants to neutralize evil as a problem for theism by detailing, at least in general, a morally sufficient reason for why a perfectly good, omniscient, and omnipotent God would allow evil. Hence, her position is opposed to skeptical theism which claims that we can have no idea of God's morally sufficient reason. Nevertheless, Stump is not presenting a theodicy. A theodicy is understood as an elaboration of *the* morally sufficient reason. Instead she is content to present *a* possibly true scenario that illustrates this morally sufficient reason. To argue in that manner is to present a defense.[27] The scenario unabashedly utilizes truths from Christianity which unaided human reason may not be able to verify.

As mentioned, what is especially relevant about Stump's latest work is her claim that her project is Thomistic, though she also claims to develop Aquinas's theodicy to deal with some of its shortcomings. But what is already puzzling is Stump's continual reference to Aquinas's "theodicy" even while she claims to be presenting only a "defense." A reader wonders if she is equivocating on her meaning of "theodicy." Or perhaps not, because it depends upon to whom one is speaking. If Stump is speaking to nontheists, as seems likely since they often raise the evil problem, then Aquinas's theodicy is a defense. But if Aquinas is speaking to fellow believers, then his theodicy is a theodicy in Stump's sense. But do nontheistic unbelievers and Christians exhaust the audiences? Might there not be nonbelievers who are theists? In particular, might there not be Thomistic metaphysicians who are not yet believers in the biblical God. In other words, these metaphysicians affirm a creator but do not yet affirm that the creator has actually communicated to humans in human history. For such metaphysicians, the ideal of a personal communication by the creator to humans is just a possibility.

It is important to remember that Aquinas did not consider metaphysics to be a sectarian study. It would be false to assume that he thought that his metaphysics could be understood just by

27. Stump, *Wandering in Darkness*, 19.

fellow Catholics. It is true that he thought that metaphysics, and philosophy in general, was very difficult and that the truths of his religious faith were a boon to correct philosophizing. This is the attitude that Pope Leo XIII later called "Christian philosophy." But in that attitude faith never supplies the premises for the philosophizing. Rather, the mode of thinking could be compared to learning mathematics by a book with the answers at the back. A disagreement with the answers at the back helps one to learn mathematical truths by driving one back to consider the numbers themselves. Likewise, Christian truths that contradict philosophical ideas direct the Christian philosopher to reconsider the facts in order to see if there is something that the philosopher may have missed either in his distraction or because of the subtlety of the evidence. But my point is that once philosophers have been brought to truth by this manner of philosophizing, they can now teach that truth to others who may not share a belief in Christianity. Likewise, someone who has been taught mathematics through books with the answers at the back can teach others who lack the mathematics book. A final analogy would be a detective who in solving a case on the basis of a hunch ends up with a body of evidence that has a life of its own, so that in court the evidence will convince others who never shared the hunch of the detective.

So, Thomists who are not Christians are a possibility. What would Stump's thinking on evil be to them? Would it be only a defense or a theodicy? In particular, given Aquinas's metaphysics, would Stump's thinking be *a* way to go or *the* way to go? I will return to these questions after a summary of Stump.

The evil that Stump will consider is suffering. Her understanding of suffering is twofold: (1) to be kept from one's flourishing, that is, one's well-being objectively understood, and (2) to have lost the desires of one's heart.[28] Stump also specifies that she is consider-

---

[28]. "What is bad about the evil a human being suffers is that it undermines (partly or entirely) her flourishing, or it deprives her (in part or in whole) of the desires of her heart, or both." Ibid., 10.

ing only the suffering of adult humans who are mentally fully functional.[29]

Taking advantage of Aquinas's thinking that love desires union with the beloved, Stump reasons that as perfectly good and loving, God would desire for his rational creatures everlasting union with him. In short, God would desire what Christians call heaven. Nevertheless, it is a fact that humans have a divided will that renders them indisposed to this union. They do will the good but they also will their own pleasure and power. Christians will account for this fact through original sin. In other words, it was not the way the perfectly good God created humans. Rather, humans came to have this condition freely.[30] The condition is quite pessimistically described by Stump as akin to a disease or cancer, and so a comparison of our current condition with being in a hospital is justifiable. That likeness in turn justifies comparing God to a doctor and suffering with medicine prescribed by the doctor. Moreover, since the medicine works either by preventing death or by curing the patient, then the divine doctor so allows suffering that God's human patients have an incentive to turn to God.[31] Or, if that turning has occurred, they have an incentive to deepen their closeness to God.[32]

The achievement of that turning, Stump calls "justification," and it is a nuanced affair.[33] God cannot bring it about unilaterally. Such action would destroy the freedom of the human will. Stump insists that no efficient cause, even a divine one, can act upon the human will without detriment to its freedom. Such is also the opinion of Aquinas, according to Stump. Aquinas is a libertarian not

---

29. Ibid., 4. In her earlier "The Problem of Evil," *Faith and Philosophy*, 2 (1985): 411, Stump tries to explain how her defense would apply to the suffering of children and even infants.

30. In "The Problem of Evil," 403, Stump extensively uses Anselm's thinking on Adam's fall. She places Aquinas in the Anselmian tradition. There is no mention of the "supernatural" state of Adam.

31. Stump, *Wandering in Darkness*, 398.   32. Ibid., 400.

33. Ibid., 158, 166–67.

a compatibilist.³⁴ But neither can the human will by itself bring about the turning. As divided, the human will cannot will psychic integration. Is this checkmate? Stump explains that if the human will freely decides to do nothing, that is, to surrender to God, God would then be allowed to remedy the dysfunction of the will. God's allowed action on the will produces in the will the act of faith.

As Aquinas understands justification by faith, a mentally normally functioning adult human person Jerome who lacks faith has a will that refuses grace until at some moment, in surrender, that refusal gives way to a state of quiescence in the will as regards the person's volitional attitude toward his past moral wrongdoing and God's goodness. When and only when Jerome's will is quiescent in this way, God infuses grace into Jerome's will. With this infusion of grace into the will, Jerome forms the global higher-order desire that detests his own past wrongdoing and desires the goodness of God.... On Aquinas's views, this higher-order desire is necessary and sufficient for justification.³⁵

Typically, justification does not immediately result in "sanctification."³⁶ Sanctification is a full integration of the human will around moral goodness. The surrendering to God may be only partial, as it was with Augustine when he ask for celibacy but said "Not yet." Also, backsliding into a divided will is always a possibility. Stump says that if sanctification is brought to completion, the completion occurs only in the afterlife. Stump is even more insistent: any response to evil that does not make mention of an afterlife is "a failure."³⁷

---

34. Ibid., 160.

35. Ibid., 166–67. Also, "If in consequence a person's will gives up this resistance and becomes quiescent, then, at that point, God puts operative grace into the will of that person. In consequence of that divinely given grace, the human will forms the global higher-order desire that is the will of faith." Ibid., 166

36. Ibid., 161.

37. Ibid., 419. Also, "I take it that this is another way of affirming the point Aquinas himself emphasized, that the notion of an afterlife is central to any attempt at theodicy (or defense) that is to have a hope of being successful," 419. Earlier on 389 Stump cites *In 1 Cor* 15:2 in which Aquinas says that if there is no resurrection of the dead, then believers would be the most miserable of people.

To be noted is Stump's insistence that in Aquinas's account of justification, the human willer is "ultimately in control of her will, because it is up to her either to refuse grace or to fail to refuse grace, and God's giving of grace depends on the state of her will."[38] Elsewhere, this ultimate control is said to render God's desires for a person "efficacious."[39] Hence, Stump admits that a more precise expression of Aquinas's theodicy is that by using suffering, God takes "the chance" of keeping a person from the worst thing and takes "the chance" of transforming a person into something glorious.[40]

Such is the "heart of Aquinas's theodicy."[41] But for Stump there are still loose ends that need to be addressed, and she believes a Thomist can do that. Even though the flourishing of our nature consists in an everlasting, loving union with God, our desires must include more than God. For God loves not just me but others. Hence, my love of God must blossom into a love of others. But now a problem emerges. A love of others will inevitably cause disappointment and that disappointment seems to curtail our flourishing. Stump expresses it poignantly:

> But a person who does not love another, his father or brother, for example, cannot be united in will with a God who does love these people. When a loved person dies, however, at least one of the desires of love for him, the desire for union with him, is frustrated. To be tranquil in the face of the death of another is therefore to be deficient with respect to one of the desires of love for him. And so, in being unmoved in the face of death of a loved person, one is not more united with God, or more in harmony with God's will but less.[42]

So how is the suffering of a broken heart to be woven into Aquinas's theodicy? Without an answer, Aquinas's theodicy looks self-defeating. It leaves one broken hearted and addresses only what is essential to human flourishing.

---

38. Ibid., 168.
39. Ibid., 164.
40. Ibid., 404.
41. Ibid., 408.
42. Ibid., 429.

Stump's solution is to return to the dynamics of love. She says, "No one who loves a human person can love her without also having some care for what she cares about, some desire for the desires of her heart."[43] But God the creator is a lover; hence, a lover of God can be confident that God will not leave us flourishing but also heartbroken. Someone whose deepest desire is for God will get back in some way his heart's desires because that is characteristic of lovers. This belief becomes the person's trust throughout his heartbrokenness. In some manner, the divine lover will also fulfill the desires of our hearts if they are woven into a desire for him. In such manner Stump completes Aquinas's theodicy.

Earlier I wondered if, because of a confusing usage of terminology, Stump was presenting a defense or a theodicy. I suggested that the confusion could be eliminated by understanding the audience. To nontheists Aquinas's theodicy is really just a defense, but to Aquinas's fellow theists it is a theodicy, that is, *the* defense. As my reader can suspect, Stump's defense leaves me feeling logically hemmed in. For from the perspective of what I understand to be the Thomistic metaphysician's knowledge both of God and the human being, what Stump calls Aquinas's theodicy is in large part one possible explanation of how evil and God can coexist. But, importantly, it is a theological possibility, a drama made possible by God gratuitously elevating the human being to another level of existence. For from the viewpoint of Aquinas's metaphysics, God already expresses his infinite love and goodness by bringing us from nonbeing to being and in giving us the natural means to attain, although with difficulty, wisdom and natural virtue. I spoke of these accomplishments in chapter 2. Elsewhere I also pointed out that the Thomistic desires for more should be assessed in the light of these achievements. It is not true that without grace the human is destitute. From the perspective of nature the human is more like a child who after a nutritional meal asks for more. The parent can

---

43. Ibid., 444.

acquiesce to the wishes of the child, but the parent does not have to acquiesce to be a good parent.

Also, as an analogical intellector of being, the human is by nature not more than a principal part of universe and only closest to being a whole, as Aquinas remarked at *C.G.* III, 112.[44] Known analogically, that is, as a sameness in difference, the *ratio entis* does not perfectly seat itself in the human intellect. Consequently, our natural dignity is compatible with activity confined to this life. In light of this knowledge of what the human being naturally is, joy is found in contributing to the whole or in seeing someone else succeed where one has failed. Similarly, a dying soldier on a battlefield can find consolation in seeing his comrades advance. Someone gets through. Hence, Stump's comments that the good from suffering must accrue to the sufferer and that a theodicy without an afterlife is a failure are too strong.[45] To return to Maritain, who in large part Stump can be seen as developing, Stump needs to deal with *ST* I, 48, 2. There Aquinas explains evil without any obvious presence of the elements of Stump's interpretation.

But if Stump would grant that her interpretation of Aquinas's theodicy is in truth only another possible philosophical defense among others to be found in and developed from Aquinas, does it succeed even in that respect? In particular, does Aquinas's theodicy assuage the broken heart? I think that there is still a problem, and it derives from Stump's understanding of the will as ultimate. For Stump our love of others should be in and through a deeper love of God who loves others. But contrary to usual Thomistic un-

---

44. At *Wandering*, 385, Stump also brings up Aquinas's commentary on Romans 8:6 in which Aquinas has every evil suffered by the saints rebounding to their own good. Aquinas's reasoning is that the good of the whole is willed for its own sake and the noblest parts of the whole partake in this ordering. Important to observe is that Aquinas is speaking of the saints, i.e., those destined to eternal glory. Hence, it is appropriate to apply to them an argument that does not necessarily apply to individual humans in the natural order. In other words, it is necessary to distinguish between a principal part that is naturally transient and a principal part that is supernaturally immortal. See my chapter 3 discussion of *C.G* III, 112 at "A Caveat in Understanding the Subject of the Consequent Good."

45. Respectively, Stump, *Wandering in Darkness*, 378 and 419.

derstandings of God as sovereign and self-sufficient, Stump admits that God is "vulnerable" in his love of humans and this vulnerability derives from human freedom: "Because God gave human beings such free will, God allowed certain things that matter to God—the salvation of all human beings—to depend on wills other than God's own. In this sense, God makes himself vulnerable to human beings."[46] Stump's thinking appears to allow an incurable heartbrokenness in God.[47] But if God can be heartbroken, and remain so, then so can we. The intractability of the problem stems from Stump's understanding of the human will as "ultimate." In a context that includes a divine providence over the very free acts of the human will, divine providence will not include this vulnerability.

Finally, what of Stump's poignant argument for the necessity of broken heartedness? In sum, our love of God entails love of neighbor. But our love of neighbor entails love of union that death frustrates. Hence, tranquility in the face of a loved one's death bespeaks a deficiency in love. If by this reflection Stump is saying that we *ought* not to be tranquil, that there is an ethical lack in not grieving, then I think she is wrong. First, our love of neighbor should be in light of how God loves us. But by using our natural powers of understanding, do we know that God loves us for eternal union with himself? I do not think that Aquinas thought that natural reason could confirm this divine intention. God could love us that way, but if God did so, it would be a supernatural act on God's part. By nature we are parts of a material cosmos. For the perfection of the universe, God or his deputies intends for the perfection of the whole the coming and going of its parts. In the light of that known divine intention and in the light of the possibility

---

46. Ibid., 123.

47. Consider this remark of process philosopher, Lewis Ford, "God cannot guarantee that evil will be overcome simply because he is not the sole agent determining the outcome of the world.... Since all these actualities are free to respond as they will, it is conceivable that most may all elect to frustrate the divine aim. The world could possibly generate into near chaos. There is no metaphysical guarantee against such." *The Lure of God* (Philadelphia: Fortress Press, 1978), 119.

of a supernatural intention, we should live in fidelity to Aquinas's natural law ethics and listen for possible further communication from the creator.

If one does believe in a supernatural divine love, then tranquility and peace are in order, not heart brokenness. To know that one's beloved is going to heaven is an undoubted antidote to sadness. As St. Paul asked, in light of our faith where is death's sting? In light of our faith, one has no excuse to be sad.

But if by her reflection Stump is saying that we *will* grieve, then she is correct. I have tried to explain how each human psyche is naturally prey to confusing the great or the small, temporally or physically, with the aura of being, so that the great and the small can be cherished too much so that their loss is psychically lacerating. This confusion is something that we have made and will continue to make. Even Christ wept for the loss of Lazarus. In any human there will be understandable sorrow. That the notion of being is playing a fauxizing role in Stump's thinking about broken heartedness is indicated by what she says about human love:

> For Aquinas... human beings are embodied, made of matter, and this fact makes us particular not only in what we are but also in what we love. There is the particular place in which a person is born, the particular time in which he grew up, the particular culture in which he lived, the particular nation, ethnicity, or people to whom he belongs: most importantly, there are the particular persons who are dear to him (or hated by him). Human beings are not like God in being capable of sharing intimately with endless numbers of people. Human beings are built for shared union in love with particular people—in fact, those few people on whom they have set their hearts.[48]

Stump's stress on particularity is an indication that the desires of the heart are prompted by "fauxized" objects, by objects that the intellect has rendered to have a value out of all proportion to the truth. Particularity is just another name for the small or minute. As

---

48. Stump, *Wandering in Darkness*, 438.

"fauxized," the loss of the desires of our heart will be piercing and painful. The tears will flow and death will have its sting. Normally, however, the sorrow will gradually pass, as the faux epiphany of being is dissolved and perspective is restored. Hence, if conformity to God's will leads us to love others in particular and our psychology invariably confuses the small with being, then as a matter of fact our lives will be marked by loss, hopefully only temporarily, of peace of mind.

In conclusion, from a theistic perspective, Stump appears to have presented more than a defense but a theodicy. Also, in terms of the categories of my work, her theodicy is personalist. But like other personalisms, it cannot claim definitiveness.

THE CONSOLATION OF RACHEL

Rachel is both sad and angry. Her sadness is evident in her weeping. Her anger is implied in her dismissal of *ST* I, 48, 2, and her refusal to be consoled. In Rachel's anger we see some of the protest of Camus and Flew. To provide some consolation to Rachel, I have to address each of her reactions.

According to Aquinas, sadness is a passion provoked by a present evil.[49] In Rachel's case, the present evil is the loss of her children. Rachel cannot find consolation because she cannot understand how to remove the evil. And she cannot understand how to remove the evil because she has a view of the human person as a whole and not as a part thereof. Accordingly, the evil cannot be made good by reference to something else. To the contrary, the evil must rebound to a good belonging to her children. But since they are no more the rebound becomes impossible. As Maritain related, Rachel is weeping for her maliciously slain children and refuses to be consoled because these young "persons" are no more. From the

---

49. "Such a passion, however, is sorrow or pain, for its subject is the already present evil [*malum iam inhaerens*], just as the object of joy is the good present and possessed [*bonum praesens et habitum*]." *C.G.* I, 89; Aquinas, *Summa contra Gentiles*, vol. I, 173. See also "Tristitia est de malo praesenti." *ST* I-II, 42, 3, ad 2m.

viewpoint of natural reason, Rachel's weeping is an overreaction. It will sound harsh. But I believe it must be said. Rachel's inconsolable sadness is created by her exaggerated view of the human person. With its own resources philosophy cannot verify the importance Rachel places on human life. The dignity to which humans are naturally entitled rests upon the intellection of being. But since this intellection is analogical, the human by unaided power never rises above the status of a principal part of the whole. Hence, with good reason Aquinas never said the human person is the most perfect thing. Rather, he said that the human person was the most perfect thing "in all of nature."[50] Hence, for Rachel to let tragedy destroy her psyche with unmitigated despair is for her to turn her back on other humans who in virtue of the presence of the *ratio boni* within them continue to call for our respect and solicitude.

But Rachel's protest is understandable. Being is playing one of its tricks. Rachel has an idea of the be all and end all. It is the idea that her children inappropriately aggrandize in her consciousness of them. Hence, their demise understandably creates weeping that philosophy cannot console. In Aquinas's philosophical psychology, such a confusion of the idea with the children is understandable. The idea of the be all and end all is the idea of being, the *ratio entis*. Once abstracted, it can sometimes become unwittingly associated with certain objects which because of their features, for example, physically or temporally, large or small, aggrandize this association. What results is a faux epiphany of being in which an object comes to possess a value out of all proportion to the truth. To contemplate the small, everything else must be removed with the result that the small stands alone with being; to contemplate

---

50. The intellection of being is a baseline for philosophical reflection. However, I often meet people who understand what Aquinas calls the state of innocence, i.e., the state in which Adam and Eve were created, as our default position. As I noted in the second section of chapter 6, the state of innocence is an effect of grace and so should be understood as supernatural and not as something owed to us as rationality is owed.

the large being can be used as a backdrop. Hence, the preciousness of being can become confused with the object.

Once one becomes familiar with the dynamic, one sees that it repeats itself over and over in human experience. It can create an endearment that stymies growth. That unfortunate result is what Scarlett O'Hara, the heroine of *Gone with the Wind*, pathetically suffered as she fought, often immorally, to resurrect her plantation of Tara that had become lost in the mists of time. At various times, all of us are Scarlett. For example, as it fades into the past, one's life and its experiences, for example, our studies in graduate school, can take on an endearing quality such that one never engages contemporary discussion nor moves beyond the ways of one's old professors. Likewise, a people's love and respect for the land of their forefathers can be so great that it creates injustices for humans existing right now.

Sometimes we have to let go. The motivation for letting go lies in the realization that what all truly love is being which is more accurately placed in people rather than in ideas or land. With that personal focus we can go on to truly honor our past teachers and forefathers even if we do something different. But it is ironic that the notion of being, in whose intellection human dignity consists, is also the very thing that can defeat the human psyche.

I think that philosophy offers two solutions to sadness. One is mentioned by Aquinas. Interestingly at *ST* I-II, 38, 1, Aquinas remarks that any pleasure is a remedy for sadness. Aquinas's psychology of the intellection of being explains why pleasure can do this. If the confusion of being with the murdered children is the cause of Rachel's sadness and if being is an abstraction from sensible data, then insofar as pleasure focuses our attention on the sensible, pleasure directs our attention away from being. That distraction should produce an alleviation of the sadness. As I mentioned in chapter 2, because the intellection of being is an abstractive affair, then being can hide itself in the process of revealing itself. Hence, Aquinas will say that most prefer sense pleasure over intellectual pleasure because so few have intellectual experience. Here the vividness of the sensible can be used to avoid the presence of being that is the cause of the sadness. Of course the consolations of sense pleasure have the dangers of addiction and immorality. Hence, it would be most important that the sense pleasures be offered to the aggrieved by true friends.

Another possibility, in my opinion, is to pit one faux epiphany against another. To the sadness of the loss of the children, there is, as Camus mentioned, the fragrance of the brushwood. The experience of the vegetation against the sea and sky rushes further to the ultimate expanse of being and so provides relief and refreshment.

Of course these solutions are temporary and superficial. The underlying confusion of being with the dead children remains and so the sadness always returns. So a second approach to Rachel's sadness is necessary. To remove the sadness a philosophical correction of the natural dignity of the human person is necessary. Intellection of being still renders the human a part of the whole, though a principal part. This philosophical estimate of the value of human life opens the possibility of redeeming suffering and death by relating them to something else. It is never the case that nothing good can come from it. Hence, Aquinas understandably relates *quandoque* evils to both natural antecedent and consequent goods. There is also the philosophically discernable possibility that *quandoque* evils are related to supernatural goods as well. Is it no small consolation to know that where our strength is insufficient to make this relation, the power of the Creator is? Griffin's claim that God's ordering of evil to good makes the evil only apparent does not dim my point. As Aquinas understands it, the divine omnipotence does not condemn God to have all the power. As stemming from God and understood as *esse subsistens*, created essences in a sense mark a new beginning with their own effects, among which are contingency like *quandoque* evils. Hence, Aquinas can say that the relation of God's will to these effects is one of permission and order only and not one of intention.

What of the anger? Aquinas understands the passion of anger to be the desire to hurt someone from a spirit of revenge.[51] In the case of Rachel, anger lies in her refusal to accept 48, 6, and that refusal reduces to the perceived injustice of treating a person as a part. Hence, Rachel demands nothing short of getting back her children. But if the truth of the human's natural status as a principle part of the whole is understood, where is the injustice? The whole of which the human is by nature a part is so fraught with contingency that no evil is surprising. For instance, Emil Fackenheim demands that philosophers face the problem of how something so uniquely evil as the Holocaust could result from people so banal as the Nazis: "And how could those who were the rule, banal ones all, place into our world a kingdom of evil without precedent, far removed from banality and fated to haunt mankind forever?"[52] Fackenheim gives up on explaining the whole by its parts and falls back on the familiar dictum that a whole is more than the sum of its parts. But should banality be so readily dismissed? In describing the banality of Hitler himself Fackenheim says, "Other than a low cunning, his one distinguishing mark is a devouring passion, and even that is mostly fed by a need, as petty as it is limitless, to show them—whom?—that the nobody is somebody."[53] Again, cannot one see again the bewitchment of another faux epiphany of being? "The nobody" is an instance of the small and so draws an association with being in the contemplation of it. The banal are prime candidates for this tragic trick. Through the play of being, it is not incongruous that banal people invest themselves with an endearment that becomes so ferocious and idiosyncratic that they feel no bounds in others.

To return to Rachel, if we remember our natural status, viz., principal parts in a cosmos naturally fraught with contingency and

---

51. "Anger [*ira*] is the appetite of another's evil for the sake of revenge [*ad vindictam*]." *C.G.* I, 90; Aquinas, *Summa contra Gentiles*, vol. I, 274. See also *ST* II-II, 158, 2.

52. Emile Fackenheim, "The Holocaust and Philosophy," *The Journal of Philosophy* 82 (1985), 513.

53. Ibid., 512–13.

with a psyche of similar nature, how can we demand that we be exempt from evil, even of the most horrendous kinds? Does not that insight remove anger and replace it with an honest resignation? Also, does not knowledge that the creator will not leave *quandoque* evil unordered to good engender some sense of justice, just as it engendered some sense of solace? If Rachel insists that she has an implacable complaint, then she should acknowledge that it is on the basis of a view of the human that is extra-philosophical; in truth the view is religiously derived. That concession should lead her to find her solace in the further information available from religion.

So in what state does the philosophizing of Aquinas leave Rachel? Without the aid of revelation to guide her, her reaction takes the form of fidelity to the precepts of Aquinas's natural law ethics. The good that we ought to do in the subject of the first principle of practical reason is not the good that we have to do or the good that we are simply free to do. This complex character of the moral good seems fulfilled in the understanding of the human as an intellector of being. For as such, the human presents itself from among all other analogates of being as a particularly intense presencing of being. Intellection enables the analogon of being to be fuller in the human than in other analogates like granite, cows, and daisies. But being is also the good; hence, the good is more intense in the human. An appreciation of this situation should ground a respect and solicitude for oneself and others that manifests the moral unseemliness of suicide, abuse, murder, stealing, lying, etc.

When God's existence becomes known, this ethic extends itself to the creator who as *esse subsistens* is the preeminent epiphany of the *ratio entis*. Hence, at I-II, 94, 2, Aquinas also speaks of the obligation to know God. At this point, if the philosopher is sufficiently attentive to the implications within being, further possibilities appear. One of these is the Christian drama of salvation.

So the human of natural virtue is a human, in the midst of the slings and arrows of contingent being, living according to the precepts of natural law and so with some measure of joy but with the hope that the creator relates to us in a more personal manner. This state of natural virtue lacks any lassitude that would render supernatural elevation of little interest to the human. The natural desires of which I spoke in chapter 6 are operating. These desires leave the human not only open to supernatural elevation but interested in the claims of various religions to have communication from the creator regarding the creator's *de facto* providence over our affairs. If philosophy begins in wonder, good philosophy incites a still richer wonder.

Selected Bibliography

Adams, Marilyn McCord and Robert Merrihew Adams, eds. *The Problem of Evil*. Oxford: Oxford University Press, 1990.

Adams, Marilyn McCord. "Horrendous Evils and the Goodness of God," In *The Problem of Evil*, edited by Marilyn McCord Adams and Robert Merrihew Adams. Oxford: Oxford University Press, 1990.

Adams, Robert Merrihew. "Middle Knowledge and the Problem of Evil." In *The Problem of Evil*, edited by Marilyn McCord Adams and Robert Merrihew Adams. Oxford: Oxford University Press, 1990.

Allen, Diogenes. "Natural Evils and the Love of God." In *The Problem of Evil*, edited by Marilyn McCord Adams and Robert Marrihew Adams. Oxford: Oxford University Press, 1990.

Anderson, James. *The Bond of Being: An Essay on Analogy and Existence*. New York: Greenwood Press, 1969.

Aquinas, Thomas. *In Aristotelis Librum de Anima Commentarium*, edited by Angelus M. Pirotta. Turin and Rome: Marietti, 1936.

———. *On Being and Essence*, translated with introduction and notes by Armand Maurer. Toronto: Pontifical Institute of Mediaeval Studies, 1968.

———. *The Disputed Questions on Truth*, vol. I, translated by Robert W. Mulligan. Chicago: Regnery, 1952

———. *The Disputed Questions on Truth*, vol. II, translated by James V. McGlynn. Chicago: Regnery, 1953.

———. *The Disputed Questions on Truth*, vol. III, translated by Robert W. Schmidt. Chicago: Regnery, 1954.

———. *On the Division and Methods of the Sciences*, translated by Armand Maurer. Toronto: Pontifical Institute of Mediaeval Studies, 1963.

———. *In Duodecim Libros Metaphysicorum Aristotelis Expositio*. M. R. Cathala and Raymundus M. Spiazzi, eds. Turin and Rome: Marietti, 1950.

———. *Expositio super Librum Boethii de Trinitate*, edited by Bruno Decker. Leiden: J. Brill, 1959.

———. *Faith, Reason and Theology*. Translated by Armand Maurer with introduction and notes of St. Thomas Aquinas, Commentary on the *De Trinitate* of Boethius, Questions 1–4. Toronto: Pontifical Institute of Mediaeval Studies, 1987.

———. *On Interpretation*, translated by Jean T. Oesterle. Milwaukee: Marquette University Press, 1962.

———. *Liber de Veritate Catholicae Fidei contra Errores Infidelium seu "Summa contra Gentiles."* Ceslaus Pera, Petrus Marc, Petrus Caramello, eds. Turin and Rome: Marietti, 1961.

———. *The Literal Exposition on Job: A Scriptural Commentary concerning Providence*, translated by Anthony Damico. Atlanta: Scholars Press, 1989.

———. *In Octo Libros Physicorum Aristotelis Expositio*, edited by P. M. Maggiolo. Turin and Rome: Marietti, 1954.

———. *Opusculum De Ente et Essentia*. Turin: Marietti, 1957.

———. *De Principiis Naturae*, edited by John J. Pauson. Fribourg: Société Philosophique, 1950.

———. *Quaestiones Disputatae de Malo*, edited by P. Bazzi. In *Quaestiones Disputatae*, vol. II, edited by Raymundus Spiazzi. Turin and Rome: Marietti, 1965.

———. *Quaestiones Disputatae de Potentia Dei*, edited by Paulus M. Pession. In *Quaestiones Disputatae*, vol. II, edited by Raymundus Spiazzi, Turin and Rome: Marietti, 1965.

———. *Quaestiones Disputate de Veritate*, edited by Raymundus Spiazzi. In *Quaestiones Disputatae*, vol. 1, edited by Raymundus Spiazzi. Turin and Rome: Marietti, 1964.

———. *Scriptum super Libros Sententiarum Magistri Petri Lombardi Episcopi Parisiensis*. Vols. 1–2, edited by Pierre Mandonnet. Paris: P. Lethielleux, 1929. Vols. 3–4, edited by Maria Fabianus Moos. Paris: P. Lethielleux, 1933–1947.

———. *Summa contra Gentiles*, vol. I, translated with introduction and notes by Anton Pegis. Notre Dame, Ind.: University of Notre Dame Press, 1975.

———. *Summa contra Gentiles*, vol. II, translated with introduction and notes by James Anderson. Notre Dame Ind.: University of Notre Dame Press, 1975.

———. *Summa contra Gentiles*, vol. III, translated with introduction and notes by Vernon J. Bourke. Notre Dame, Ind.: University of Notre Dame Press, 1975.

———. *Summa contra Gentiles*, vol. IV, translated with introduction and notes by Charles O'Neil. Notre Dame, Ind.: University of Notre Dame Press, 1975.

———. *Summa Theologiae*. Edited by Ottawa Institute of Mediaeval Studies. Ottawa: Collège Dominicain d'Ottawa, 1941.

———. *Summa Theologica*, translated by Fathers of the English Dominican Province. N.Y.: Benzinger Brothers, 1947–48.

Barrett, William. *Irrational Man: A Study in Existential Philosophy*. Garden City, N.Y.: Doubleday & Company, Inc., 1962.

Bradley, Denis J. M. *Aquinas on the Twofold Human Good: Reason and Human Happiness in Aquinas's Moral Science*. Washington, D.C.: The Catholic University of America Press, 1997.

Brown, Montague. "Aquinas on the Resurrection of the Body." *The Thomist* 56 (1992): 165–207.

Camus, Albert. *The Plague*, translated by Stuart Gilbert. New York: Alfred A. Knopf, 1948.

Catan, John R., ed. *St. Thomas Aquinas on the Existence of God: The Collected Papers of Joseph Owens*. Albany: State University of New York Press, 1980.

Chesterton, G. K. *Orthodoxy*. New York: John Lane Company, 1914.

Connellan, Cohn. *Why Does Evil Exist?* Hicksville, N.Y.: Exposition Press, Inc., 1974.

Copleston, F. C. *Aquinas*. Baltimore: Penguin Books, 1961.

Crosby, John. "Is All Evil Really Only Privation?" *Proceedings of the American Catholic Philosophical Association* 75 (2001): 197–210.

———. "Is It Possible Knowingly to Do Evil?" *Proceedings of the American Catholic Philosophical Association* 74 (2001): 325–33.

Curran, Charles E., ed. *Absolutes in Moral Theology*. Washington, D.C.: Corpus Books, 1968.

Davies, Brian. *The Reality of God and the Problem of Evil*. London: Continuum, 2006.

Dawson, Christopher. *Progress and Religion: An Historical Inquiry*. Washington, D.C.: The Catholic University of America Press, 2001.

Donnelly, P. J. "Discussion of the Supernatural Order." *Theological Studies*, 9 (1948): 213–49.

Dostoevsky, Fyodor. *The Brothers Karamazov*, translated by Andrew R. MacAndrew. New York: Bantam Books, 1970.

Fackenheim, Emile. "The Holocaust and Philosophy." *Journal of Philosophy* 82 (1985): 505–14.

Flew. Anthony. "Theology and Falsification," *New Essays in Philosophical Theology*. New York: The Macmillan Company, 1964

Garrigou-Lagrange, Reginald. *God: His Existence and His Nature*, translated by Dom Bede Rose. St. Louis: B. Herder Book Co., 1939.

Gerson, Lloyd P., ed. *Graceful Reason: Essays Presented to Joseph Owens*. Toronto: Pontifical Institute of Mediaeval Studies, 1983.

Gilson, Etienne. *The Christian Philosophy of St. Thomas Aquinas*, translated by L. K. Shook. Notre Dame, Ind.: University of Notre Dame Press, 1994.

Green, T. H. and T. H. Grose, eds. *David Hume: The Philosophical Works*. Darmstadt: Scientia Verlag Aalen, 1964.

Griffin, David R. *Evil Revisited: Responses and Reconsiderations*. Albany: State University of New York Press, 1991.

———. *God, Power, and Evil: A Process Theodicy*. Westminster, Ky.: John Knox Press, 2004.

Hasker, William. "On Regretting the Evils of This World." In *The Problem of Evil: Selected Readings*, edited by Michael L. Peterson. Notre Dame, Ind.: University of Notre Dame Press, 1992.

Henle, Robert J. *Method in Metaphysics*. Milwaukee: Marquette University Press, 1980.

Hick, John. *Evil and the God of Love*. New York: Harper & Row, Publishers, 1978, rev. ed.

Hume, David. *Dialogues Concerning Natural Religion and Other Writings*, edited by Dorothy Coleman. Cambridge: Cambridge University Press, 2007.

———. *David Hume: The Philosophical Works*, edited by T. H. Green and T. H. Grose. Darmstadt: Scientia Verlag Aalen, 1964.

———. *A Treatise of Human Nature*. In *David Hume: The Philosophical Works*, edited by T. H. Green and T. H. Grose. Darmstadt: Scientia Verlag Aalen, 1964.

Journet, Charles. *The Meaning of Evil*, translated by Michael Barry. New York: P. J. Kenedy, 1963.

Kant, Immanuel. *Groundwork of the Metaphysics of Morals*, translated by Mary Gregor. Cambridge: Cambridge University Press, 1998.

———. *Critique of Practical Reason*, In *Critique of Practical Reason and other Writings in Moral Philosophy*, translated and edited by Lewis White Beck. Chicago: The University of Chicago Press, 1949.

Kenny, Anthony. *The Five Ways: St. Thomas Aquinas' Proofs of God's Existence*. New York: Schocken Books, 1969.

Kirn, Arthur G., ed. *G. B. Phelan: Selected Papers*. Toronto: Pontifical Institute of Mediaeval Studies, 1967.

Klubertanz, George P. *St. Thomas on Analogy*. Chicago: Loyola University Press, 1960.

Knasas, John F. X. "Aquinas and Finite Gods." *Proceedings of the American Catholic Philosophical Association* 53 (1979): 88–97.

———. "Super God: Divine Infinity and Human Self-Determination." *Proceedings of the American Catholic Philosophical Association* 55 (1981): 197–209.

———. "*Contra* Spinoza: Aquinas on God's Free Will." *American Catholic Philosophical Quarterly* 76 (2002): 417–29.

———. *Being and Some Twentieth-Century Thomists*. New York: Fordham University Press, 2003.

———. "Does the Catholic Church Teach That There Is No One True Philosophy?" *Angelicum* 80 (2003): 417–35.

———. "Haldane's Analytic Thomism and Aquinas's *Actus Essendi*." In *Analytical Thomism: Traditions in Dialogue*, edited by Craig Paterson and Matthew S. Pugh. Burlington, Vt.: Ashgate Publishing Company, 2006.

Kushner, Harold S. *Why Do Bad Things Happen to Good People?* New York: Avon Books, 1981.

Lee, Patrick. "Permanence of the Ten Commandments: St. Thomas and His Modern Commentators." *Theological Studies* 42 (1981): 422–43.

Loemaker, Leroy E., trans. and ed. *Gottfried Wilhelm Leibniz: Philosophical*

Papers and Letters. Dordrecht, Holland: D. Reidel Publishing Company, 1976.

Mackie, J. L. "Evil and Omnipotence." In *The Problem of Evil*, edited by Marilyn McCord Adams and Robert Merrihew Adams. Oxford: Oxford University Press, 1990.

Maritain, Jacques. *The Degrees of Knowledge*, translated by Gerald B. Phelan. New York: Charles Scribner's Sons, 1959.

———. *God and the Permission of Evil*. Milwaukee: Bruce Publishing Co., 1966.

———. *The Person and the Common Good*. Notre Dame, Ind.: University of Notre Dame Press, 1966.

———. *A Preface to Metaphysics: Seven Lectures on Being*. New York: Mentor Omega Book, 1962.

———. *The Sin of the Angel*. Westminster, Md.: The Newman Press, 1959.

———. *St. Thomas and the Problem of Evil*. Milwaukee: Marquette University Press, 1942.

Martin, Michael. "Reichenbach on Natural Evil." *Religious Studies* 24 (1988): 91–99.

McEvoy, James. "The Other as Oneself: Friendship and Love in the Thought of St. Thomas Aquinas." In *Thomas Aquinas: Approaches to Truth*, edited by James McEvoy and Michael Dunne. Dublin: Four Courts Press, 2002.

——— and Michael Dunne, eds. *Thomas Aquinas: Approaches to Truth*. Dublin: Four Courts Press, 2002.

McKeon, Richard, ed. *The Basic Works of Aristotle*. New York: Random House, 1970.

Milhaven, John G. "Moral Absolutes and Thomas Aquinas." In *Absolutes in Moral Theology*, edited by Charles E. Curran. Washington, D.C.: Corpus Books, 1968.

Miller, Barry. *The Fullness of Being: A New Paradigm for Existence*. Notre Dame, Ind.: University of Notre Dame Press, 2002.

O'Connor, William R. *The Natural Desire for God*. Milwaukee: Marquette University Press, 1948.

Owens, Joseph. "The Accidental and Essential Character of Being in the Doctrine of St. Thomas Aquinas." In *St. Thomas Aquinas on the Existence of God: the Collected Papers of Joseph Owens*, edited by John R. Catan. Albany: State University of New York Press, 1980.

———. "Analogy as a Thomistic Approach to Being." *Mediaeval Studies* 24 (1962): 302–22.

———. "Aquinas: 'Darkness of Ignorance' in the Most Refined Notion of God." *Southwestern Journal of Philosophy* 5 (1974): 93–110.

———. "Soul as Agent in Aquinas." *The New Scholasticism* 48 (1974): 40–72.

———. *An Elementary Christian Metaphysics*. Houston: Center for Thomistic Studies, 1985.

———. "Towards a Philosophy of Medieval Studies." *The Etienne Gilson Series 9*. Toronto: Pontifical Institute of Mediaeval Studies, 1986.

Paterson, Craig, and Matthew S. Pugh, eds. *Analytical Thomism: Traditions in Dialogue*. Burlington, Vt.: Ashgate Publishing Company, 2006.

Pegis, Anton, ed. *The Basic Writings of St. Thomas Aquinas*. New York: Random House, 1945.

———. "Molina and Human Freedom." In *Jesuit Thinkers of the Renaissance*, edited by Gerard Smith. Milwaukee: Marquette University Press, 1939.

———. "Penitus Manet Ignotum." *Mediaeval Studies* 27 (1965): 212–26.

Penelhum, Terence. "Divine Goodness and the Problem of Evil." In *The Problem of Evil*, edited by Marilyn McCord Adams and Robert Merriweather Adams. Oxford: Oxford University Press, 1990.

Peterson, Michael L., ed. *The Problem of Evil: Selected Readings*. Notre Dame, Ind.: University of Notre Dame Press, 1992.

Phelan, Gerald B. "St. Thomas and Analogy." In *G. B. Phelan: Selected Papers*, edited by Arthur G. Kirn. Toronto: Pontifical Institute of Medieval Studies, 1967.

Plantinga, Alvin. "God, Evil, and the Metaphysics of Freedom." In *The Problem of Evil*, edited by Marilyn McCord Adams and Robert Merriweather Adams. Oxford: Oxford University Press, 1990.

Portalié, Eugène. *A Guide to the Thought of Saint Augustine*, translated by Ralph J. Bastian. Chicago: Regnery, 1960.

Quinn, John. "The Third Way to God: A New Approach." *The Thomist* 42 (1978): 50–68.

Reichenbach, Bruce. *Evil and a Good God*. New York: Fordham University Press, 1982.

Rousseau, Mary. "The Natural Meaning of Death in the *Summa Theolo-*

giae." *Proceedings of the American Catholic Philosophical Association* 52 (1978): 87–95.

Rousselot, Pierre. *The Intellectualism of St. Thomas*, translated by James E. O'Mahony. New York: Sheed and Ward, 1935.

Rowan, John P. *Commentary on the Metaphysics of Aristotle*. Notre Dame, Ind.: Dumb Ox Books, 1995.

Rowe, William. *The Cosmological Argument*. Princeton: Princeton University Press, 1975.

———. "Evil and Theodicy." In *William L. Rowe on Philosophy of Religion: Selected Writings*, edited by Nick Trakakis. Burlington, Vt.: Ashgate Publishing Company, 2007.

St. Amour, Paul. "The Scale-Wielding God and the Limits of Philosophical Theodicy." *Proceedings of the American Catholic Philosophical Association* 74 (2000): 259–72.

Smith, Gerard, ed. *Jesuit Thinkers of the Renaissance*. Milwaukee: Marquette University Press, 1939.

———. *Freedom in Molina*. Chicago: Loyola University Press, 1966.

Stump, Eleonore. "The Problem of Evil." *Faith and Philosophy* 2 (1985): 392–423.

———. *Wandering in Darkness: Narrative and the Problem of Suffering*. Oxford: Clarendon Press, 2010.

Swinburne, Richard. *The Existence of God*. Oxford: Clarendon Press, 1979.

Trakakis, Nick, ed. *William L. Rowe on Philosophy of Religion: Selected Writings*. Burlington, Vt.: Ashgate Publishing Company, 2007.

Weisheipl, James. *Friar Thomas D'Aquino: His Life, Thought, and Work*. Garden City, N.Y.: Doubleday & Company, Inc., 1974.

Wippel, John. "Quidditative Knowledge of God According to Thomas Aquinas." In *Graceful Reason: Essays Presented to Joseph Owens*, edited by Lloyd P. Gerson. Toronto: Pontifical Institute of Medieval Studies, 1983.

Index

Abraham and Isaac incident, 110–19
Adams, Marilyn McCord, 155–56; horrendous evils, 155, nontranscendent goods, 155
Adams, Robert Merrihew: knowledge of counterfactuals, 223–24
Allen, Diogenes, 195
Anger, 290–91
Antecedent good, 57, 146–48, 150
Aquinas, Thomas: absolute consideration, 38n24; *agens fortissimum*, 227; angelic sin, 162n17, 237n60; bent leg analogy, 242; carpenter analogy, 241; chance events, 174; concession to Plato, 187; contemplation of truth, 251; contingency and providence, 176–78, 227; *esse commune* (also *esse formale, ratio essendi*), 186, 272–75; evil as privation, 124–26; evil proves God, 126–31, 141–44; formal distinction, 48; freedom of the will, 26, 62; God and contradictions, 131; God and evil choices, 231–32; God and evils, 87–95; God and free choice, 215–20, 226–30; God as subsistent *esse*, 36, 139; grace, 8, 81; happiness and motions of the will, 43; *implicit* intellection, 32; inequality in things, 48; monsters, 53, 92; natural desires, 182–93; natural knowledge of God, 33; negative judgment, 274; no best world, 52; no demonstration of resurrection, 84; nonconsideration of the rule, 234–35, 240; no philosophical demonstration of original sin, 82; original sin, 83–85; philosophical knowledge of God in metaphysics, 35; *quandoque* evils and God's will, 59, 146; quidditative knowledge of cause, 271; sin, 233–38; state of innocence, 68; subject of first practical principle, 27; twofold order to good, 114; virtual presence, 51; world's reflection of divine infinity, 52

Brothers Karamazov, The: "Rebellion" disquisition, 178–82
Brown, Montague, 83

Camus, Albert, 12–15, 158
Cause *per accidens*, 58–59
Chance events, 175; in divine providence, 176–78
Chesterton, G. K., 201n12
Christian philosophy, 278
Clarke, Samuel, 133–34
Concept: analogical and univocal, 22, 185

301

Connellan, Cohn, 2n2
Consequent good, 58–59, 148–50; necessity of, 60; subject of, 61–69
Contraception, 29
Copleston, F. C., 131
Cosmological theodicy, 153, 194–262
Crosby, John: objection to evil as privation, 131–32; willing evil, 238–40

Davies, Brian, 23n7, 129n10; 139n36, 144n46, 264–76; God as essentially good, 275; God as incomprehensible, 265, 267; individual-quiddity distinction, 265; "like from like" thesis, 266–67, 269
Dawson, Christopher, 162n18
Death: as natural defect, 75–77, 145–46; possible supernatural override of, 80, 120
Donnelly, P. J., 183n58

Effect: knowing essence of cause, 129; *per se* vs. *per accidens*, 37n22
Epictetus, 196–97
Epiphany of being, 43, 291
Esse, 36; for accidents, 216; as proper effect, 128–29, 269; as *sui generis* attribute, 140
Evil: natural corruption, 75–77, 145, 232–33; no definitive Thomistic explanation, 151–52, 260; pain objection, 126; privation, 124–26; sin, 233–38; summary of Aquinas, 145–52; types of, 145
Existence neutral, 38n24

Fackenheim, 290
Flew, Anthony, 12, 69, 158
Ford, Lewis, 284n47
Free will defense: Aquinas, 215–20, 244–45, 256; Mackie, 214; Plantinga, 221–23; Reichenbach, 252–53; Stump, 281
Friendship, 30–31

Garrigou-Lagrange, Reginald: on Molina, 224n51; sufficient reason, 136–40
Gilson, Etienne, 270n16
Grace, 8, 81
Griffin, David Ray, 1n2, 52n8, 167–78; on Aquinas, 173–74; on Knasas, 229n54; objection to Hick, 168–72

Hartshorne, Charles, 24
Hasker, William, 158–61
Heidegger, Martin, 39
Hick, John, 161–67; afterlife, 163; eternal damnation, 161n16; evil and God's will, 165; Holocaust, 171; original sin, 161, 164; sin of Satan, 162; soul-making, 162, 167
Holocaust, 171, 290
Human: closer to the whole, 65; closest to existing always, 66; contemplator of truth, 251; dignity of, 195; as intellector of being, 28, 283, 291; master of its acts, 62; as principal part, 46, 64–65; self-awareness, 237; targets apparent good, 232–38
Hume, David, 28, 140n38, 201–6

Incorruptibility vs. immortality distinction, 66

Job commentary: inscrutability of divine providence, 85–86
Journet, Charles, 2n3, 52n8, 97–104
Joy: caused by *ratio boni*, 17

Kant, Immanuel: existence not a predicate, 140, 217n38; person as end, 10; starry heavens, 13

Kenny, Anthony, 37n22; objection to "like follows like," 128
Knasas, John F. X., 35n21, 69n24, 141n42, 183n58, 227n52
Kushner, Harold S., 1n2, 87n22

Lee, Patrick, 104–9
Leibniz, Gottfried Wilhelm, 51

Mackie, J. L., 209–15; omnipotence paradox, 214, 221n46
Maritain, Jacques, 144, 241n66, 283; interpretation of Aquinas's evil text, 2–4; person as a part, 9; person as a whole, 4; quidditative knowledge of God, 270n17
Martin, Michael, 257n89
McEvoy, James, 30n15
Metaphysics: as implicit, 35–40
Milhaven, John G.: moral absolutes, 113
Miller, Barry, 256n86
Monogamy, 29
Moral necessity, 27, 239, 291

Natural desire: for everlasting life, 192–93; for God, 183–89; for happiness, 189–92; none in vain, 191
Nonprecisive abstraction, 20
Notion of being. *See Ratio entis*

O'Connor, William R., 183n58
Onimus, Jean, 14n29
Original sin, 45, 83–85, 150
Owens, Joseph: analogy as sameness in difference, 23n5; 38n24, 66n21; *esse* for accidents, 143n45, 216n38; no quidditative knowledge of God, 270n16

Passion, 235, 286, 288–90
Pegis, Anton C., 224n51, 270n16

Penelhum, Terence, 130n11
Personalist theodicy, 154, 155–93
Phelan, Gerald B., 23n5
Plantinga, Alvin, 220–25; God's knowledge of counterfactuals, 223–24; "Leibniz's lapse," 220; significant freedom, 221–22; transworld depravity, 222
Pope Benedict XVI, 112
Portalié, Eugène, 224n51
Praeter intentionem: ambiguity of, 89–92; Journet, 97; Lee, 105
Presence: essential and actual, 30n14
Punishment, 94–95, 106–8, 150, 161n16

Quandoque evil: definition, 46; explanation, 53, 146–47; frequency of, 69–73; God, 92; Hick, 164
Quietism, 230
Quinn, John, 55n10, 77n3, 144n46

Ratio boni: Crosby, 238; first object of the will, 17, 18; happiness, 189
Ratio entis: as *ratio boni,* 17, 23; free choice as *quoddam ens,* 217; nongeneric, 21, 142; taken from *esse,* 143; two tricks of, 32–33, 40, 287, 290
Regensburg address, 112
Reichenbach, Bruce, 47n1, 56n11, 252–62; God not morally good, 130; knowledge of counterfactuals, 253–54; omnipotence paradox, 221n46; theodicy for moral evil, 252–56; theodicy for natural evils, 257–62
Religion, possibility of, 121
Retorsion, 137–38
Rousseau, Mary, 67n21
Rowe, William, 37n22, 140n38; pointless evils, 206–9; sufficient reason, 133–35

Sadness, 286–89
Schlink, Basilea, 197–99
Sexual embrace, 29, 117
Smith, Gerard, 224n51
St. Amour, Paul, 153n1, 183n58
Stump, Eleonore, 180n54, 276–86; broken heart, 282, 283–85; divided will, 279; on Hick, 162n18, 165n26; justification, 279; meaning of suffering, 278; resurrection, 280, 283; sanctification, 280; on Swinburne, 247; theodicy vs. defense, 277, 282
Sufficient reason, principle of: Aquinas, 135–36, 138–40; Pius XII and *Humani generis*, 136; Rowe's objections, 134–35

Swinburne, Richard, 245–51; afterlife, 250; choice of destiny, 245; inductive knowledge, 246; natural evils, 246

Theodicy: cosmological and personalist, 153

Universal physical cause, 55, 76–77

Weil, Simone, 199–200
Willing evil *per accidens*: ambiguity of, 89–92; God, 87–89, 145; Lee, 105
Wippel, John, 271n17

Yaffe, Martin D., 86n22

Aquinas and the Cry of Rachel: Thomistic Reflections on the Problem of Evil was designed in Meta (serif and sans) and composed by Kachergis Book Design of Pittsboro, North Carolina. It was printed on 60-pound House Natural Smooth and bound by Sheridan Books of Ann Arbor, Michigan.

www.ingramcontent.com/pod-product-compliance
Lightning Source LLC
Chambersburg PA
CBHW020315010526
44107CB00054B/1854